FORCE AND FREEDOM

AMERICA IN THE NINETEENTH CENTURY

Series editors:
Brian DeLay, Steven Hahn, Amy Dru Stanley

America in the Nineteenth Century proposes a rigorous rethinking of this most formative period in U.S. history. Books in the series will be wide-ranging and eclectic, with an interest in politics at all levels, culture and capitalism, race and slavery, law, gender, and the environment, and regional and transnational history. The series aims to expand the scope of nineteenth-century historiography by bringing classic questions into dialogue with innovative perspectives, approaches, and methodologies.

FORCE
AND
FREEDOM

BLACK ABOLITIONISTS
—— *and the* ——
POLITICS *of* VIOLENCE

KELLIE CARTER JACKSON

PENN

UNIVERSITY OF PENNSYLVANIA PRESS

PHILADELPHIA

Copyright © 2019 University of Pennsylvania Press

All rights reserved. Except for brief quotations used
for purposes of review or scholarly citation, none of this
book may be reproduced in any form by any means without
written permission from the publisher.

Published by
University of Pennsylvania Press
Philadelphia, Pennsylvania 19104-4112
www.upenn.edu/pennpress

Printed in the United States of America on acid-free paper
1 3 5 7 9 10 8 6 4 2

A Cataloging-in-Publication record is available from the Library of Congress
ISBN 978-0-8122-5115-9

For
Nathaniel Emmitt Jackson
Psalms 37:4

CONTENTS

The Philosophy of Force

> Our white brethren cannot understand us unless we speak
> to them in their own language; they recognize only the
> philosophy of force.
>
> —James McCune Smith

Since August 1, 1834, free black Americans often celebrated Emancipation Day with parades, food, bazaars, and speeches, much like the Fourth of July. While the day marked the legal abolition of slavery in the British West Indies, it also represented what was possible for America: the eventual nonviolent abolition of slavery. However, for the well-known physician and abolitionist James McCune Smith, August 1 was incomplete, at best, and a farce, at worst. He refused to celebrate the holiday and criticized those who did. The son of former slaves, McCune Smith wrote an essay that appeared in *Frederick Douglass Paper* in August 1856. In the essay, he condemned British emancipation as merely a faulty compromise between slaves and their white masters, whom the British government generously compensated for their loss of property, thereby legitimizing the notion that slaves were less than human. Yet the government made virtually no effort to compensate the enslaved. "A paltry twenty thousand pounds was appropriated for the education of the freed men," McCune Smith lamented. "That is all given to the former slave in consideration of the robbery and embruting [*sic*] which has been perpetuated on him for centuries."[1]

What vexed McCune Smith the most was the notion that British emancipation had been "a boon conferred" rather than "a right seized upon and held." Consequently, he mocked celebrants by mimicking an old 1848 blackface minstrel song, "Masa gib me holiday." Were black Americans to hope for abolition as a gift from slave owners acting of their own free will? According to McCune Smith, true freedom could not be bestowed; it had to be won. Violent upheaval was "the order of things." Teaching children to celebrate *given freedom* needed to stop, he insisted, as this was not the kind of freedom worth having. "Our freedom must be won and the sooner we wake up to the fact, the better," he warned his readers.[2]

Harkening back to the electric feeling that inspired numerous slave rebellions, McCune Smith subsequently praised leaders such as Denmark Vesey, Nat Turner, and the brave men and women who fought during the Christiana Resistance of 1851. These violent acts effectively shed light on the future of black Americans, he contended. "Our white brethren cannot understand us unless we speak to them in their own language; they recognize only the philosophy of force," he explained. According to McCune Smith, expecting white Americans to embrace black humanity required physical engagement. "They will never recognize our manhood until we knock them down a time or two," he exclaimed.[3] Black resistance and violence was central to understanding their antidote to American slavery.

Force and Freedom

In the history of the movement to abolish slavery, the shift toward violence among African Americans remains largely unaddressed. In addition, the ways in which black abolitionists utilized violence deserves a more sustained and nuanced analysis. Black resistance was central to abolitionism.[4] Accordingly, *Force and Freedom: Black Abolitionists and the Politics of Violence* actively examines one of the perennial questions in political thought: is violence a valid means of producing social change? Specifically, this study addresses how black abolitionists answered this question. Black abolitionist ideology not only explains how the politics of violence paved the way for the Civil War, but how the politics of violence helped prepare the nation to view black people as equal Americans with inalienable rights. *Force and Freedom* is the first of its kind to offer a close look at the complex and varied ways violence was deployed by antebellum black activists.[5]

While praising the efforts of a few notable men and women abolitionists, most contemporary discussions of the subject routinely lament that nothing good can come from political violence.[6] On the contrary, few good things can be acquired from those in power except by force, often violent force. A retreat from engaging in a complex understanding of the political purposes of violence limits both how we see and make use of the past. Within the field, there is a propensity to privilege the performance of nonviolence and deny the possibility and utility of violence as the great accelerator in American emancipation.

Historiography typically follows the chronological pattern of moral suasion in the 1830s, political abolition in the 1840s, and separatism and emigration in the 1850s. Some historians see the shift from moral suasion to violence as one of declension, with African Americans giving in to despair in the wake of the Fugitive Slave Act of 1850. Others see the antebellum period as the moment in which the maturation of a black nationalist consciousness calcified. I align my work with the more recent scholarship of Manisha Sinha, Patrick Rael, Matthew Clavin, and W. Caleb McDaniel, who see this moment as part of the creation of an alternative revolutionary tradition in an age of revolution. I see black abolitionism as a movement that began almost at the inception of Atlantic world slavery and understood the idea and experience of violence more than any other group.

Force and Freedom examines the political and social tensions preceding the American Civil War, as well as the conditions that led many black abolitionists to believe slavery could be abolished only through violent measures. By exploring black abolitionists' shift from a campaign of moral persuasion in the 1830s to their push for more combative and violent strategies to end American slavery in the 1850s, I explain the various moments that cultivated their desire for force. The purpose of this study is fourfold: First, I draw scholarly attention to why black abolitionist leaders prioritized violence over nonviolence as a means for liberation. Second, I explore the factors that precipitated and accelerated this change of perspective toward the use of violence. Third, I address the ways in which black leaders arrived at a place of mutual agreement, differing with the tactics of various white abolitionist leaders who evoked and employed violence. Fourth, I reveal how the expanding influence of the black abolitionist movement—from its early orators, to the black press, to the formation of militia groups—illustrates the power of black abolitionists to mobilize their communities, compel national action, and draw international attention. Within the racially charged context of antebellum America, I draw attention to the immense importance of violence to imagining emancipation and, in turn, freedom into being.

Why Violence?

Force and Freedom could just as easily be expressed as force *for* freedom. The paradox of using force and violence to bring about freedom and ensure peace is common within our own western political context. Violence is the double-edged sword of democracy. In the quest for freedom, violence becomes a necessary liberating force when it is the only remaining option. Understanding political violence is often about understanding an ideology of last resorts. In many ways, this study is an analysis of "last resorts" among black Americans. This study asks: should the enslaved or free black people be forced to obey laws that do not grant them the rights to shape such laws?

Throughout the book, I refer to violence as political or use the phrase "political violence," by which I mean forceful or deadly acts that operate around a political agenda or motivation to produce change. I understand history as struggles for power and contestations over meaning, influence, and governance. Everything about slavery and its abolition was contested. White planters and politicians perceived abolitionists' and African Americans' aggression as a threat to their own power. And though some scholars may not recognize leaders of slave rebellions or black abolitionists as politicians, their roles were indeed political.[7]

Additionally, violence became a political language for African American abolitionists. That is to say, black leaders addressed how violence became a way of communicating and provoking political and social change. Along the lines of McCune Smith's "philosophy of force," imagining violence as a language helps scholars of nineteenth-century African American history understand both how power is maintained and how power is disseminated through conventional and unconventional channels.

The era of revolutions set an early example for understanding violence as both a rhetorical and physical weapon to maintain the status quo, as well as the means to overthrow it. The historian François Furstenberg argues that, during the nineteenth century, Patrick Henry's famous mandate "Give me liberty or give me death" was the greatest revolutionary slogan of all time.[8] Thus the idea among black abolitionists that freedom denied should be taken by force was not new. The contagious egalitarian language of the eighteenth and nineteenth century erupted in a set of expectations and bore serious consequences. The revolutionary rhetoric and force deployed by the Founding Fathers offered black abolitionists an opportunity to present themselves as equal men whose struggle mirrored that of American revolutionaries. Inadvertently, the Founding Fathers supplied the language and ideology for black abolitionists to rationalize a violent overthrow of slavery. Meanwhile, Haitian revolutionaries provided the precedent.

The successful overthrow of slavery during the Haitian Revolution supplied the first example of a black revolutionary victory achieved through violence.[9] For black abolitionists, an independent Haiti represented the impossible made possible. The Haitian Revolution, and the slave rebellions more generally, served to illustrate the fact that political violence was a direct and inevitable consequence of slavery and oppression. Black abolitionists offered the Haitian Revolution as a constant reminder of how they could overthrow the institution of slavery in America. For the enslaved and black leadership, violence as a political language meant that Haiti was more than a noun; it was a verb. These examples imbued black Americans with the confidence to assert that equality and authority was not divine, hereditary, or accidental but that most societies and individual conditions could be logically engineered.[10] In other words, a radical change in society and social structure could be produced, even by those possessing the least access to power. Thus violence had a democratizing effect; it created opportunities for any enslaved or oppressed free person to engage in a political and physical pushback to their oppressive conditions. In short, black resistance to slavery offered Americans an opportunity to perfect democracy.

The son of former slaves, James Theodore Holly was an abolitionist who later emigrated to the island of Haiti, which became its own black independent nation in 1803. In the 1850s, in pointing to the hypocrisy of American independence, Holly described the inspiration that Haiti offered to black reformers. "The revolution of this country [America] was only the revolt of a people already comparatively free, independent, and highly enlightened," he posited. Meanwhile, "the Haitian Revolution was a revolt of an uneducated and menial class of slaves, against their tyrannical oppressors who not only imposed an absolute tax on their unrequited labor, but also usurped their very bodies." Holly did not believe that American colonists could rightly call themselves oppressed. For Holly, revolutions required a sense of legitimacy greater than the 1773 Tea Act. In other words, "a three pence per pound tax on tea" was not a sufficient grievance.[11] With an equal level of seriousness and humor, he wrote, "The obstacles to surmount, and the difficulties to contend against, in the American revolution, when compared to those of the Haytian, were, (to use a homely but classic phrase,) but a 'tempest in a teapot.'" For black abolitionists, the American and Haitian Revolutions involved more than a set of enlightened principles: each provided the rationale and means through which to accomplish abolition.

Many black leaders began to argue that violent political discourse was completely in line with American religious traditions and early liberal republican views.[12] In a letter published in the *North Star,* for example, fugitive slaves declared, "If the American revolutionists had excuse for shedding but one drop of blood, then have the American slaves excuse for making blood to flow 'even unto the horse-bridles.'"[13] For them, words such as "freedom," "liberty," "resistance," and "slavery" created dichotomies that functioned and thrived on urgency. Phrases used during the revolution, such as "rebellion to tyrants was obedience to God" and the well-known axiom "he who would be free must himself strike the first blow," carried with them a set of beliefs that, for those yearning for their own freedom, connected politics and political discourse with violence.

Changing Views

During the 1830s, the formal beginning of the abolitionist movement emerged out of a sense of religious fervor and optimism. Spiritual revival and a belief that Christ's return was imminent engendered a second Great Awakening, which influenced the belief among abolitionists that moral suasion coupled with nonviolent resistance was the best and surest way to abolish slavery. Many of the early abolitionists believed that moral suasion would work to end slavery.

The white abolitionist William Lloyd Garrison emerged as a leading proponent of nonviolent ideology and nonpolitical action within the antislavery movement. In the face of angry mobs, arson attacks, and other acts of brutality, Garrison instructed abolitionists to "turn the other cheek." And, for some time, they did. All efforts outside nonresistance were shunned, even in self-defense. Yet, twenty years into the abolitionist movement, American slavery had expanded, the enslaved population had doubled, and abolitionists were no closer to freedom than when they began the American Antislavery Society in 1833. For black leadership, the notion of nonresistance popularized by Garrison had all but collapsed. During the two decades, abolitionists devoted to the campaign for emancipation and leaders of the antislavery movement had become morally exhausted. At each turn, it appeared that the Slave Power—

a term used to describe the dominating political, economic, and social influence of slaveholders—wielded unlimited control over the fate of black Americans. Effectively, none of the new laws established during the antebellum period served to revive abolitionist optimism.

If nonviolent resistance and moral suasion constructed the house that Garrison built, black Americans were merely renters. They never fully owned nonresistance principles. Within the movement, black abolitionists, black freedmen, and the enslaved were most susceptible to the brunt of proslavery violence.[14] When white anti-abolitionist mobs attacked, it was predominantly black businesses, homes, and churches that were destroyed. Anti-abolitionist mobs regarded any institution in the black community as a target of political, economic, and social competition. For example, Philadelphia, "the City of Brotherly Love," experienced seven major antiblack and anti-abolitionist riots over the course of the 1830s and 1840s. Even the state of Maine, with its extremely small black population, experienced anti-abolitionist aggression.[15] These violent acts and sentiments inspired an increased militancy among black abolitionists. Simply put, force emerged because moral suasion failed to protect black people and produce liberation.

For abolitionists, the world changed after 1850. With the passing of the 1850 Fugitive Slave Law, it was not difficult to abandon moral suasion in the face of a slave catcher. For former and fugitive slaves, pacifism was no longer an ideology they could afford. Even freeborn black leaders all claimed they were prepared to resort to arms in defiance of the Fugitive Slave Law and the Supreme Court's 1857 decision in the Dred Scott case, which voided any rights African Americans held as enslaved or free people. As conditions declined for black Americans, black abolitionists grew more isolated and began to warn people that violence was inevitable. With tensions rising, in 1859 a radical abolitionist newspaper, the *Anglo-African Magazine*, boldly declared that, eventually, Americans would have to choose between facing the bloodiest slave rebellion by black Americans or the armed attacks by white allies: "So, people of the South, people of the North! Men and brethren, choose ye which method of emancipation you prefer—Nat Turner or John Brown's."[16]

The strategy of abolition was a long and winding road. A moral campaign alone required a change of the heart, conscience, and will. An abolitionist campaign with a political bent called for a restructuring of power and political systems. The abolition of slavery had to both stand for morality and institute real social and political change. Accordingly, the history of abolition through the lens of black leadership is one of the best ways to understand how radical social movements compel and produce political change.

The willingness among black abolitionist leaders to embrace violence was not merely a result of frustration but, after years of practicing nonresistance under white leadership, a calculated pivot. While black radical authors such as David Walker and Henry Highland Garnet served as publishing pioneers, they were not exceptional in their regard for the utility of force. Lewis Hayden, Jermain Loguen, Harriet Tubman, Robert Purvis, Maria Stewart, Peter H. Clark, and many others believed in armed defense and armed resistance to combat the institution of slavery. But the moment of transition from moral suasion to violence was different for each activist and was inspired by personal experience as well as political philosophy. For Frederick Douglass, the constant threat of mob attacks compelled him to engage in physical altercations with several men in Pendleton, Indiana, marking a shift in his philosophy of nonviolence. For Charles Remond, the Fugitive Slave Law of 1850 required that abolitionists reimagine their positions on violence in the face of recapture or kidnapping. For William Parker, region was a factor. Living in close proximity to the border states demanded constant vigilance against slave catchers. For Lewis Hayden, witnessing the recapture of the fugitive slave Anthony Burns in Boston brought him to commit murder. All throughout the movement, the complexity of the abolitionist's offensive and defensive strategy was both multifaceted and fluid. Distinguishing what some black abolitionists viewed as the inevitability of violence and implementing such violence were two very different processes.

Within the historiography, there is also a propensity to gender violence as masculine and gender slave owners as male, but more often than reported, women employed similar motivations for force. Few black women publicly challenged traditional family norms or spoke contrary to nonresistance during the first two decades of the antislavery movement. But gradually, the political climate gave rise to women's need to address their grievances. Women's contributions to the antislavery movement at all levels cannot be underestimated. By the 1850s, leading abolitionist women, including Mary Ann Shadd Cary, Frances Ellen Watkins Harper, Sarah Remond, Harriet Purvis, and Sojourner Truth, assumed stronger stances in the aid of fugitive slaves and self-defense. It is well recorded that Harriet Tubman and other women were not above packing a pistol for their journeys out of bondage. Black women confronted slave catchers, corroborated on collective and protective violence, and even contemplated emigration in search of better opportunities outside the United States. The difficult decisions being made by black families required shared sacrifice. Within my work, I examine women's responses not separately, but collectively, within a movement that pivoted equally on their influence, rhetoric, and action.

Centering Black Abolitionists in the Movement

This significant shift among black leadership, particularly post-1850, allows a new interpretation of black protest thought. The entire decade created a space for black abolitionists to convince their white allies that moral suasion was insufficient to combat the Slave Power. Black leadership believed that "protective violence," or self-defense among black abolitionists and their allies, as well as the threat of violence disrupted Northern apathy and heightened Southern paranoia. Slaveholders had used force and violence to exploit black Americans, and, in return, black Americans recognized the necessity of engaging force and violence to express and combat their powerlessness. Furthermore, black leadership pushed the North to see that an antislavery war was better than a proslavery peace.[17]

More than an account of the ideologies and actions of politicians, this book reveals how the enslaved and black leaders used force to engage and expand a political agenda. It is neither about the divisive and reductive political factions of eastern abolitionists versus western abolitionists nor about Garrisonians versus political abolitionists. For too long these binaries have placed more attention on white oppositional ideologies. This work focuses on how black leadership served as the engine for the movement and set the tone for envisioning freedom and enfranchisement.

Moving black abolitionists from the periphery to the center of abolitionist historiography highlights the influence of black activism in accelerating violence at the local, state, and national levels. Several scholars have contended that most antebellum studies that focus on black Americans offer an institutional approach that examines the larger causes, connections, and consequences of slavery. Because of this view, there is a tendency to analyze black Americans collectively or solely in the context of their relationship to slavery in the South or to segregation in the North. While this method has added greatly to historical scholarship and our understanding of the past, it does not do enough to examine black people as individuals, as "whole and complex persons."[18] This approach, in turn, prevents readers from appreciating the humanity of black people. The difficult decision for black Americans to consider political violence over moral suasion invokes a sense of silenced humanity. *Force and Freedom* takes readers beyond the honorable polities of moral suasion and the romanticism of the Underground Railroad and into an exploration of the agonizing decisions, strategies, and actions of those charged with the arduous task of creating political and social reform without an official (or recognized) political voice.

Force and Freedom not only reveals why black abolitionists mattered in the antislavery movement but also charts their broader significance to American history. Black abolitionists were instrumental as both the subjects and founders of the antislavery movement. Black leaders served as the primary catalysts for recruiting white followers to abolitionism and for investing the movement with its dual commitment to ending slavery and ending racism. Yet, aside from Frederick Douglass and Harriet Tubman, black abolitionists are routinely forgotten in public memory. Manisha Sinha contends that, within previous historiography, there has been a tendency to look at American abolitionism as composed largely of white men who promoted moral suasion on the one hand and paternalism on the other. Slavery has been generalized as a "white man's burden" to eradicate evil. This notion presents a myopic view of history in which the struggle of black men and women is erased from the quest for freedom. Sinha rightly observes, "The roots of black abolitionist historiography that dealt with the growth of black radical tradition and African American's intellectual engagement with the problems of slavery and racism lay firmly among black abolitionists themselves."[19] With their contributions, America was forced to face the rights of black people as a national priority for the first time.

The Influence of Black Abolitionists Over Time

Additionally, *Force and Freedom* has larger implications for understanding social and political movements across time. Abolitionists expanded how people understood human rights. Reforms in the realms of, but not limited to, gender, labor, capital, citizenship, criminality, empire, and nation all owe a debt to the efforts and tactics that abolitionists championed. In the long trajectory of black freedom struggles, black abolitionists remain the standard by which scholars have examined the Civil Rights movement, the Black Power movement, and even Black Lives Matter.[20] In the twentieth century, we might see similar language concerning the promotion of armed black self-defense in Robert F. Williams's 1962 text, *Negroes with Guns* and his disagreements with the nonviolent strategists of the Civil Rights movement. Much like the David Walker of his time, Williams's remarks and writing were largely rejected, but that does not lessen the fact that black activists have always understood violence politically and rhetorically. In fact, in 1968, Martin Luther King Jr. gave a speech entitled "The Other America," in which he declared, "A riot is the language of the unheard."[21] Though King remained committed to "militant, powerful, massive, non-violence as the most potent weapon" in the struggle for justice and freedom, he also remained empathetic to the struggle for survival facing black people in the United States. He explained how oppressive conditions left individuals with few alternatives. Meanwhile, engaging in violent rebellions was the fastest way to generate a response to their oppression. To this day, riots, rebellion, and violence serve as usable a past for historians. Riots are public. Riots are chaotic. Riots have a way of magnifying not merely flaws in the system but also the strength of those in opposition.

From the beginning of the antislavery movement, abolitionists understood this concept well. The ideological stance in the writings and speeches of the antislavery activists William Wells Brown, Maria Stewart, Charles Remond, and Mary Shadd Cary, to name a few, could just as easily have been sentiments echoed by contemporary civil rights leaders a hundred years later. The phrase "freedom now" was never more urgent than in the decades leading up to the Civil War. The radical nature of the abolitionist movement was apparent, and referring to someone as an "abolitionist" was tantamount to labeling someone a Communist in the 1950s. Likewise, it is difficult to understand contemporary social movements without acknowledging the framework early black reformers provided.

Moving chronologically, each chapter of *Force and Freedom* addresses the critical buildup to the Civil War and the pivotal circumstances that influenced political violence. Chapter 1 examines the limitations of nonviolence by charting the rise and decline of moral suasion and Garrisonian nonresistance in the 1830s and 1840s, as well as the circumstances that led black abolitionists to become frustrated with moral suasion. Chapter 2 begins with a description of the much-deplored Fugitive Slave Law and the factors that led many black Americans to choose "fight or flight" in the face of slave catchers. Aside from invigorating a waning antislavery movement, the Fugitive Slave Law's greatest contribution was its ability to accelerate antebellum political violence, particularly in Boston, New York, and the border state of Pennsylvania, among other locales. Chapter 3 spans the years of the Kansas-Nebraska Act and the Dred Scott Supreme Court case and addresses the political struggles black abolitionists endured while trying to implement aggressive strategies of force and political violence. Chapter 4 explores John Brown's raid on Harpers Ferry and black involvement in the ill-fated campaign. While the biographical works on Brown are too numerous to count, little work has been conducted regarding the powerful and subversive ways African Americans influenced and invested in Brown's attempt to bring about radical change. The fifth and final chapter highlights black abolitionist responses on the eve of the Civil War. National partisanship proved to be one of the greatest factors in determining the pace at which abolitionists pushed for reform, and in many ways it foreshadowed the war. Both free and enslaved black Americans exerted a powerful influence on the social and political landscape in the period leading up to the Civil War and forever altered the trajectory of American history and American protest movements.

*   *   *

When the black abolitionist and minister Joshua Easton spoke at a Massachusetts Anti-Slavery Society meeting in 1837, he declared, "Abolitionists may attack slaveholding, but there is a danger still that the spirit of slavery will survive, in the form of prejudice, after the system is overturned. Our warfare ought not to be against slavery alone, but against the spirit which makes color a mark of degradation."[22] While black reformers continually regarded emancipation as a starting point, for many the core of white supremacy was not chattel slavery, but antiblackness. Combating the political, economic, and social power of white people meant overturning the system that required the degradation of black people and the promotion of whiteness. To this day, Easton's warning feels timely.

If those in power can speak a language based only on the philosophy of force, then the acquisition of equal rights will always require rethinking nonviolence. In some ways, McCune Smith's words were prophetic: black men and women in the United States won their freedom with their own hands. They stole away themselves and their loved ones, physically fought against their enemies, and lost many battles, but they won the war. Some gave the ultimate sacrifice, only finding freedom through death. They continually proved their own humanity in the face of a barbaric system. However, McCune Smith's final proclamation proved shortsighted. He believed that after

DR. JAMES McCUNE SMITH,
First regularly-educated Colored Physician in the United
States. (See page 325.)

Figure 1. "Dr. James McCune Smith, first regularly-educated colored physician in the United States." Courtesy of the Manuscripts, Archives, and Rare Books Division, Schomburg Center for Research in Black Culture, New York Public Library.

black people gave their enemies a good fight, white Americans would "hug us as men and brethren."[23] He called this brutish reconciliation a "holy love of human brotherhood which fills our hearts and fires our imagination." While, in the end, North and South were reunited as one, white Northerners and Southerners extended a hand of holy love and human brotherhood only to each other. Black Americans were never welcomed into this family. In freedoms won and in freedoms given, the day of "holy love of human brotherhood" has not yet arrived.

CHAPTER 1

Forcing Freedom

The Limits of Moral Suasion

No oppressed people have ever secured their liberty without resistance.
—Henry Highland Garnet

The success of the Haitian Revolution convinced black abolitionists that the ending of slavery would entail a revolution and that revolutions entailed violence. Thus, antebellum history is replete with examples of black Americans inspired by the newly liberated and independent Haiti. In 1800, a slave named Gabriel living in Richmond, Virginia, planned a bold conspiracy against slave owners in collaboration with both white and black Americans. His plan is often cited as an attempt to replicate the events that brought down slavery in Saint-Domingue.[1] However, Gabriel's plot was discovered and foiled, leading to mass executions. In 1811, Charles Deslondes, a former overseer and a free mulatto from Saint-Domingue, led hundreds of slaves living in the German Coast (a region located above New Orleans and on the east side of the Mississippi River) to revolt in one of the largest slave rebellions in American history. Donning their planter's military uniforms, leaders of the rebellion mounted horses and marched militia-style to convey authority. It is estimated that between two hundred and five hundred slaves were involved in the German Coast rebellion. The revolt was overthrown in its infancy and ended with its leaders and accomplices decapitated. The rebels' heads were mounted on stakes along the road leading into New Orleans as a warning to stave off potential uprisings.[2] In 1822, Denmark Vesey, an African American who had lived for a short time in Saint-Domingue, plotted another slave insurrection, this time in Charleston, South Carolina. Although Vesey reportedly had promised his followers the help of Haitian soldiers once they had overthrown the city of Charleston, the alleged rebellion was thwarted before it could take place. While these rebellions failed, what remains important was the choice to use orchestrated violence to overthrow slavery. In each instance, the enslaved believed violence was the most strategic tool to combatting their oppression.[3]

The rebellious climate created by the American and Haitian revolutions coupled with republican ideology provided enslaved and free African Americans with a sense of optimism that was unprecedented.[4] Black abolitionists looked to the examples of violence against the enslaved inflicted by white American forefathers and of black Haitians who used violence to liberate their nation. They saw violence as a legitimate response to the institution of slavery and as a pathway to liberation. This view runs contrary to past historiography that argues that the politicization of black abolitionists has more to do with the American Colonization Society (ACS; a group interested in sending black Americans back to African colonies established in Liberia and Sierra Leone). However, this argument is not only incomplete but continually places black leadership outside of the intellectual, ideological, and tactical debates regarding abolition and plans for their own enfranchisement.[5] In many ways, the ACS was created in response to free black Americans, black resistance and rebellion, and the failure of abolition to spread beyond New York and Pennsylvania.[6]

Tactics regarding abolition were constantly being contested by black leaders, especially when it came to the idea of moral suasion. Persuading a slave society of the evils of bondage was one thing; not responding to that evil with violence felt counterintuitive. For black abolitionists, pacifism was too restrictive. Nonresistance would not and could not restore the humanity of black Americans alone, which alongside abolishing slavery, was the central goal of black Americans. For some, political and violent force was required. How else might white Southerners and Northerners see black people as people, if not by force? Although the American slave rebellions of the early 1800s were foiled or failed, the success of the Haitian Revolution rendered white supremacy vulnerable and thereby surmountable. Among black abolitionists, all roads pointed toward the island of Haiti and the call for America to live up to its principle of all men created equal. The success of the Haitian Revolution also proved that a black revolutionary tradition existed and was deeply rooted both inside and outside the United States.[7]

William Lloyd Garrison was the founder of the New England Anti-Slavery Society and the American Anti-Slavery Society. As a white abolitionist, Garrison's brand of nonresistance was continually challenged by incidents of white-on-black violence and in turn created disenchantment among black leaders who no longer saw Garrison's form of agitation as effective or exhaustive. What became most important for black abolitionists was the need to contest methods that proved ineffective. Accordingly, the early years of the abolitionist movement questions the utility and limits of moral suasion. The ideological weapons of black leadership during the first two decades of the movement were clearly demonstrated through historical precedent, radical rhetoric, and the burgeoning threat of violent resistance. Prior to the turbulent 1850s, the goals of black abolitionists were best illustrated and understood by examining the radical speeches and language used to express discontent and their defensive rationale and reactions to the world around them.

David Walker's Appeal to the Use of Violence

In black abolitionist thought, David Walker's *Appeal* and Henry Highland Garnet's *Address to the Slaves* serve as the bookends to a conflict and conversation long in the making and culminating with their joint publication in 1848. In 1829, two years before Garrison's *Liberator* was founded and four years before the American Anti-Slavery Society became an organization, David Walker was circulating his ideas and vision for ultimate emancipation. Born free in North Carolina, Walker lived for a time in Charleston, South Carolina. While living in Charleston, it is highly probable that he was aware of the Denmark Vesey conspiracy to overthrow slave plantations and was influenced by rebellious sentiments among black Americans. He would have also been cognizant of the events regarding Haiti and the belief that Haiti supported American slave rebellions.[8] Walker likely also knew of Haitian president Jean-Pierre Boyer's attempts to recruit black Americans to emigrate to the island throughout the 1820s.[9] Yet, instead of heading to Haiti, Walker took his ideas north to Boston where in 1825 he opened a used clothing store. From the rebellious climate of the slaveholding South to the organized abolitionist movements of the North, every region in which he lived influenced Walker.[10] He became involved in the African Methodist Episcopal Church and spoke out against colonization. It seemed everything around him propelled him toward activism and abolition through both a political and a spiritual lens. His interactions within Charleston's intricate network of black leaders and ministers connected to local, national, and international happenings were an example of Walker's potential to institute change. In a very short time, Walker became a prominent abolitionist who defended slave rebellions and called for black pride in his writings. In 1829, Walker published his famous *Appeal in IV Articles*. His heavily circulated and widely discussed pamphlet argued that if white Americans were to abolish slavery and change their racist views concerning black inferiority, then black and white Americans could live harmoniously.

Walker understood that violence was employed by white oppressors to maintain slavery and power. Although Walker believed in the legitimacy of political violence to combat oppression, his deepest desire was for reconciliation. The historian Alfred Hunt attests that "Walker was one of the first protesters against slavery to make the point that became the sine qua non of twentieth-century anticolonial leaders such as Franz Fanon: Taking one's own destiny into one's hands was an act of manhood that created self-respect as well as freedom."[11] Walker rationalized violence only as a form of self-defense, a forceful attempt to establish justice and equality.

In his short *Appeal*, Walker referred to Haiti several times; it was known that he had closely followed the events on the island. Undoubtedly, the Haitian Revolution encouraged Walker to contemplate political violence at both the local and national levels. Walker wrote to the enslaved and free black Americans alike to protect themselves from their masters with violence. Keenly aware of the injustice and hypocrisy slavery created, Walker urged: "Therefore, if there is an *attempt* made by us, kill or be killed. Now, I ask you, had you not rather be killed than to be a slave to a tyrant, who takes the life of your mother, wife, and dear little children? Look upon your mother, wife and children, and answer God Almighty; and believe this, that it is no more harm for you to kill a man, who is trying to kill you, than it is for you to take a drink of water when thirsty."[12] Walker posed the following question to the enslaved: "Are we MEN!!—I ask you, O my brethren! are we MEN?" This gendered appeal stands in stark contrast to the nonthreatening abolitionist slogan "Am I not a Brother?" portraying a shackled black man pleading for his liberation. Walker called for white Americans to see black humanity as a form of manliness and for the enslaved to be motivated by manliness as a justification for self-defense. He assured his readers that the Lord would provide them a leader the like of Hannibal and of Toussaint in Haiti, and advised them to read the history of Haiti. He added that he did not need to refer to antiquity for a story of freedom; he needed only reference the "glory of the blacks and terror of tyrants" in Haiti. This precedent, he wrote, would be enough to convince the most "avaricious and stupid of wretches." Walker never minced words.[13]

The historian Peter Hinks rehabilitates Walker from scholars who portrayed Walker's calls for violence as atypical from his moral-suasionist abolitionist peers. Hinks understands Walker's *Appeal* as a platform for social uplift and as a necessary sophisticated analysis of last resorts. For Walker, when all other means had been exhausted to maintain one's family or well-being, the oppressed had an obligation to defend themselves as best they could. Walker represented the values, beliefs, and aspirations of a band of black reformers in the late 1820s who were outraged by the persistence of slavery and believed that violent resistance should not be excluded to end it.[14] Empowerment and increased political awareness was the essence of the *Appeal*.

Walker's rationale is best explained as a reiteration of liberal-republican ideology coupled with evangelical principles. He too, had co-opted the principles of the Founding Fathers' ideology and employed it to defend his inalienable rights as a person, and in particular as a Christian. In addition, it was Southerners like Walker who brought to the North a clear notion that armed black resistance founded on the word of God and on the underground organizational structures already existing by many enslaved people was possible. In the 1820s, he represented a new generation of black political leaders who possessed a broad-based commitment to social uplift and enfranchisement. That commitment could not be separated from the desire to do away with racist institutions and perceptions built on denying access and equality for black people.[15]

Walker's words were circulated up and down the Eastern Seaboard and as far west as New Orleans. While it has been suggested that Walker had pamphlets sewn into the lining of the clothes he sold from his shop, he more likely utilized the intricate network of black sailors in port cities who transported goods and ideas from town to town. Free, literate, and mobile black Americans had the greatest impact in getting the word to the enslaved and other free black communities. The words were intended to be read out loud to enable literate ministers, mobile black laborers, and black seamen to disseminate the message to large groups. A Boston newspaper claimed, "Since the publication of that flagitious pamphlet . . . we have noticed a marked difference in the deportment of our colored population. It is evident they have this pamphlet, nay, *we know* that the larger portion of them have read it, or *heard* it read, and that they glory in its principles, as if it were a star in the east, guiding them to freedom and emancipation."[16] The pamphlet acted in concert with an insurrectionist spirit that could direct black Northerners and Southerners. The white abolitionist and minister Samuel J. May exclaimed, "The excitement which had become so general and so furious against the Abolitionists throughout the slaveholding States was owing in no small measure to . . . David Walker."[17] As a result, legislatures as far away as Louisiana tightened literacy laws.

A little over a year after the publication of the pamphlet, Walker was a marked man. In the South, Walker had a hefty bounty on his head, wanted dead or alive by slaveholders. And, by June 28, 1830 the thirty-three-year-old was dead. Scholars are not clear as to what led to Walker's death. Many suspected poisoning, due to the large rewards offered by Southern slaveholders for his murder, but the most likely conclusion was lung fever, of which his daughter had died a week prior. According to the *Boston Daily Courier*, seven people in the city had died all in the same week to lung complications.[18] Nevertheless, the death of Walker did not curb the spirit for reform among abolitionists and the enslaved. In Boston, another newspaper, the *Liberator*, was finding its own voice and hoping to expand upon and beyond Walker's ideas, primarily by using moral suasion to put nonviolence at the forefront of the abolitionist agenda.

Garrison's Liberator: The Moral Argument

At the start of a new year, January 1, 1831, the white abolitionist William Lloyd Garrison began publishing his own weekly abolitionist newspaper, the *Liberator*. Later that year, Garrison founded the New England Anti-Slavery Society. The next year, he cofounded the American Anti-Slavery Society. Born in Newburyport, Massachusetts, Garrison became involved in the abolitionist movement at twenty-five years of age. He began a short stint working with the American Colonization movement but quickly rejected the views of an organization whose sole purpose was to send black Americans "back" to Africa. He then moved to Baltimore, where he wrote for Benjamin Lundy's publication the *Genius of Universal Emancipation* but eventually left and returned to Boston to start his own paper. Garrison kept the need for immediate abolition at the forefront of his agenda, rejecting too the gradualist approach that supported emancipation somewhere in the unforeseeable future and likely culminated with indentured servitude. Running his own newspaper allowed Garrison to distribute a militant tone and to argue in favor of immediate emancipation.

In addition to being an abolitionist, Garrison was a pacifist. His tactics of moral suasion established the notion that immediate emancipation could be achieved by convincing Americans of the sinfulness of slavery. Moral suasion was intended to appeal to the conscience and compel one to repentance, particularly in the wake of the second Great Awakening. The notion of nonviolence cannot be separated from its Quaker influence on the abolitionist movement. Garrison believed in pacifism; on religious grounds he was wholly opposed to violence. The American Anti-Slavery Society officially stated in its Declaration of Sentiments that "carnal weapons for the deliverance from bondage" either by the enslaved or by one acting on behalf of the enslaved was unacceptable. Furthermore, if moral suasion was an offensive position, then nonresistance was a defensive tactic. Nonresistants were strict pacifists and staunchly religious; they renounced all resorts to violence and war. The coupling of these principles promoted by Garrison instructed members to fight moral corruption with moral truth. It was believed that together moral suasion and nonresistance could effectively abolish slavery.

Though Garrison was a pacifist, he never disparaged Walker; he catered to the attentive audiences of black Americans Walker had cultivated with his pamphlet. Courting the base of supportive readers was essential for survival, particularly the survival of a press. Garrison's stance against colonization and his call for social reform appealed to black readers, who made up the bulk of his subscribers. In the first five months of his paper's existence, nearly all five hundred readers of the *Liberator* were African American. By 1834, black readers made up three-fourths of the twenty-three hundred subscribers and over a dozen black agents who delivered the paper. The *Liberator* was just as much black America's as it was Garrison's. Even Garrison lauded that the paper "belongs especially to the people of color—it is their organ."[19]

Unfortunately, as was the case for Walker, Garrison's activism and radical sentiments often placed him in danger. Once he issued his newspaper, Georgia offered $5,000 to anyone who would capture and carry Garrison to the state for trial. Many Southern states had passed laws preventing the circulation of "incendiary" abolitionist literature. He faced ridicule, threats, and mobs, yet he remained a staunch proponent of turning the other cheek in the face of opposition. For Garrison, nonresistance was about condemning the use of violent force in war and even self-defense. In 1833, Garrison wrote part of the constitution of the American Anti-Slavery Society, in which he included a clause that rejected any use of violence, claiming, "Ours forbids the doing of evil that good may come, and lead us to reject, and to entreat the oppressed to reject, the use of carnal weapons for deliverance from bondage; relying solely upon those which are spiritual, and mighty through God to the pulling down of strong bonds." He explained his firm belief in moral suasion by giving his own call and response, asking, "What is able to overthrow the present system of slavery?" and answering, "An enlightened, consolidated, and wisely-directed *public opinion.*" He asked and answered again: "How this shall be secured? By disseminating LIGHT—by preaching the TRUTH. For this purpose we established *The Liberator,* as a medium though which LIGHT and TRUTH might obtain a wide circulation."[20] Some abolitionists believed that they could elevate the human race by pleading for Christian and moral duty and that their cry for justice would eventually be heard. For Garrison, the means and ends of American abolition were rooted in Christian principles.

In 1835, the American Anti-Slavery Society issued a statement promising not to give the "slightest aid to slave insurrections." The group claimed that if they could reach the enslaved, "they would advise them to be quiet and peaceful."[21] Abolitionists supported the model of peaceful British emancipation in the West Indies, even though rebellion had been the primary catalyst for emancipation. The Baptist War was the largest and most violent slave rebellion in Jamaican history. With Jamaica as the crown jewel of the British Empire in the Caribbean, no one wanted to be Haiti.[22] As much as white abolitionists attempted to avoid violence, many were beginning to see what the enslaved and black abolitionists already understood: slavery begets violence. And the American South had no desire to follow the model of the British Empire.

The historian Aileen Kraditor argues that Garrison "distinguished between principles, which must never be compromised, and policy, which to serve principle must be flexible." She adds that "the common ground of the Garrisonians was the belief that the antislavery platform must be kept broad enough to hold abolitionists of all varieties so long as they agreed that slavery was sinful and must be immediately abandoned." Kraditor contends that in the seventeen years from 1834 to 1850, the majority of the tactical problems of the abolitionist movement could be broken into ideologies that were both supported and refuted by various leaders, particularly among black abolitionists.[23] The practice of self-defense and violence and its utility was constantly questioned. It was during these formative years that the expectations of the abolitionist movement solidified into what it would become for black and white activists.

In March of 1831, at a meeting in Philadelphia, the black abolitionist leaders Frederick A. Hinton, William Whipper, and James Cornish resolved that they were "cheerfully" in accord with the views and sentiments of Garrison. They promised to give dignified support to his paper and to "exercise every means in our power to give them [Garrison's ideas] a more extensive circulation." While critics charged Garrison with fanaticism, black abolitionists praised Garrison's "efficient and unwavering advocacy of human rights." They added, "While such fanaticism breathes the spirit of truth, honesty, and justice, may it be our lot to be cast in its precious mould."[24] For the first time, the black community had an ally that was not pushing colonization or a gradual approach to emancipation. While Walker's *Appeal* grounded black leaders' ideological framework, Garrison was hoping to develop their practices. Abolitionists understood that the reformer's job was to make the truth widely known and that public opinion would do the rest.[25] Garrison firmly believed that people could be persuaded to abolish slavery through nonresistance and moral suasion.

Such leaders encouraged enslaved people to be patient. In 1835, the Massachusetts Antislavery Society affirmed that the enslaved would be redeemed "by the patient endurance in their wrongs . . . the slaves will hasten the day of their peaceful deliverance from the yoke of bondage . . . whereas by violent and bloody measures they will prolong their servitude, and expose themselves to destruction."[26] Moral suasion was intended to make the slave owner fear not the enslaved, but God. Furthermore, abolitionists appealed not only to the slave owner, but to the nation, imploring its people to turn from their offensive and grievous ways. In a letter to the *Liberator*, one abolitionist wrote that a just God had declared vengeance was His and wondered how slave owners could pretend that the pain they had caused Africans would not result in divine retribution.[27]

Certain that God would administer judgment for the sins of slavery, black abolitionists endeavored to convince the ministers and elders of churches to adopt the cause of perseverance and moral reform. They believed that if they trained undisciplined youth in moral pursuits, then they would be able to convince people everywhere that true happiness comes through moral elevation.[28] Patience, long-suffering, and an appeal to the sensible and moral self lay at the foundation of these abolitionists. In many ways, emancipation was a religious experience: full confirmation of the goodness of man's potential, if he would but right his wrongs. The abolitionist newspaper the *National Enquirer* echoed such sentiments. The paper called upon its readers to "endeavor to enlist the sympathies and benevolence of the Christian, moral, and political world. Without regard to creeds, we shall only ask for the fulfillment of Christian duty, as the surest method of extending righteousness and justice." The newspaper made it clear that it intended to procure the abolition of slavery and racism. The *National Enquirer* selected valuable subjects for rallying points: education, temperance, economy, and universal liberty. The editor's hope was to have his readers, in theory and practice, become thoroughly acquainted with these subjects in preparation for future action.[29] These values and the accompanying moralism fed into Americans' optimistic belief in improvement and empowerment.

The reason for the embrace of Garrison's principles over Walker's forceful resistance by black leadership was simple: practicality. If a movement of black and white abolitionists was to be successful, compromise was paramount. Black leaders were willing to set aside violence for white abolitionists who were willing to set aside colonization. Moral reform appealed to black activists because it appealed to their white allies, who had only recently taken up the stance of immediacy in regard to abolishing slavery. Looking back on the movement, in 1846, black Bostonian leaders acknowledged, "We had good enough doctrine before Garrison, but we wanted a good example" to present to white audiences.[30] Other black leaders concluded that moral suasion promoted peace and harmony "as a measure necessary to aid in effecting the total abolition of slavery."[31] Black abolitionists contended they would advocate for the cause of peace, "believing that whatever tends to the destruction of human life, is at variance with the precepts of the Gospel, and at enmity with the well being of individuals as well as society."[32] In other words, in order to be successful, abolitionist principles had to be aligned with biblical principles because no one would question the authority of the Bible. Perhaps more than anything, black leadership was happy to have allies who supported them. If their tactics proved successful, then violence could be left out of the conversation Walker facilitated just a few years ago.

Weighing Moral Suasion and Violence
as Abolitionists' Tools

As patience became part of the platform, some leaders argued that in the face of oppression, patience was not a virtue but a vice. Dr. Franklin, a patron of the *Liberator*, wrote the following in a letter to the editor in 1831: "There are ways to try men's patience; and I say that treading on the toes of human creatures with sharp instruments, and searing their bodies with hot irons, for centuries, it cannot be expected that they will exhibit the submission of Job."[33] Along similar lines, in 1831, "A colored Philadelphian" wrote to the *Liberator*: "When we take a retrospective view of things, and hear of almost every nation fighting for its liberty, is it to be expected that the African race will continue always in the degraded state they now are? No. The time is fast approaching when the words 'Fight for liberty, or die in the attempt,' will be sounded by every African ear throughout the world."[34] His and Franklin's observations proved correct.

On August 21, 1831, Nat Turner's rebellion in Southampton County, Virginia, sent shock waves throughout the country. Turner originally planned his own rebellion to begin on July 4, an ironic selection given the national holiday. But due to illness, Turner pushed the date back. Turner was intelligent, literate, and highly religious. He spoke of visions he received and believed his actions were divine and intended by God. The day of the rebellion and on his orders, a group of fellow slaves traveled from plantation to plantation with instructions to kill all of the white people. The rebelling slaves killed slave masters and their families with hatchets, axes, knives, and other blunt objects instead of firearms so as not attract others to their attention. When Turner and his brigade of slaves finally met resistance from white militia, they had already slain sixty white men, women, and children. The rebels saw their violence as just compensation for the oppression they had endured. Their violence was more than an act of defiance; it was retribution and revolution. It took two days to stop the rebellion and, astonishingly, Turner escaped. He remained on the run for months before he was captured. He was tried, convicted, and sentenced to death by the authorities. In the aftermath of the rebellion, the local militias killed three free black people and more than a hundred enslaved persons, some by lynching. Turner's rebellion recognized and used the principles of force to achieve freedom, and black abolitionists did not fail to notice his impact on African American resistance to slavery. The rebellion echoed the fear and brutality white planters and their families experienced during Haiti's revolution.

In response to Turner's rebellion, an unknown black man wrote a letter to the *Liberator*. He wanted to see slavery abolished without bloodshed and abhorred the thought of a Saint-Domingue-like uprising. His hope, then, was that the white people of the United States would have an epiphany, as had the Egyptians who imprisoned the Israelites, and in the face of past rebellions and rumors realize that it was in their best interest to let the slaves go free. The unidentified man sincerely hoped that the impetus of truth and moral suasion would be sufficient to assist the great work of human rights, without the use of force and with an active faith in the goodness of men's hearts.[35]

Another article in the *Liberator*, titled "Causes of Slave Insurrections," stated that such rebellions were inevitable wherever men were held in bondage. It was basically a matter of human nature: "Negroes, like other men, have a spirit which rebels against tyranny and oppression."[36] Though Turner's insurrection failed, its impact was powerful. Even Garrison believed Turner's justification was no different than that of "our [fore]fathers in slaughtering the British."[37] If the Founding Fathers could commence a revolution against Great Britain for what appeared to the abolitionists to be superficial reasons, surely the enslaved could rise up against real oppression and the tyranny of American slavery. He claimed also that it was indeed Haiti—and not the United States—that lived up to the principles of freedom and liberty for all. While Garrison contended that the slaves had every right to revolt, however, he made it clear that he took no part in their revolts, and specifically in Turner's revolt. Despite his empathy for the enslaved, he refused to concede that political violence was the solution.[38] Garrison feared slave rebellions would only create more burdens for the enslaved, such as violent backlash, increased sales (spurring the breakup of families), and tighter restrictions, particularly because the revolts had a propensity to fail. It was impossible for successful rebellion in America to look like that in Haiti. Moreover, as a staunch supporter of nonviolence, he did not desire to emancipate slaves at the expense of the planters' safety. At a National Negro Convention Garrison exclaimed, "I believe you [black Americans] have stronger reasons for dreading a Southern insurrection than the whites themselves."[39] In other words, Garrison knew, as did all black Americans, that the repercussions of slave rebellions were harsh and extreme. Rebellions entailed risks that most African Americans were simply not willing to take, particularly those living in relative freedom.

While moral suasion was intended to persuade slaveholders of their wrongs, it often appeared that Garrison was also pleading more with black Americans to be persuaded against retaliation. In the first edition of the *Liberator*, Samuel J. May argued that Garrison had repudiated violence "as wrong in principle and disastrous in policy." Garrison's opinions on this point were generally embraced by his followers and explicitly declared by the American Anti-Slavery Society, which stated in 1833 that people of the South and North should be assured of the organization's pacific principles. According to May, Garrison claimed, "We hoped to abolish the institution of slavery by convinilcing [sic] slaveholders and their abettors of the exceeding wickedness of the system." They had sent letters and pamphlets to Southern friends, minsters, and political officials they knew. However, Garrison specifically claimed that "in no case did we send our publications to slaves."[40] In contrast, the genius of Walker's *Appeal* is that it spoke directly to the enslaved and white Americans simultaneously. In the spirit of preventing violence, white abolitionists were neglecting the very base upon which their campaign was built.

Like many African Americans, the abolitionist Joseph C. Holly, older brother of the emigrationist James Theodore Holly, embodied the diversity and complex nature of black abolitionism. He was born to free parents in Washington, DC, settled in Brooklyn, New York, and became a shoemaker. In many ways, Holly was the quintessential activist: he gave speeches for the American Anti-Slavery Society and lectured independently, he confronted the issue of racism with the same fervor with which he combated slavery, he endorsed black newspapers, he assisted fugitive slaves, and he helped to free black families from slavery by raising money for their purchase. Holly took a strong ideological stance toward making sure black Americans secured their own uplift, but he also encouraged the help of white allies to aid in black employment. Holly supported Garrisonian principles but also supported political abolitionists, those who sought to use the government and politics to accelerate changes for the movement. Holly did not see moral suasion and reverence for Toussaint Louverture, Nat Turner, and the defense of slave violence as mutually exclusive.[41] Among black and white abolitionists, the subject of slave revolts had become a divisive topic. Most abolitionist leaders opposed advocating slave rebellions like Turner's, but Holly could not be persuaded to abandon the pivotal events that shaped black radical thought. Many black leaders thought moral suasion and defense were not completely irreconcilable; one could value both principles as offensive and defensive tactics against proponents of slavery. Violence and self-defense might have been options of last resort, but they were always an option. Holly was nothing if not pragmatic.

Violence Rises in the Face of Moral Suasion

Nat Turner's violent slave rebellion in Southampton, Virginia, ushered in the tumultuous 1830s. The abolitionists' "peace principles" were severely tested during the great "mob years" of anti-abolitionist campaigns. During a ten-year period, cities erupted in violence across the country. The rise is crime and mob violence was brought on by a number of factors, such as the increased growth of urban cities; an insurgence of foreign immigration, which spurred bitter ethnic and religious tensions; and the burgeoning abolitionist movement, which fed racist anti-negro sentiments.[42] For example, in 1834 in New York City, the white abolitionist Lewis Tappan fled the city with his family under threats of attack. Upon finding his home empty, rioters removed Tappan's furniture and set it on fire. For free black Americans, the violence was worse. Their homes and churches were often demolished or set on fire. The African-American Episcopal priest Peter Williams Jr.'s home was severely damaged and his place of worship, St. Philip's African Episcopal Church, was completely destroyed.[43] The lists go on: there were at least 115 incidents of mob attacks against free black Americans and abolitionists during the 1830s. This is an astounding shift considering there were only 21 recorded incidents in the 1820s and just 7 violent confrontations in the 1810s.

Nothing was more difficult than to adhere to nonviolence in the face of an angry mob. In all sections of the country, abolitionists found themselves subjected to bitter, and sometimes injurious, physical attack. The riots made the 1830s the most violent decade prior to the Civil War. In many cases the underlying causes for these riots were racism and the idea that abolitionists sought miscegenation, the greatest fear of anti-abolitionists. The terror evoked by the thought of mixing the races resulted in the targeting and lynching of many black men, as anti-abolitionists sought to preserve the status quo.[44] The 1830s also saw widespread mob violence against abolitionists and African Americans in the North, as social and political struggles over slavery began to dominate the nation. Despite the many attacks suffered by both African Americans and white abolitionists, a correspondent who wrote for the *Liberator* proclaimed, "Among the friends of moral reform . . . the belief is prevailing more and more that our Saviour meant to inculcate the doctrine of never fighting in self-defense."[45] For Garrison, pacifism was not only strategic—it was Christ-like. In nearly every case of anti-abolitionist violence, the response of the abolitionists was nonviolent.[46]

However, African Americans realized that they were the most vulnerable to the brunt of proslavery violence. Pacifism may have been Christlike, but in the face of mob it was also a sure path to martyrdom. Black schools were burned down. Black businesses were destroyed. In October of 1834, anti-abolitionist rioting destroyed forty-five homes in Philadelphia's black community. Moral suasionist ideology weakened as proslavery violence became more intense, particularly in cities hard hit by anti-abolitionist mobs, such as Philadelphia, New York, and Boston. Black leaders began to place more emphasis on the values of self-defense than of morality. Protecting one's livelihood for self-improvement trumped turning the other cheek in the face of a burning business. Other abolitionists, who could not bring themselves to persuade audiences to embrace peace, remembered Walker's radical sentiments and sought to intimidate with the memories of rebellion.

Influenced by Walker, Maria Stewart was a schoolteacher and public speaker living in Boston. She was the first African American woman to lecture on women's rights and served as a contributor to the *Liberator*. Stewart was also the first black woman to publicly acknowledge and echo the sentiments of Walker's *Appeal*. She declared, "African rights and liberty is a subject that ought to fire the breast of every free man of color in these United States, and excite in his bosom a lively, deep, decided, and heart-felt interest."[47] Stewart posed the question, "where are the names of our illustrious ones?" Stewart acknowledged that she could point to a list of white heroes, but where were the heroes in the black community? She called on black leadership to take a more aggressive stance. For Stewart, progress was not merely about recognizing black heroes but also of making sure their ideals and contributions were carried out by succeeding generations. In 1835, she issued a rallying cry to black Americans: "Far be it from me to recommend to you, either to kill, burn, or destroy. But improve yourselves, express yourselves, rise!" Stewart was instructing black people to take matters into their own hands for advancement and protection. For an African American woman to use the words "kill, burn, destroy" in a speech was quite radical, perhaps unprecedented. Stewart's purpose was to echo Walker—"Though Walker sleeps, yet he lives and his name shall be had in ever-lasting remembrance." She concluded that she was enlisted in holy warfare and that she intended to fight until her voice expired in death.[48] Stewart recognized the consequences of political violence and believed many would inevitably suffer for pleading the cause of oppressed black people. Without hesitation, she boldly declared, "And I shall glory in being one of her martyrs."[49] Defense of black rights would not be left up to men alone. When it came to self-determination and enfranchisement, freedom was not gendered. Stewart saw herself as much a part of Walker's vision as any black man. When and if the enslaved and free black Americans would rise up, it would undoubtedly include both men and women.

Nevertheless, white abolitionists continued to underestimate how much of an impact black radical leadership had on black thinking. In 1835, white abolitionists held a public debate in Boston on the question "would the slaves be justified in resorting to physical violence to obtain their freedom?" The debate likely stemmed from a growing conversation about the utility of force and violence among black activists and followers. The combative atmosphere in which abolitionists often found themselves compelled them to consider violence at the very least on behalf of the enslaved; never mind that the enslaved did not need permission or affirmation from abolitionists to rebel. The *Liberator* reported on the gathering, at which Reverend Samuel May opened the debate by arguing for the negative. "According to the dictates of unenlightened and unsanctified human nature," May claimed, the enslaved would be justified in attempting violently to liberate themselves in secular terms. However, according to May, the principles of the Gospel and the precepts of Jesus Christ did not allow the enslaved to resort to violence. May continued, "The spirit of the Gospel is one of forbearance, of long suffering, of forgiveness." The rest of the meeting's attendees seemed to be of one accord. They believed slave rebellions could be justified but simultaneously saw rebellion as immoral. These were sentiments developed by men who had never been enslaved or experienced the harsh reality of such a life. The very debate stemmed from a place of privilege never afforded to black Americans. Nevertheless, the attendees were so fully in agreement it appeared that the question at hand was not a topic worth debating, until a man known as Mr. Weeks began to argue in favor of the enslaved's resorting to physical violence. While little is known of Mr. Weeks, the *Liberator* claimed that the gathering rebuked him unanimously for his suggestion.[50] If white leadership was unwilling to envision black violence, how would they respond to white abolitionists who considered taking up arms in self-defense? It was not long before they too would face with their own mortality in the face of a mob.

Fighting Words and the Murder of Elijah Lovejoy

In the summer of 1835, Southern states passed laws to keep antislavery petitions and literature out of slave territory. Additionally, the South instituted
the "gag rule," which prohibited antislavery discussions from taking place in
Congress from 1835 to 1844. After Walker and Nat Turner, rhetoric likely to
incite slave rebellion (and proslavery violence) was just as much a threat as a
slave rebellion. And, if language was a weapon, then the white abolitionist
and Presbyterian minister Elijah Lovejoy's printing press was an arsenal. Living in Alton, Illinois, proslavery mobs destroyed four of Lovejoy's printing
presses. Lovejoy admitted in the *Liberator* that "a loaded musket is standing
at my bedside, while my two brothers, in an adjoining room, have *three others*, together with *pistols, cartridges,* etc." Lovejoy explained that he had "inex-
pressible reluctance" to engage in violence or resort to self-defense. Yet, after
having lost several printing presses, he understood that there would be no
policing protection for his property. He declared, "There is at present no
safety for me, and no defense in this place either in the laws or the protecting
aegis of public sentiment."[51] When an angry mob set fire to Lovejoy's press on
November 7, 1837, Lovejoy attempted to defend his property and disperse the
mob by threatening to shoot, but before he could, Lovejoy was shot and
killed. The proslavery mob destroyed his press one final time by breaking it
into pieces and throwing it in the river.

As soon as the news of Lovejoy's death spread, white abolitionists and
Garrisonians accused Lovejoy of neglecting Christian principles. William
Goodell, a white abolitionist and founder of the New York State Anti-Slavery
Society, criticized Lovejoy's actions. Goodell believed that the mob would not
have killed Lovejoy if he had not taken up arms. He contended that the entire
episode could have had "a more thrilling and abiding effect" if Lovejoy had
not acted in self-defense—although, perhaps not for Lovejoy. These were the
cowardly laments of a man who could not bring himself to confrontation,
and Goodell admitted he was afraid. He recalled later that he had feared that
abolitionists might be tempted to use violence to defend themselves and produce inevitable bloodshed, "in which the abolitionists would be almost certain to be overpowered."[52] Goodell was not alone in his rejection of Lovejoy's
actions, but it would have been better to accept violence in the form of self-
defense than to accept and tout nonviolence as a shield for impotence.[53]

As a pacifist, Garrison claimed he was "shocked" that Lovejoy, a Presbyterian minister, had taken up arms in self-defense. Because he had resorted to such means, Garrison claimed that while Lovejoy "was certainly a martyr—strictly speaking—he was not . . . a Christian martyr." Garrison's biographer Henry Mayer stresses the importance for the abolitionist leader to maintain Christian ethics as the center of the movement. Just two years earlier, Garrison himself had been attacked by a mob in Boston. The anti-abolitionist mob tied a rope around Garrison's waist and dragged him through the streets of Boston. If given the opportunity, the mob would have surely lynched him, but authorities intervened by placing Garrison in a city jail for his own safety. Garrison had wanted Lovejoy to exert the resolve he had exhibited: nonresistance to the point of death. Presenting the situation through a Garrisonian lens, Mayer asks, "What kind of abolitionist movement could exist if people lauded the printer who died with a rifle in his hands and shunned the printer who upheld the Bible as the standard of government?"[54]

A year after Lovejoy's murder in Alton, black people living in the area found themselves at the mercy of mobs, riots, and individual attacks. Fearful that the violence would continue unchecked, a group of them began to collect arms in the local hall. When members of one mob learned of the collection of arms by the black community, they plotted to attack the hall. A white abolitionist named Thomas Shipley, known for his ability to defuse an altercation, became aware of the mob's plans. Shipley attempted to prevent open violence by meeting with the black people who were gathered in the hall. Because Shipley was known as a friend to the black population, he convinced them not to resort to violence, as doing so would only "increase their trouble." The African Americans aborted their plans and left the hall, but probably not without resolve to take matters into their own hands if the violence persisted. Shipley reported the leaders of the white mob to the authorities and they were arrested.[55] These were the sorts of stories white abolitionists could cite as examples of the strength of nonresistance. But this story also validated the idea that these local black Americans living in Alton were not completely wedded to the notion of nonviolence. What if Shipley had not intervened? Black Americans knew what the consequences of fighting back could mean, but sometimes not responding only left more at stake. The acquiescence to back down from a fight was rarely ever countered with the arrest of white attackers. Shipley's efforts were the exception, not the rule.

The abolition of slavery and the establishment of equality for black people was a dual calling. Black leadership could not have abolition without equality or have equality without abolition, and moral suasion could accomplish neither. The abolitionist Peter Paul Simmons highlighted this important idea in his speech before his black brethren at the African Clarkson Association. He declared, "The basis of the manumission society was to elevate Africans by morals, and this has been formed upwards of a half century, and what has been done? Our people were slaves then and are the same today." He concluded that free black Americans living in the North were no exception: "This northern freedom is nothing but a nickname for northern slavery."[56] The freedom African Americans experienced in the North was nothing like that experienced by their white counterparts. Racial discrimination prevented many black men from obtaining respectable employment and benefiting from Northern economic expansion. Due to large increases in immigration, free black Americans found themselves competing with immigrants for menial jobs that involved little or no skill. While black leadership pushed for equality alongside abolition, the socioeconomic status of many black Americans remained stagnant. Most African Americans were marginalized laborers and largely impoverished.[57] Only a small number of black men could receive an education that would allow them to become lawyers, teachers, physicians, or ministers. Most black women were only able to help sustain their families by working as domestics or housekeepers.

In addition to African Americans' dismal economic opportunities, their chances of obtaining political influence were nearly nonexistent. For example, in New York, black men needed to own $250 worth of property to vote. In 1835, New York City had an estimated black population of 15,061, of which only 86 were eligible to vote. Twenty years later, in 1855, only 100 of the 11,640 black people living in New York City could cast ballots.[58] In 1838, fueled by fear of an increasing black population in their state, Pennsylvania's constitutional convention restricted voting rights to "white" men. In Indiana, Illinois, Iowa, and Oregon, there was no need to discuss the voting rights of black men—because African Americans were prohibited from entering the territory.[59] Ultimately, by excluding black people from the workforce, denying them their voting rights, and alienating free African Americans from American society, Northerners indirectly cultivated black people's forceful resistance.[60] As frustrations grew, black abolitionists began to turn against moral suasion in growing numbers. For them, abolition had to be accompanied by political and economic opportunity. Moral suasion and nonviolence offered no practical benefits. Black abolitionists were prepared to accept any force, including violence, that could provide and institute real change in their political and socioeconomic status.

Thus, black leadership understood that neither nonresistance nor moral suasion addressed black equality and the rights and privileges afforded only to white Americans. Despite Garrison's popular ideology, freedom within the American narrative was perpetually linked to the idea that violence was a virtue when resisting tyranny.[61] Black leaders passed down these ideals from generation to generation and based them on the principles of freedoms taken, not given. Revolutionary liberal and republican values, combined with religious traditions, demonstrated the capacity for black abolitionists to address and combat their current circumstances within their movement.

Practical Abolitionism Allows
Self-Defense and Civil Disobedience

Perhaps few knew more about what was at stake than Lewis W. Woodson, a minister in the AME church who was considered by some as the father of Black Nationalism. As Martin Delany's mentor, Woodson put forth an ideological-pragmatic-spiritual program for the collective elevation of African Americans. As a firm believer in self-determination, Woodson believed that black Americans should take primary responsibility for their own uplift, rather than relying on white Americans or seeking their counsel. He realized that even if slavery were abolished, such victories would be insufficient to alter the political position of black Americans. For his people to succeed, Woodson contended, black people needed to form a collective racial front against exploitation in general.[62] For Woodson, separatism, a movement to form separate political, social, cultural, and spiritual institutions for black people that were perpetually dominated by whites, was a viable alternative for the black community and promoted the transformation necessary for black people's economic prosperity and freedom. He called on African Americans to collectively produce a moral revolution.[63] To do so, black abolitionists would not only have to persuade people of the evils of slavery but also drastically alter their myopic perceptions of black Americans. But first, black leaders needed to turn inward and empower their collective body from within. For example, it was black abolitionists who led the way in Underground Railroad and the successful escapes of fugitive slaves. During his lifetime, David Ruggles, a black antislavery activist, aided more than six hundred African Americans in attaining freedom through the Underground Railroad.[64] Ruggles was responsible for the escape of Frederick Douglass and other prominent black leaders. His model of "practical abolitionism", a term coined by the historian Graham Russell Gao Hodges, advocated civil disobedience and simultaneously enforced self-defense against kidnappers.[65] Ruggles's actions set him apart from nearly all his contemporary abolitionists and foretold of the violent struggles brewing throughout the antebellum period.

Phillip A. Bell, a black journalist and founder of the *Weekly Advocate*, eloquently summarized the ideology of violence, its political language, and the model of Ruggles: "What language shall we adopt in portraying the manly conduct of such characters as reside among us? . . . We hazard nothing when we boldly assert, that there is not a crime of greater magnitude—no enormity more foul, than that of making a Slave of a Freeman among us." For Bell, death was too soft a punishment for slaveholders and slave catchers. Bell was willing to concede a diversity of opinions within the movement, but regarding self-defense, he demanded complete unity. "Imitate the conduct of a Ruggles," he commanded, "and be as one man in the firm and unalterable determination to maintain your just rights, and defend your property and persons against all attacks of men."[66] Bell recognized that the abolitionist movement, despite Garrison's beliefs, could not be separated from its political implications. Nonviolence was not only irrational in light of the African American experience, but it also ran counter to liberal republican values. Bell had a clear sense of black self-determination shaped by his activism and his experience of living in the Northeast. Bell was born to free black parents in New York City and attended the city's Free African Schools. He joined the group that formed the New York *Weekly Advocate*, later renamed the *Colored American*, and became the paper's first General Agent and part-time editor. He also partnered with Samuel Cornish (America's first black editor) while at the paper in writing articles to aid the abolitionist cause.

Simmons also ran in the same circles as Bell and Ruggles and later published works in the *Colored American*. In the same speech he gave before the African Clarkson Association of New York City, he reflected sentiments similar to Bell's and of other black activists who wanted more than moral suasion and moral elevation as a path to freedom and equality. He asked, "Why is it, that we never hear of a physical and a political elevation?" His response was straightforward, because both call for "united strength." For Simmons, physical and political efforts were the only methods left to adopt. Inaction only led to another generation of enslaved people. "No," declared Simmons, "We must show ACTION! ACTION! ACTION!"[67] Simmons clearly understood how abolition could not be separated from political, social, and even economic ideals. Though measures had been taken by Congress to keep the abolition issue at bay, by the 1840s slavery had become deeply political. With Turner's rebellion, the growth of mob violence against black communities, and the murder of Lovejoy, campaigns for nonviolence were collapsing and a once-promising coalition between black and white leaders was in decline, leading to the emergence of an independent movement among marginalized and militant African Americans. Furthermore, the ideological transformations of abolitionists such as Henry Highland Garnet and Frederick Douglass led to significant turning points among black leadership. As these key leaders found empowerment in political violence in ways that nonviolence failed to provide, others sought to follow suit.

Violence Becomes a Necessary Means for Black Abolitionists

Henry Highland Garnet was among those who led the charge against moral suasion and toward political action and self-defense. Many know Garnet for his famous "Address to the Slaves" speech given in 1843. However, Garnet's conversion from moral suasion to revolutionary violence arose from earlier experiences. He was born into slavery in New Market, Maryland, in 1815. When he was almost ten years old, he and his parents escaped. When a slave agent attempted to seize his family in New York City, Garnet's father got away by jumping off a roof, and Garnet armed himself with a knife for constant protection.[68] Nearly ten years later, when slavery ended in New York, black families were eager to have their children educated so they could escape menial labor. Thus, a young Garnet, along with Thomas Sydney and Alexander Crummell (later an abolitionist and minister), were sent from New York to attend the Noyes Academy, an experimental interracial school in Canaan, New Hampshire. The Noyes Academy was established in 1835, and George Kimball, a white abolitionist who helped to build the Congregational Church, was one of its principal founders. Kimball intended the school to be a place for children of all races to attend. The first class was composed of twenty-eight white students and fourteen black students.

However, on August 10, 1835, opponents of interracial education attacked the school. For two days, over three hundred residents wrapped chains around the schoolhouse with the declared intent to "drag the nigger school off its foundation and through town."[69] White men from the surrounding communities used more than ninety oxen to drag the school into the river and eventually set the building's remnants on fire. But destroying the school alone did not seem sufficient. The mob began to fire shots at the students' boardinghouse. It was during this attack that Garnet picked up a shotgun and began to fire back to defend the remaining students and get them to safety. At the time, the black population of New Hampshire was about 607 out of an estimated population of 269,000.[70] Nevertheless, the fear of miscegenation was fixed in the mind of the mob. John Harris, a witness and Noyes trustee, described the assault as "a monument of violence."[71]

Nineteen years old during the Canaan attack, Garnet found the experience to be transformative. The event led him to believe that violence, particularly self-defense, was necessary. Accordingly, when Garnet, at twenty-seven years old, delivered his "Address to the Slaves" at the National Negro Convention in Albany, he spoke from personal experience. The historian Steven H. Shiffrin claims that historians have erroneously portrayed Garnet as having entertained a lifelong commitment to revolutionary violence. Evidence for Shiffrin's position can be seen in a speech Garnet gave to the Massachusetts Liberty Party State Convention in January of 1842, declaring, "I cannot harbor the thought for a moment that . . . [the slaves'] deliverance will be brought about by violence. No; our country will not be so deaf to the cries of the oppressed; so regardless of the commands of God. . . . No, the time for a last stern struggle has not yet come."[72] An article in the *National Reformer*, a newspaper founded by William Whipper (the wealthiest African American of his day and an advocate of nonviolence and racial integration), claimed that Garnet was aware of the importance of nonviolence. Garnet, Whipper asserted, would prefer to see slavery abolished peacefully; however, he had no confidence that the abolitionists would succeed by advocating for their cause on moral grounds.[73] Yet, Shiffrin makes it clear that, while no conclusive evidence can pinpoint what changed Garnet's stance, he believes that Garnet's fugitive slave status and the Supreme Court decision of *Prigg v. Pennsylvania* in 1842, a decision that made it easier for slaveholders to recover runaway slaves, were determining factors in changing Garnet's mind.

In a response to the Prigg decision, Garnet delivered his most famous speech at the National Negro Convention in Buffalo, New York in 1843. His fiery speech not only shocked the delegates in attendance but also marked a turning point in how the abolition of slavery should be approached. Garnet lectured, "Fellow men! Patient sufferers! behold your dearest rights crushed to the earth! See your sons murdered, and your wives, mothers, and sisters doomed to prostitution. In the name of the merciful God, and by all that life is worth, let it no longer be a debatable question whether it is better to choose *Liberty or death*." He followed these remarks by reminding his audience of the heroes they had in Denmark Vesey, Toussaint Louverture, Nat Turner, Joseph Cinque, and Madison Washington, all of whom had fought for black people's freedom through rebellion. Garnet referred to these men as "Patriots" and "Noble men." Assuming that the consequences for ending slavery would have to be violent and charged, he insisted that those who listened would be better off dead than living as slaves; he asserted that a violent course was their only hope, as slavery could not be eradicated without bloodshed.[74] No doubt at the top of his lungs, Garnet voiced the same fiery word three times: "Resistance! Resistance! Resistance!" "No oppressed people," Garnet claimed, "have ever secured their liberty without resistance." In his speech he affirmed, "that the time had come to resort to this course"; that other means had failed, and would fail; that abolitionists, who were very benevolent men, had done about all that they could do; that non-resistance was ridiculous, and not to be thought of, even for the present, by the slaves.[75]

For Garnet, moral suasion and the legal system equivocally failed black Americans. *Prigg vs. Pennsylvania* was a sign that the system was indeed created for the protection of white men only. If the right to freedom could be overturned in Pennsylvania—home of the Quakers and "Brotherly Love"— where else could one be safe? Furthermore, Garnet refused to be condemned by Garrison. "If it has come to this," Garnet replied, "that I must think and act as you do, because you are an abolitionist, or be exterminated by your thunder, then I do not hesitate to say that your abolitionism is abject slavery."[76] Garnet was over having white men dictate his and other African Americans' responses. White leadership could not be trusted to take the movement far enough and fast enough for Garnet. Nevertheless, because Garnet's speech was so radical, fellow black leaders voted on whether it should be published. Frederick Douglass, along with Charles Remond, an early black orator and activist for the movement born free in Massachusetts, represented those who strongly opposed its being published. Douglass contended that although it was acceptable to forward slaves' rights to achieve freedom by force, it was not acceptable for Garnet to claim that force was the only means by which slavery could be eradicated. He continued to argue that the *only* realistic hope for freedom lay in taking the high road rather than using violence.[77]

Interestingly, Garnet's resolution to call for slaves to rebel lost by one vote: nineteen to eighteen delegates. But the close count revealed dissention among the delegates and the weakening of the moral suasion position. The vote was also symbolic of a change of heart within the abolitionist movement. If black abolitionists could come within just one vote of publishing a speech that endorsed slave rebellions, how much closer were they to abandoning moral suasion? Garnet's speech was also effective because it was based on the premise that slavery was so evil it was necessary to resist it on religious grounds, meaning a religious obligation prevented the notion from being dismissed. Shiffrin writes: "To disagree with Garnet's conclusion, an audience which had met to decry slavery would have to say that slavery was not *that* evil. In short, a group of people who prided themselves on being militant activists against slavery would for the first time have to view themselves as moderates."[78] No steadfast abolitionist was willing view himself or herself as conservative in the campaign to abolish slavery.

For six years, from 1843 to 1849, debates between black leadership remained intense. Many saw the Mexican American War (1846–1848) as an attempt to expand slavery and its territory. Thus, an environment of war and violent means never waned. Douglass and Garnet had become rivals over who controlled the dominant voice among black leadership. In an article in the *North Star*, Garnet challenged Douglass openly, exclaiming, "You publish that I have no faith in the use of moral means for the extinction of American slavery. I believe with all my heart in such means—and I believe that political power ought to be used for that end and that when rightly used, it is strictly moral." He added, "I also believe that the slave has a moral right to use his physical power to obtain his liberty—my motto is, give me liberty or give me death. Dare you, Frederick Douglass, say otherwise! Speak plainly—I am 'calling you out.' "[79] Garnet wanted to make it clear that Douglass could not deny the righteousness of self-defense or the republican ideology of the forefathers. Garnet acknowledged that he and Douglass were both born into slavery and suffered greatly from it. He felt Douglass was being at the very least disingenuous to suggest moral suasion as a strategy and was baffled that any former slave would tell people to "bow down to the unreasonable and unnatural dogmas of non-resistance." Then Garnet shared his harshest feelings about the matter: "Whoever the colored fugitive may be that advocates such trash, he is either a coward, a hypocrite, a fool, or a knave." He claimed that someone like Douglass could not be trusted because he was more invested in his own celebrity. "Whenever pressed by the hunger of fame," Garnet quipped, "He would sell a thousand birth-rights for a mess of pottage." It is important to note that while Garnet had trouble getting his speech published, Douglass's first narrative was quite a success. Published in 1845, the first printing sold over 5,000 copies within four months. Subsequently, six more editions were published between 1845 and 1849. Garnet believed that Douglass was compromising not just his beliefs, but black abolitionists' principles for fame. He claimed his values shifted like the "colors of the chameleon", and were as "changeable as the weathercock."[80] Garnet spared Douglass nothing in this critique. What Garnet could dismiss in Garrison as a white man, he abhorred in Douglass.

Black abolitionists such as Woodson and Garnet considered black liberation to be intrinsically connected to political and spiritual redemption. Garnet's "Address to the Slaves" acknowledged that if the enslaved were to free themselves, violence would have to be an integral part of their liberation struggle. The black liberation ideology of these abolitionists also maintained that the enslaved's efforts would be blessed by God.[81] This does not mean that black abolitionists condoned all-out violence, but self-defense was up for debate in a way that it had not been since the tragedy of Elijah Lovejoy's death. Black Americans did not have the luxury of being able to separate moral and political aspects of the struggle against slavery that Garrison did. Many of them were simply doing what they could to move the cause forward, even as they struggled to survive. While not every black leader had reached the conclusions of Walker, Woodson, and Garnet, others such as Douglass could not be convinced until they faced their own transformative experiences.

Early in the movement, Douglass firmly agreed with Garrison. He refused to condone slave rebellions and worked hard to convince his fellow black abolitionists to refrain from encouraging actions that he believed would be catastrophic.[82] The scholar Leslie Friedman Goldman argues that "Douglass really believed that persuasion and moral example—moral suasion, as he called it—would be more effective in saving the slaves than would wild resorts to bloodshed." Goldman adds that early in his career, Douglass "actually believed that the slaveholders would be shamed by a transformed public opinion into giving up their own slaves."[83] During the first five years Douglass worked for Garrison, he expressed the certainty that the American people needed only to be *enlightened* about the horrible oppression of slavery. Douglass pushed for patience.

Nonetheless, in 1843, the same year that Douglass opposed Garnet's address, he, too, found himself on the side of violence. Douglass was giving a lecture with several abolitionists friends when a mob of began to disrupt the event. Nearly sixty well-armed men began to threaten the speakers and ordered them to be silent; it was clear they had come to fight. The rioters then began to tear down the speaker's platform and charge the stage. One of the presenters, William A. White, was hit repeatedly in the head, and several of his teeth were knocked out before he fell to the ground. Douglass attempted to fight his way through the crowds with a stick, but he was overcome and pummeled over and over again as he lay prostrate on the ground. When the attackers finally rode off, Douglass was unconscious and his right hand was broken. Neal Hardy, a Quaker, revived Douglass and nursed him at his home. Because Douglass's broken bones were not properly set, his hand never recovered its natural strength and dexterity.[84] In 1893, toward the end of Douglass's life, he recalled the incident in an unpublished letter and explained, "I was Non-Resistant til I got to fighting with a mob at Pendleton, Ind: in 1843. . . . I fell never to rise again, and yet I cannot feel I did wrong."[85] Those who have studied Douglass—and his evolving views on violence—believe that while he supported self-defense, he remained opposed to violence as a weapon of reform.[86] For those who are familiar with Douglass's narrative, his hallmark "fight with Mr. Covey" was a turning point. Douglass refused to be broken or whipped by Covey, and a two-hour blow-for-blow fight ensued in which Covey finally conceded. As a result, Douglass was never whipped again. Because he wrote about his experience with such "glowing terms," he became a prime example of a man who would not shun self-defense.[87] Few black abolitionists practiced the notion of nonresistance and moral suasion when facing a mob attack or a personal assault. Black abolitionists utilized both accommodation and resistance as collective strategies for survival. And while it was much easier to be nonviolent in word than in deed, black abolitionists could make clear distinctions between occasions that were appropriate for violent resistance and those that were not. For instance, in the report of the Committee on Abolition of the National Negro Convention in October 1847, Douglass offered what he believed to be a rational view concerning violence, "The slave is in the minority, a small minority, the oppressors are an overwhelming majority." He contended that the enslaved people had no rights, whereas white Americans possessed every legal and deadly advantage to keep them oppressed.[88] Douglass explained that under these circumstances, black leadership had the responsibility to develop the best means of abolishing slavery. He urged the committee to see the rationale for employing violent resistance because the committee believed that resorting to bloodshed would be "the perfection of folly, suicidal in the extreme, and abominably wicked."[89] Leaders of the abolitionist movement equated violence with

FIGHTING THE MOB IN INDIANA.

Figure 2. "Fighting the Mob in Indiana." Courtesy of the Photographs and Prints Division, Schomburg Center for Research in Black Culture, New York Public Library.

sin. Furthermore, the repercussions of slave rebellions almost always proved deadly for both the guilty and the innocent. But an anti-abolitionist mob was not a slave rebellion, and Douglass understood this firsthand.

By the end of the 1840s, abolition was still not imminent, and Douglass realized he would have to take a different approach. His breaking point, the point at which he moved beyond self-defense to political violence, may have come in 1847 after he met John Brown in Springfield, Massachusetts. Douglass recalled that he had become less hopeful about the peaceful abolition of slavery and more impressed by Brown's convictions. During an antislavery convention in Salem, Ohio, Douglass was sharply rebuked by Sojourner Truth when he insinuated that slavery could be destroyed only by bloodshed. "Frederick, is God dead?" Truth asked. "No," he answered, and "because God is not dead slavery can only end in blood." Douglass acknowledged that Truth was of the Garrison school of nonresistance, but it was not long before she too "became an advocate of the sword," when the war for the maintenance of the Union was declared.[90]

Douglass's frustration in the movement was beginning to make its way into his speeches. And though they would not come to fruition until much later, he along with John Brown began to spread the intellectual seeds of violent dissent. That same year, Douglass stepped into his own even more by establishing his own antislavery newspaper, the *North Star*, with its motto: "Right is of no Sex—Truth is of no Color—God is the Father of us all, and we are all brethren." When Douglass established the *North Star*, it symbolized a step toward self-determination, black separatism, and a stepping out beyond the prominent tutelage of Garrison. Samuel R. Ward, the black abolitionist minister and editor of the *Farmer and Northern Star* and Boston's *Impartial Citizen*, claimed that perhaps Douglass's and Garrison's public disputes revealed Garrison's own "hostility toward black manliness and independence," a charge Garrison strongly denied.[91]

Garrison stated in his own paper that "a good deal of anxiety is felt and expressed by many of his [Douglass'] old and most reliable friends, in view of this change in his sentiments; and he appears to be keenly sensitive to any criticism from that quarter—construing that criticism, as he appears to do, into an impeachment of his motives." Garrison did not approve of Douglass's relationship with Gerrit Smith and the Liberty Party or his interpretation of the US Constitution. Douglass had become political and Garrison believed it was impossible to reconcile government, politics, and slavery. After quibbling about the fact that Douglass had changed the name of his paper from

the *North Star* to his own name (the *Frederick Douglass Paper*), an act he saw
as egotistical, Garrison lamented that ultimately he and his friends were sorry
to see Douglass leave for what he saw as faulty politics. "It is not a question of
purity of motives, but of soundness and vitality of position; and we see no
cause why the discussion should not be conducted, on both sides, in an ami-
cable and magnanimous spirit." Garrison also dismissed the claim that Douglass left because all of the white editors on staff were financially compensated
and Douglass was not. But Garrison retorted that this notion was simply "an
unkind fling."[92] Nevertheless, the loss of Douglass was a major setback for the
Garrison camp and all who continued to tout moral suasion. For white abolitionists, Douglass was their greatest public relations tool, their representation
for recruitment to the movement.

By 1849, Douglass had changed his ideological stance even more. He declared, "Slaveholders have no rights more than any other thief or pirate. They
have forfeited even the right to live, and if the slave should put every one of
them to the sword tomorrow, who dare pronounce the penalty dispropor-
tioned to the crime?"[93] Filled with righteous indignation, Douglass became
frustrated and impatient. He recognized that more than twenty years into the
movement, American abolitionists had accomplished little. Douglass was always strategic. It is likely he understood that justifying slave revolts or slave
violence was a way of threatening slave revolts without blatantly encouraging
them. Furthermore, black abolitionists had become frustrated with the
movement's ineffectiveness and dominant white leadership. As the true subjects and founders of abolitionism, black leaders wanted control and agency
in the movement that belonged to them. Douglass and Garnet understood
violence as a rational response to oppression, a belief that echoed sentiments
proudly hailed during the Revolutionary era. No one could deny the parallel
between the principles of black abolitionists and those of the Founding Fathers, nor could anyone ignore the outcome of the American Revolution or
the Haitian Revolution: an oppressed colony that had engaged in a violent
war had won its independence and freedom. Even Garrison had to acknowledge that the patriots achieved American independence—not with moral
suasion or electoral politics, but with violence.

Lines Drawn in the Quest for Equality

In August of 1845, J. W. C. Pennington, a former slave and a Presbyterian minister, preached his farewell sermon at the Fifth Congregational Church in Hartford, Connecticut. Pennington declared that the nation was still taking shape. He stated, "I am still a young man. . . . And the last half of the present century will be our great moral battle day. I go to prepare for that."[94] Although it was perhaps not his intention, Pennington and almost all Americans would surely face a "moral battle" in the last half of the nineteenth century. If one thing was clear, it was that the campaign for moral suasion was significantly weakened. No one knew what the future of America held for black Americans, but few were willing to wait and see. Black abolitionists, like Pennington, set out in search of more forceful tactics.

In some ways, time was the decider. Time proved how much had changed and how much had not. It was two decades into the movement and the abolitionists were no closer to abolishing slavery than the day they started. If anything, the institution of slavery was stronger. And the more people held onto slavery, the more black leaders let go of their beliefs in the utility of nonresistance. In 1847, the *Liberator* regretfully reported a speech by Charles L. Remond, a former proponent of nonresistance, in which he urged the enslaved to "RISE AT ONCE, en masse, and THROW OFF THEIR FETTERS."[95] That same year, the Troy National Convention proposed the motion: "This Convention recommends to our people the propriety of instructing their sons in the art of war."[96] Although the motion failed, incidents like Garnet's speech marked a shift in the abolitionist ideology. The fact that the resolution for "instructing sons in the art of war" could be entertained was one more crack in the foundation of nonviolence. As early as 1841, the Maine and New Hampshire abolitionist conventions had refused to denounce violence in support of freeing the slaves. Eight years later, both New England states were even more fervent in their approval of support for the enslaved, even at the cost of physical violence and bloodshed. At the Ohio state convention in 1849, members recommended ordering five hundred copies of two of the most notorious writings of the antebellum period for purchase and distribution: David Walker's *Appeal* and Garnet's "Address to the Slaves." The two writings were printed together in one volume in 1848.[97] By promoting "two of the most radical calls to violence," black abolitionists were taking bold steps and distancing themselves from moral suasion.[98] Walker and Garnet's were not merely exceptional texts, they typified or put into words the central development of the period.

Resistance among black abolitionists began to affect their white counterparts as well. By the late 1840s, one by one, white abolitionists had begun to question the efficacy of moral suasion. By 1845, Gerrit Smith, a radical white abolitionist and philanthropist from New York, had grown to doubt that slavery would "die a peaceful death."[99] Similarly, Theodore Parker, a white minister, declared around the same time, "War is an utter violation of Christianity. If war be right, then Christianity is wrong, false, a lie. Every man who understands Christianity knows that war is wrong."[100] But in a letter to his fellow minister Francis Cobb, Parker wrote: "I think we should agree about war. I hate it, I deplore it, yet see its necessity. All the great charters of humanity have been writ in blood, and must continue to be so for some centuries."[101] Leaders of the movement were beginning to understand that violence was not merely insidious or even vengeful but potentially a political tool that could be used to achieve a greater good.

Historically, perhaps the question of the 1830s and '40s should have been: Why nonviolence? Why moral suasion? Moral suasion was useful, but as slave owners won more and more legal and political gains, moral suasion proved ineffective as a tool largely because it did not address equality. Overall, the limitations of nonviolence were fourfold: first, nonresistance demonstrated that white elites were out of touch with the concerns of the black community. Continued discrimination, disenfranchisement, kidnappings, unemployment, growing segregation, and increased violence plagued black communities. Often black success courted violence. Real change that would result in a new social structure required more than verbal persuasion or moral elevation by African Americans. For black Americans to obtain the right to vote, own land, or maintain a living wage, they needed political and economic intervention. Second, moral suasion failed because it required the unstated assumption that black people were equal. Despite black success in the pulpit and the press, black Americans could not convince their counterparts to abandon racial prejudices. Peter Paul Simmons argued that the only thing moral reform had achieved was in creating "a conspicuous scarecrow designed expressly . . . to hinder our people from acting collectively for themselves."[102] In other words, moral suasion was nothing more than an emotional decoy that could never sufficiently frighten or endanger slaveholders and the institution of slavery. Even William Whipper, a proud advocate for moral suasion, lamented that it was "not for lack of elevation, but complexion that deprived the man of color equal treatment."[103] Third, given the longevity and prosperity of slavery, abolitionists were not speaking to a waning slave economy built on tobacco at the end of the eighteenth century. Cotton was king and its economic stronghold dictated not only the life expectancy of the enslaved (life expectancy rates among the enslaved rose and fell with the price of cotton) but also the political power of slaveholders to secure its dominance. Economically, nonviolence could do nothing to curb the world's insatiable demand for cotton. As the enslaved population grew, the only threat planters feared was rebellion. Fourth, and finally, the principles and rhetoric of republican ideology, which included calls to take up arms against tyranny, were powerful. Because of Haiti, Garrison could never fully capture the hearts and minds of black Americans. Because of Haiti, David Walker and Henry Highland Garnet had voices that could not be silenced. Undoubtedly the desire for freedom among the enslaved existed before 1791. However, when the sons and daughters of Haiti struck for freedom, as Douglass notes in his speech on Haiti at the World's Fair in 1893, "they struck for the freedom of every black man in the world."[104] The possibilities of violent rebellion cannot be underestimated; it was a common wind blowing and circulating all throughout the black Atlantic.

Freedoms given would always play second fiddle to freedoms won. Waiting for slavery to simply end of its own accord or out of the benevolence of planters proved fruitless. In order for the movement to progress, it could not remain static; it had to evolve. If black abolitionists were going to produce real change, they had embrace political protest and collective political violence.[105] Essentially, they had to force freedom.

CHAPTER 2

Fight, Flight, and Fugitives

The Fugitive Slave Law and Violence

> The only way to make the Fugitive Slave Law a dead letter is to make half a dozen or more dead kidnappers. The man who takes the office of a bloodhound ought to be treated as a bloodhound.
>
> —Frederick Douglass

In the spring of 1850, Charles Lenox Remond, the famed orator and abolitionist from Massachusetts, lectured to a small crowd of attendees at the Ford Street Baptist Church on the current position of black people in America. He talked about the Fugitive Slave Bill (then before Congress), the anticipated action of the Compromise Committee (which was composed of thirteen men set to draft legislation based on Senator Henry Clay's proposals to ease sectional tension between slave states and free states), the debate regarding annexation of Cuba and of Canada, and the revival of the colonization movement. Perhaps, for Remond, what he saw that was most troubling was the increased influence of the Slave Power, a term used during the antebellum period to describe the political and economic power of the slaveholding class.[1] He believed that the 1850s ushered in "a new and dangerous phase" particularly for the abolitionist movement. According to the *North Star*, Remond chided his audience for their "inactivity and indifference" to the degradation of their race in general. He insisted that black Americans perpetuated their own oppression by their apathy. In the face of a rapidly changing political climate and the growth of slavery creeping further across US territory, black people would have to become more forceful in their pursuits of emancipation and equality.[2] For Remond, black reformers needed to possess two essential qualities to combat slavery and racism: the will to agitate and the readiness to risk physical assault.

New legislation changed everything, even for those who wanted to remain dispassionate. The one factor that pushed black leadership and their followers to immediate action was the Fugitive Slave Law. The law did something quite remarkable for the abolitionist movement, and in particular, African Americans: it made violence a necessary alternative. This is best illustrated by major abolitionist centers such as Pennsylvania, New York, and Massachusetts.[3] In a sense, all three states vied for the honor of being the place where the Fugitive Slave Law could, in effect, be unenforceable. Some of the most famous confrontations regarding the law involve the Christiana Resistance of 1851 in Pennsylvania, the Jerry Rescue in Syracuse, New York, and the capture and return of Anthony Burns in Boston, Massachusetts. In addition, the individual stories of runaway slaves who employed the tools of violence to gain freedom are both revealing and gripping.

Some of the most compelling examples of political violence occurred through resistance, self-defense, and collective defense against the law. The enslaved continued to resist through running away despite the law, while free black Americans resisted by engaging in various forms of civil, and sometimes not so civil, disobedience to protect their liberty. Self-defense was even more important in the face of a slave catcher. History reveals that it was not always the fugitives who risked their lives, but the slave catcher who attempted to capture those in question. Additionally, collective defense led to the development of black vigilance groups determined to protect fugitives and even seek out kidnappers who threatened to return them. The individual or collective actions of black Americans shaped both the conversations and the course of sectional tensions.

The law essentially required black Americans to become political and active in their own defense by patronizing antislavery newspapers, joining black antislavery societies, producing autobiographical accounts of their enslavement and escape, attending conventions that agitated for their civil and political rights, and organizing resistance to the Fugitive Slave Law, leading to higher levels of black militancy. Local abolitionist communities transitioned into national hotbeds of abolitionist activism as result of the Fugitive Slave Law. Indeed, the law's greatest contribution was the acceleration of antebellum political violence.

The Fugitive Slave Law

Just several months after Remond's lecture, on September 18, 1850, Congress enacted a much more aggressive Fugitive Slave Law. The law had been on the books since 1793 and required the return of runaway slaves. In section 2, clause 3 of the United States Constitution, the Fugitive Slave Clause stated that no enslaved persons living in a slave state could escape to a free state and be considered discharged of their service or labor. The law required that a fugitive slave be returned to his or her rightful owners and that slave owners maintained their property rights in both the slaveholding South and through-out the country. A fugitive slave was still a slave and therefore could be re-turned to their rightful owner at any time from any state. Furthermore, any child born of a fugitive mother was also considered property of the slave owner.

The law, however, was rarely enforced, perhaps most notably when even President George Washington could not secure the return of his former slave Ona Judge after several attempts.[4] For decades, fugitives had used the North as a safe haven, and they intended to protect their newfound livelihoods. By 1850, an estimated one thousand runaway slaves per year were escaping to major cities or free territories where they could begin new lives.[5] Many en-slaved people sought new identities or raised the money to purchase their freedom after they fled. These self-emancipated men and women enriched their lives through marriage and education of their children. Their goal was simple: to live an antislavery life.[6]

The law was also fraught with controversy over states' rights versus fed-eral law because many Northern states sought to protect runaways and free black people from kidnapping. Due to years of confrontation between slave states and free states, Senators Henry Clay of Kentucky and Daniel Webster of Massachusetts composed the Compromise of 1850 to prevent the Union from erupting over political tension regarding slavery. Under the leadership of Stephen A. Douglass of Illinois, the 1850 compromise required five provi-sions: California would enter the Union as a free state, slavery would be per-mitted in Utah and New Mexico, the slave trade in Washington DC would be prohibited (although slavery was still legal), and finally the Fugitive Slave Law would be revised and revamped to ensure its enforcement.

The strengthened Fugitive Slave Law of 1850 was different in many ways. For one, it had teeth—there were several serious consequences for anyone who obstructed the return of fugitive slaves. First, the superior court of each state had the power to appoint commissioners who were responsible for reclaiming and returning fugitive slaves to their masters. Second, the court officials obtained compensation according to the judge's decision: $10 if the judge returned the slave to the proclaimed owner and $5 if the judge decided there was insufficient proof to do so. Third, if a court commissioner refused to fulfill his responsibility to return fugitive slaves, he could face upward of $1,000 in fines. Moreover, if the fugitive in question escaped from the nonconsenting commissioner, he would be subject to additional fines for the market value of the slave. Fourth, the bill declared: "All good citizens are hereby commanded to aid and assist in the prompt and efficient execution of the law." The Fugitive Slave Law launched a nationwide debate and disturbed what many Northerners and abolitionists saw as their own "status quo" by requiring white and black Northerners to aid in returning fugitive slaves, which forced them to become de facto employees working on behalf of Southern planters.[7] Any person who knowingly hindered the arrest of a fugitive slave could be fined more than $1,000 and jailed for six months. To reclaim an enslaved person, the owner needed only to make his plea to a court commissioner and the process could begin. Once captured, the accused had no right to trial by jury. The edict made clear that no hearing under this act could allow the testimony of the alleged fugitive to be admitted as evidence; except in cases involving mistaken identity, the master's testimony was all that was allowed.[8]

The new law was also retroactive. If an enslaved person had escaped as a child or had lived longer free than in bondage, it did not matter. These provisions put the lives of every African American throughout the country in jeopardy. Frederick Douglass wrote, "Colored people who had been free all their lives felt themselves very insecure in their freedom." He explained that the law required only the oaths of "any two villains" for a man born free to legally be consigned to slavery for life. Thus, even free black Americans were susceptible to kidnapping or false accusations. Douglass added, "While the law was a terror to the free, it was still a greater terror to the escaped bondman." For fugitives, he declared there was "[no] peace. Asleep or awake, at work or at rest, in church or market, he was liable to surprise and capture."[9] It is likely that many former enslaved people feared that one day in a crowd they would recognize a familiar face—or, worse still, be recognized themselves. No one had become more relentless than the slave catcher, and slaveholders were unyielding in their efforts to reclaim their property. In a newspaper article, the former slave and abolitionist William Wells Brown parodied biblical scripture when he claimed, "Resist the [devil], and, it is said he will run away from you, resist the slaveholder and he will run to you."[10] According to this line of thinking, slaveholders were worse than the devil and everything about the new law favored the slave owner.

The revised Fugitive Slave Law was the proslavery reaction to years of personal liberty laws, slave runaways, and vigilance committee activity. As black frustrations grew throughout the 1840s, activists turned to more practical measures, such as politics and fugitive slave efforts. Every radical speech, pamphlet, or heroic escape served to generate proslavery fears and certainly inspired the revamping of the Fugitive Slave Law. In this way, we see how radical abolitionism worked: not by changing hearts and minds but by causing a paranoid South to overreact in ways that garnered sympathy for abolitionism. The South looked like a bully, especially to those who still espoused nonresistance.

Arguably, this was just what the abolitionist movement needed. The law resurrected the movement, which had been fatigued by years of stagnant advancement toward immediate abolition. The passage of the Fugitive Slave Law was the final turning point in a failed campaign for moral suasion and signaled the need for radical political advocacy that Garrison often opposed. Furthermore, it became clear that the new law could not be combated without force. Black abolitionists fully expected to do just that.

The Rise of Black Militancy

During the spring and summer of 1850, while the Fugitive Slave bill was still pending in Congress, both black and white abolitionists and their allies met frequently to urge the defeat of the most heinous aspect of the 1850 Compromise. They gathered in cities from Pittsburgh to Portland. The growing militancy of black American activists in the 1850s was apparent at almost every state and local meeting of black leaders. The resolutions recorded by members of these meetings and conventions left little doubt that many participants desired a radical response, even military action against the United States, in order to achieve emancipation and equality. Labeled by scholars as Negro Nationalism or Black Nationalism, these leaders addressed a growing demand for self-determination, self-protection, and self-expression. "More radical, more self-contained, and more independent" described the character of black abolitionists in the North for all of the 1850s.[11] This, in turn, set the pace for combating the Fugitive Slave Law all around the country. Black leadership spoke with a renewed sense of urgency and force. The Fugitive Slave Law turned the runaway into one of the most controversial and political figures of the 1850s. Runaway stories could take on a celebrity quality depending on the level of risk, ingenuity, and willingness to engage in violence. Thus, violence became the new political language for the oppressed—a language that drew the strongest response from both black leaders' enemies and their allies.

Within one month after the passage of the 1850 law, protest meetings were being held in the cities of Brooklyn, Philadelphia, Providence, and Boston and numerous other places where delegates vowed to use violence in defying the law.[12] Black people in New York took to public protest. The official newspaper of the American Antislavery Society, the *National Anti-Slavery Standard*, demanded, "Shall we resist Oppression, Shall we defend our Liberties? Shall we be FREEMEN or SLAVE?" The newspaper openly encouraged enslaved people to defend themselves "with the surest and most deadly weapons, including bowie knives and revolvers." Furthermore, the newspaper made it clear that defense would be a group effort. One New York antislavery meeting resolved members to be each other's keeper and to "strike dead the first man who dares to lay his hand upon a brother to throw him into bondage."[13] Many black Americans made the commitment through a pledge. At black conventions held all around the country, leaders encouraged their members not to rule out the use of violent resistance to the "runaway law." In fact, in a September meeting, one of the resolutions stated that runaway slaves were "justifiable in resorting to any means, even if it be the taking of the life of him who seeks to deprive of us of what is dearer than life." Other resolutions vowed to "take the scalp of any government hound, that dares follow on our track," to "slay them [slave catchers] as we would any other legalized land pirates" should they approach a slave's family.[14] Collectively and individually, each speech, escape, meeting, resolution, and conflict regarding slavery during the 1850s built upon the last, fueling an environment that made the antebellum period one of the most violent eras in US history. Black leaders were committed to making the act of enforcing the law a dangerous endeavor.

The Christiana Resistance in Pennsylvania

Because of the proximity of Pennsylvania to the bordering slave state of Maryland, many runaways sought safety and freedom over the Pennsylvania state line. In fact, Pennsylvania had the highest percentage of runaways living within the state.[15] However, slave catchers, well aware of this, monitored the area and made quite a business of returning runaways. Notoriously known as the Gag Gang, a group of men who operated in the Christiana area, a border town, were successful at terrorizing black Americans and carrying suspected fugitives back into Maryland. In response to Gag Gang kidnappings and the general assault on black residents, people like William Parker became infuriated and formed his own group, the Lancaster Black Self-Protection Society.[16]

Parker was a local activist and former fugitive himself, having run away with his brother, Charles, from Anne Arundel County, Maryland. Parker vowed that he would form an organization for fugitive slaves for mutual protection against slaveholders and kidnappers. "I thought," declared Parker, "that, if I had the power, they should soon be as free as I was, and I formed a resolution that I would assist in liberating everyone within my reach at the risk of my life, and that I would devise some plan for their entire liberation."[17] Parker was not alone. In a collective stance, a group of fugitive slaves formed the protection society and resolved to "prevent any of brethren being taken back to slavery, [even] at the risk of our own lives."[18]

As a leader in his community, Parker set an example for how the law should be regarded. He promised he would knock down the first slaveholder who drew a pistol on him.[19] And he did. On one particular night, some men burst into his home wanting to know about runaways and threatened Parker with a gun. He grabbed a pair of heavy tongs and struck one of the intruders across the face and neck, knocking the man off his feet. For a few minutes the intruder laid there senseless, but afterward rose up and walked out of Parker's house with his comrades and without a word. It is likely they were more afraid of a black man who as unafraid to take them on in the face of gun.[20] Parker was emphatic when he declared, "My rights as freeman were . . . secured by my own right arm."[21]

Parker routinely proved that he was serious about enforcing the protection of his community as well. He encouraged the black residents and white allies not only to confront kidnappers but also to "seek revenge on those who betray the escaped slaves."[22] For instance, he wrote about an episode in which a local man by the name of Allen Williams betrayed a runaway slave. Parker, along with the Black Self-Protection Society, agreed that for his acts Williams should die. As a result, Williams was severely attacked and beaten but somehow managed to escape with his life. When Parker's group confronted another betrayer in a brutal attack, he also escaped, but Parker claimed the man ran "as if the spirit of his evil deeds was after him."[23] Parker was acting in full agreement with the well-known words of Frederick Douglass, "The man who takes the office of a bloodhound ought to be treated as a bloodhound."[24]

On September 11, 1851, Parker's reputation brought four fugitive slaves (Noah Buley, Nelson Ford, George Ford, and Joshua Hammond) to his door. The men sought safe haven at Parker's home in Christiana, on their continued path north. Willingly, Parker agreed to house and protect them. It was not long after their arrival that Edward Gorsuch, the Maryland slaveholder in search of his slaves, arrived with his son, his nephew, a deputy marshal, and his assistants to claim his enslaved property. When Gorsuch and his men confronted Parker at his home, words were exchanged. Parker recounted the standoff between Gorsuch and Kline, the US Marshal:

> I told them all [the four fugitive slaves] not to be afraid, nor to give up to any slaveholder, but to fight until death.
>
> "Yes," said Kline, "I have heard many a negro talk as big as you, and then have taken him; and I'll take you."
>
> You have not taken me yet, I replied; and if you undertake it you will have your name recorded in history for this day's work.
>
> Mr. Gorsuch then spoke, and said,—"Come, Mr. Kline, let's go up stairs and take them. We can take them. Come, follow me, I'll go up and get my property. What's in the way? The law is in my favor, and the people are in my favor."
>
> At that he began to ascend the stair; but I said to him [Gorsuch],— See here, old man, you can come up, but you can't go down again. Once up here, you are mine.[25]

To some extent, Parker was wrong about Gorsuch and Kline, for it was Parker and his wife, Eliza, whose actions would have their names recorded in history as heroes. What followed was one of the most significant violent altercations before the Civil War. As the men's conversation escalated, Eliza alerted members of the Black Self-Protection Society by blowing a horn, a prearranged signal to prepare for slave catchers. Gorsuch's men had been instructed to

Figure 3. "The Tragedy at Christiana." From William Still, *The Underground Railroad* (Philadelphia: Porter & Coats, 1872). Courtesy of the Library Company of Philadelphia.

shoot at anyone who blew a horn. Although they shot at Eliza numerous times, she hid behind a stone wall and was protected. Meanwhile, Parker began heaving pitchforks and axes at the men in an attempt to run them off. Within moments, eighty black men and women along with two Quakers arrived on the scene. Armed with guns and farm equipment, they surrounded Gorsuch's men and the marshal. Outnumbered and out-armed, the marshal fled in terror as shots were fired. In the end, Gorsuch, unwavering, stood his ground but was killed, while his son was severely wounded.[26] Parker made it clear that Gorsuch's death came at the hands of his own slaves. "His slave struck him the first and second blows; then three or four sprang upon him, and, when he became helpless, [they] left him to pursue others."[27]

It is important to note that protective violence was not left to men alone. Parker also attested that, eventually, "the women put an end to him [Gorsuch]."[28] With the exception of Eliza, the nameless and faceless women within this story reveal the remarkable role women played in employing violence.

Women had no trouble putting an end to Gorsuch, and the fact that Parker declares that multiple women were involved validates the solidarity among black residents regarding violent response across the sexes. Both black men and women were susceptible to kidnapping and assault. Exploited by the sexual violence of slavery, women were equally tasked to take revenge on their representative oppressor. Thus, Christiana is also significant because it represents a collective act of defiance in which both men and women acted heroically. Had it not been for Eliza's quick thinking to alert the Black Self-Protection Society, this resistance could have ended quite differently. Instead, the four fugitive slaves and Parker fled to Canada, while thirty-five black people and five white people were arrested for treason and held in the Moyamensing Prison in Philadelphia to await trial. The Christiana Resistance became national news, and a symbol of the political transformation of a black community bound together by protective collectivism. Border towns within Pennsylvania went down in history not only as places where black Americans suffered violence but also as places where they managed to use violence to redeem their sense of self, community, and value.

Later, Frederick Douglass wrote about Parker and the four escaped men who had stopped by his home in Rochester on the way to Canada. "I could not," he proclaimed, "look upon them as murderers. To me, they were heroic defenders of the just rights of man against mansteaders and murderers. So I fed them, and sheltered them in my house."[29] Douglass admitted that had the authorities come to his house that night, his "home would have been stained with blood."[30] He then accompanied Parker and his men as they boarded a steamer headed to Toronto. Once on the ship, Parker presented Douglass with the revolver that fell from Gorsuch's hand when he died. Parker described the weapon as "a token of gratitude and a memento of the battle for Liberty at Christiana." With that, Douglass declared, "I returned to my home with a sense of relief which I cannot stop here to describe."[31] Christiana was a major victory in the fight against the Slave Power. The charges against the accused were dropped, and Parker and his wife Eliza lived out the rest of their days on a fifty-acre settlement in Buxton, Ontario. As much as Douglass is admired as a national leader, the local leadership of Parker expands our understanding of the pivotal contributions of other black abolitionists, for whom someone like Douglass plays a supporting role.

The political ramifications the Christiana Resistance traveled far and wide. Internationally, the influx of black Americans into Canada was causing the diplomatic relationship with the US to become hostile. Canada was not interested in aiding the US in the return of fugitive slaves. The Christiana Resistance also came at a great cost. The US government spent $50,000 ($1.47 million in 2012 dollars) trying to find justice for Gorsuch to no avail. Nearly every political faction had an opinion about who was to blame. Non-radical white abolitionists attempted to distance themselves from the event, claiming that the black residents of Christiana were "acting independently of the guidance by whites."[32] To the black leadership's credit, this was largely true and necessary to move beyond the failed practices of moral suasion and white paternalism. Yet, Democrats saw the resistance as a tool to berate their enemies and presented false or exaggerated details to be reprinted throughout Southern newspapers. In particular, the Democratic Party blamed Pennsylvania governor William F. Johnston for the increase in violence committed by black people. Democrats were determined to defeat Johnston, a Whig, in the October election. By exploiting racial tensions regarding slavery, his opponents argued that Johnston was partisan to black residents and abolitionists because he would not support the Fugitive Slave Law and refused to repeal the state's 1847 anti-kidnapping act.[33] Democrats also accused Johnston and the state's "notorious abolitionists" of responsibility in Gorsuch's death.[34]

However, the North blamed slaveholders for their own demise. The *New York Independent* attributed Gorsuch's death to all advocates of the Fugitive Slave Law: "The framers of this law counted upon the utter degradation of the negro race—their manliness and heroism—to render feasible execution" and, according to the paper, they fool-heartedly "anticipated no resistance from a race cowed down by centuries of oppression, and trained to servility."[35] Gravely mistaken, Southerners were beginning to discover that "men, however abject, who have tasted liberty, soon learn to prize it, and are ready to defend it."[36] More than any other event, next to John Brown's raid, tensions from Christiana helped to precipitate the coming of the Civil War. According to the scholar Thomas Slaughtery, the soil of the Civil War was fertilized with Gorsuch's blood.[37]

Protection of the family unit was of the utmost importance, for it was the one thing no enslaved person could prevent in slavery: the separation of husband and wife, parent and child, sibling and kin. Black residents living in Bradford Country, Pennsylvania, determined, "Before we will submit to be dragged into southern bondage by the man-stealers of the South, we will die in defense of our right to liberty."[38] Black men, in particular, felt entitled to defend themselves and protect their families; they looked forward to proving their manhood, strength, and courage, of which, for so many years, they had been robbed during enslavement.

In Pittsburgh, Martin Delany was a prominent abolitionist and proponent of emigration. In 1854, he led the National Emigration Convention that met in Cleveland, Ohio, and published his famous manifesto, "The Political Destiny of the Colored Race on the American Continent." Delany denounced partnering with white abolitionists and encouraged black Americans to leave for the Caribbean or South America. For Delany, flight had always been his strategy to resist oppression. But in lieu of the law, violence was not off the table either. He threatened: "If he [slave catcher] crosses the threshold of my door, and I do not lay him a lifeless corpse at my feet, I hope the grave may refuse my body a resting place, and the righteous Heaven my spirit a home."[39] Violence was not only becoming an option in ways that were not possible during the precious decade, but it many ways it had become the only option for those who could not leave.

Robert Purvis, president of the Pennsylvania Anti-Slavery Society, was moved to violence as well at the onset of the Fugitive Slave Law. Born free in Charleston, South Carolina, Purvis moved to Pennsylvania and attended abolitionist schools. He was educated at Amherst College and returned to Philadelphia to settle with quite a bit of wealth, inherited from his English father. The total estate he shared with his two brothers was estimated at $250,000.[40] Purvis, like many black abolitionists began his activism as a Garrisonian. He helped establish the American Anti-Slavery Society in Philadelphia and signed its Declaration of Sentiments. Yet, from 1852 to 1857, during the height of the enforcement of the Fugitive Slave Law, Purvis became the chairman of the General Vigilance Committee and used his home as a station for the Underground Railroad. On October 17, 1850, at an annual Pennsylvania Anti-Slavery Society meeting held at West Chester, Purvis declared, "Should any wretch enter my dwelling, any pale-faced spectre among ye, to execute this law on me or mine, I'll seek his life, I'll shed his blood." Like many black husbands and fathers, Purvis believed that nonresistance was not an option when it came to his family. Purvis said to pacifists in particular: "What can I do when my family are assaulted by kidnappers? I would fly, and by every means endeavor to avoid it, but when the extremity comes I welcome death rather than slavery, and by what means God and nature have given me, I will defend myself and my family."[41] The white abolitionist and minister Parker Pillsbury, who developed a reputation for approaching hostile crowds with nonresistant tactics, was shocked by the strong outbursts the new law created. He claimed circumstances were extreme when such a law could move a man like Purvis to such defiance and talk of violence.[42]

To protect fugitive slaves from capture, Pennsylvanian black leaders employed strategies that ranged from threats to actual violence. For example, when a black man by the name of Henry Garnett was arrested in Philadelphia, local black residents encouraged one another to "arm themselves . . . and shoot down officers of the law."[43] From then on rumors spread that "from parts of Pennsylvania . . . armed negroes prowled around in search of slave catchers."[44] Violent incidents involving fugitives increased in number. Throughout Pennsylvania, Parker acknowledged, Southerners were provoking people to take up protective defense. He claimed that slave catchers "did not hesitate to break open doors, and to enter, without ceremony, the houses of colored men; and when refused admission, or when a manly and determined spirit was shown, they would present pistols, and strike and knock down men and women indiscriminately."[45] He recounted the story of a black girl who was living under the care of the well-known abolitionist Moses Whitson. Three men claimed the girl belonged to them. They tied her up and attempted to take her back to Maryland. A black man and neighbor named Benjamin Whipper began to sound the alarm. A number of men joined Parker in tracking the kidnappers to a place called Gap Hill. They ambushed the slave catchers, freed the girl, beat the men, and told them to get out of town. They beat the men so severely that two of the slave catchers later died in Lancaster as a result of their wounds, and the one who managed to make it back to Maryland died shortly thereafter.[46]

This was far from the only incident of organized defense against slave catchers. In 1852, when a Baltimore policeman attempted to arrest a fugitive slave in Columbia, Pennsylvania, the officer was surrounded by a crowd of angry black residents. The fugitive slave then bit the officer to free himself. It was reported that the officer barely escaped back to Maryland with his life.[47] This was not a case of self-defense but of collective defense. Corporately, black people were willing to engage in violence and risk their lives to ensure the protection of their communities. There remain countless stories of black men and women and their allies employing the use of axes, pistols, rifles, and the like to combat slave catchers in the region.

Collective defense was used against black slave catchers as well. Black men served as the most treacherous of slave catchers, earning trust only to cash in later. The *Pittsburgh Gazette* reported the story of a black man named Joseph Walker who was accused of betraying a fugitive girl to her master and robbing her of all the money she possessed: $7.00.[48] Betrayal could not be tolerated among members of the black community. Walker was sent a letter and warned to leave the city, but he did not heed the advice. Then one night, Walker was "met by a couple of persons" at one or two o'clock in the morning.[49] According to the newspaper, the men placed a bag over Walker's head led him to the forest about a mile outside of town and brutally flogged him. The *Gazette* reported, "If the charges be true, he deserved all he got and more." However, Walker managed to hear the names Dimmey and Green during his attack. Later, a man by the name of Robert Green was arrested on charges of battery and assault and was held on $100 bail for Walker's assault.[50] It is not known what happened to Green, but this and many other stories of protective violence gave black Pennsylvanians a reputation throughout the area and beyond: "put an end to man-stealing in Pennsylvania forever."[51]

The Jerry Rescue in New York

Pennsylvania was not alone in its resistance to the Fugitive Slave Law. In New York, just one week after President Millard Fillmore signed the bill into law, fugitive slaves and their allies gathered to defy it. New Yorker Benjamin Stanley, a very dark-complexioned man from North Carolina and rumored to be of distant relation to Edward Stanley, a member of Congress, made a passionate address before a meeting of black leaders. He advised his listeners to prepare to receive family and friends with "bruised arms and broken heads." To great cheers, Stanley recommended arming the enslaved with bowie knives and revolvers and arming themselves like men coming to the rescue of those in trouble. "Yes that is the word—you must do the work," declared Stanley. "You must do it, and show that a population of twenty-five thousand colored people will not allow the fugitive to be conveyed back to bondage." He claimed that New York must be the battleground, adding (among great cheers), "We cannot battle at the South, and therefore it must be done here."[52] According to Stanley, if New York was not worth fighting for, no other city or state was worth the effort. The audience erupted in applause at each statement he made regarding the use of violent force and collective defense. Stanley asked, "Will you stand by and see one of your own color thrown back into chains and Slavery?" Again, the audience began to shout out echoes of "No, no" and "Never!" He concluded that if a fugitive slave could not obtain a bowie knife or arms to defend himself, then he should shout out when seized by slave catchers, for no one would stand by peacefully and allow him to be carried away. For Stanley, collectivism and self-defense was everything. He acknowledged "how much better is it for the fugitive slave to stay here, and, if he must die, to die with his friends."[53]

Much like Pennsylvania, New York owed much of its conflict to the politics of proximity. Cities such as Syracuse, Rochester, and Buffalo were close to the Canadian border and it was fairly easy to travel to and from them via foot or ferry. Syracuse played a major role as a depot on the Underground Railroad. The city was a safe haven for fugitive slaves and abolitionists. Just five days after the law passed, the town's free black community called a meeting at the African Congregational Church.[54] The *Syracuse Standard,* one of the largest local newspapers reported, "The fugitive slave law is causing some excitement among the colored population here, who have organized and assembled and armed themselves to resist any attempts on their liberty."[55]

It became increasingly difficult for white Americans to counsel black Americans on issues of resistance. Samuel R. Ward, founder of the Syracuse antislavery newspaper, *Impartial Citizen,* explained how James Mott, a white abolitionist and the husband of Lucretia Mott, took issue with the resistance that Ward recommended to black men. While Ward believed Mott's heart was "full of sympathy with us," and his "determination to disobey the Whig Hunker law" was as strong as ever, he was one of many who could not bring themselves to endorse actions that might incite violence. Ward's own position was that "for black men to resist the law, even unto blood and death, is, to my mind a duty as . . . liberty itself. . . . That non-resistants should feel and advise otherwise is according to their principles; but they must be black men, before they can feel for and advise black men."[56]

In 1850, the fugitive turned abolitionist and community leader Jermain Wesley Loguen gave a speech concerning the Fugitive Slave Law. He recounted his experiences and claimed that neither he nor black Americans in general needed counsel or encouragement to defend themselves. Born into slavery in Tennessee, Loguen escaped, fled to Canada, and later settled in Syracuse.[57] Loguen was a stationmaster for the Underground Railroad in Syracuse and a minister, who later became bishop, in the African Methodist Episcopal Zion Church. He declared: "I was a slave; I knew the dangers I was exposed to. I had made up my mind as to the course I was to take. . . . They [fugitive slaves] had taken their stand—they would not be taken back to slavery. If to shoot down their assailants should forfeit their lives, such result was the least of evil. They will have their liberties or die in their defense. What is life to me if I am to be a slave in Tennessee."[58] For Loguen, a return to slavery was out of the question. The only alternative was to continue to flee or fight for one's liberty. He challenged his audience and the city of Syracuse to become a safe haven for fugitive slaves. Loguen was not afraid of repercussions but insinuated that it was federal officials who should be cautious. He stated, "I tell you the people of Syracuse and of the whole North must meet this tyranny and crush it by force, or be crushed by it." He added, "The time has come to change the tones of submission into tones of defiance,—and to tell Mr. Fillmore and Mr. Webster, if they propose to execute this measure upon us, to send on their bloodhounds."[59]

As Loguen concluded his speech he maintained, "Whatever may be your decision, my ground is taken. I have declared it everywhere. It is known over the state and out of the state—over the line in the north, and over the line in the South. I don't respect this law—I don't fear it—I won't obey it! It outlaws me, and I outlaw it, and the men who attempt to enforce it on me."[60] Loguen's fiery words represented the essence of black resistance. They made it abundantly clear that federal agents would have to exhibit overwhelming force in order to quell the protests that would ensue from capture. Black abolitionists living in Syracuse believed their position would serve as an inspiration in Auburn, Rochester, Utica, and Buffalo and eventually all the northern cities. Loguen proclaimed, "May God grant that Syracuse be the honored spot, when it shall send an earthquake voice through the land![61]

In the spring of 1851, the words of resistance were tested. The secretary of state and former senator from Massachusetts Daniel Webster traveled to Syracuse to give a speech concerning the new and controversial law. Webster warned, "They say the law will not be executed. Let them take care, for those are pretty bold assertions. The law must be executed, not only in carrying back the slave, but against those guilty of treasonable practices in resisting its execution. Depend on it, the law will be executed in its spirit and to its letter." In an attempt to put Syracuse on notice, Webster added that citizens should expect the enforcement of the law "in the midst of the next Anti-slavery Convention, if the occasion shall arise."[62] Webster had no idea how quickly his predictions would become reality. On October 1, 1851, when the antislavery Liberty Party was holding its New York State convention, William Henry, a forty-year-old runaway slave from Missouri, also known as Jerry, was violently arrested for theft. However, when his fugitive status was uncovered, he was imprisoned in accordance with the Fugitive Slave Law.

Crowds of people gathered to witness Jerry's arrest, and many more crowded the courthouse to agitate for his release. From the moment black leaders of the community were informed, they plotted to rescue Jerry from his jail cell. Rumors rapidly spread that a rescue was to take place after dark. The *New York Tribune* reported: "The chief movers of the crowd appeared to be negroes."[63] In preparation for the protest, Loguen worried that white supporters might back out of their promise to aid in the rescue, so he charged the black community to show up at the jail in large numbers. Loguen declared: "If white men won't fight, let fugitives and black men smite down Marshals and Commissioners—anybody who holds Jerry—and rescue him or perish."[64] Loguen asked the people of Syracuse whether they would enforce the Fugitive Slave Law: "[Will you] permit the government to return to me and other fugitives who have sought asylum among you, to the Hell of slavery. The question is with you."[65] Among black abolitionists, Loguen had no need to ask the question. Black Americans were vigilant in their attempts to keep fugitive slaves from being returned and took it upon themselves to seize control of their community.

The story and rescue of Jerry was a dynamic portrait of civil disobedience and collectivism. The first attempt to rescue Jerry failed: he escaped the building but was quickly recaptured. So black and white leaders met to coordinate a successful rescue that would ensure Jerry's release. Remarkably, a crowd of two to three thousand, white and black, came to aid in Jerry's ultimate liberation. Armed with clubs, axes, and iron rods, men gathered outside the courthouse. A white abolitionist, Charles Wheaton, was said to have placed such tools outside of his hardware store to help people arm themselves. A young and muscular black man by the name of Randall, holding an iron bar, placed himself in front of the double doors of the entrance to the courthouse; his stance perhaps daring officials to oppose him. In preparation for storming the building, a group of people secured a large beam to use as a battering ram. Hundreds of protestors stormed the building, despite shots fired by deputy marshals. The crowd would not and could not be deterred. Friends of Jerry were able to seize him and lead him to a safe house amid the commotion. The friends then secretly disguised Jerry as a woman and placed him on a ship to Canada. The former fugitive slave lived in Canada as a free man until his death a few years later.[66]

While the black population was small, an estimated 350 black people out of 21,900, the white population made extreme efforts to oppose the law alongside African Americans. Many prominent white abolitionists supported the black leaders' call for opposition to the law. Among the most outspoken was Gerrit Smith, a philanthropist, politician, and social activist from Utica, New York. When the Liberty Party held its New York State convention in Syracuse, its members decided to focus much of their discussion on the recent Jerry Rescue. Smith praised Syracuse for its cooperative defiance of the law and put forth resolutions that called "for the punishment of those who participated in the capture of a fugitive slave as kidnappers." He urged white people to support black resistance, "even if they have to take a life."[67]

On the very next day after Jerry's rescue, Smith responded to Webster, who he called "that base and infamous enemy of the human race" in remarks made to members of the Liberty Party convention. Smith applauded "the mighty uprising of 2,500 brave men, before whom the half-dozen kidnappers were 'as tow'" and introduced the following resolution, adopted at the Liberty Party convention: "*Resolved*, That we rejoice that the City of Syracuse—the anti-slavery city of Syracuse—the city of anti-slavery conventions, our beloved and glorious city of Syracuse—still remains undisgraced by the fulfillment of the satanic prediction of the satanic Daniel Webster."[68]

Indeed, Webster's declaration was in effect, a challenge. Had he not proclaimed the enforcement of the law during an antislavery convention, perhaps white abolitionists and allies might not have felt so passionate about breaking it. To standup to the Fugitive Slave Law was to take a political stance that inferred insubordination to the Slave Power. In 1852, Smith won election to Congress. Douglass equated his victory to Syracuse resistance. He claimed Smith would go to Congress with "the Jerry Level" in his hand.[69]

In addition, the white abolitionist Reverend Samuel J. May delivered a speech two weeks after the Jerry Rescue and stated that when people saw a man being dragged through the streets, chained and treated like he was the worst of felons, all because he claimed his right to humanity, they were outraged.[70] Prior to this incident, May was a self-proclaimed pacifist, but in a letter to Garrison he confessed, "When I saw poor Jerry in the hands of the official kidnappers, I could not preach nonresistance very earnestly to the crowd who were clamoring for his release." May rationalized to Garrison that given the circumstances, the Fugitive Slave law presented him and the movement with little choice as it related to action. He acknowledged that if they could not "kill this infernal Law, it will kill us." Politically, the Fugitive Slave Law was the one step that in effect united all factions, from Garrisonians to Whigs, to Free Soilers, to Democrats, to black leadership. For the first time, collaboration seemed feasible and violence, particularly against slave catchers, was attractive. Circumstances reached a pinnacle that May saw as a "death-grapple."[71]

The law forced all people to weigh their risks, their level of involvement, and their commitment to their values. A black vigilance committee was in existence prior to the rescue, but its role inspired the formation of an interracial vigilance committee shortly after the passage of the Fugitive Slave Law. It was this interracial committee, composed of thirteen men "who pledged to interfere with any attempt to enforce the law in Syracuse" that helped to organize the rescue. When the Fugitive Slave Law came to Syracuse, the bravery and cohesion of the black community alongside the leaders of the white community who pledged support and protection made the rescue a success. Among the thirteen were Jermain Loguen, Charles Wheaton, Lyman Clary, Vivus Smith, Charles Sedgewick, Hiram Putnam, Elias Leavenworth, Abner Bates, George Barnes, Patrick Agan, Robert Raymond, and John Thomas.[72] These respected leading men were lawyers, newspaper editors, ministers, politicians, and even a physician. If these reputable men were willing to risk their livelihoods, what kind of an impact could they have on persons with much less to lose? While a number of people did not favor political violence or even abolition, the Fugitive Slave Law persuaded formerly apathetic people to pledge their support and promise their protection to runaway slaves. These actions were based more on defiance against the Slave Power than morality. The law was an affront to Northern sensibilities; it forced white Northern Americans to comply with the political and economic interests of slave owners in which they refused to be of service.

Thus, the Jerry Rescue made several significant contributions to the abolitionist movement. First, after the rescue, several trials were held to appropriate blame for Jerry's escape. These trials kept the issue of the Fugitive Slave Law in the public eye for almost two years, giving abolitionists the platform and publicity they needed. Second, people who might not have taken an interest in the antislavery movement previously were now paying attention to the new ways in which such laws affected them. Jerry was a constant reminder of how the city had come together for the cause of a fugitive slave. Third, not only was the law not successfully enforced, but also Syracuse became a place where fugitive slaves could seek assistance and shelter without fear of repercussions. Syracuse was able to prove Webster wrong. As Loguen hoped, Jerry's rescue served as a model and as a threat to future slave catchers and to the slavery system as a whole. Most important, Syracuse accepted the utility of forceful and even violent resistance to the Fugitive Slave Law. Resistance would no longer be merely rhetorical; the event became a ritual. Indeed, yearly celebrations of Jerry Rescue Day took place on October 1 in the black community from 1852 to 1860.

Throughout the 1850s the general public in the North became more receptive to the abolitionist message. In an editorial in the *Frederick Douglass' Paper*, Loguen wrote about his travels from Syracuse to southwest Pennsylvania. He traveled from city to city, from meeting to meeting, discussing the Fugitive Slave Law. Loguen remarked, "I never saw the time during the last ten years that I have been in the antislavery field when the public ear was so ready and willing to hear on American Slavery." Loguen believed the law was, in a way, "what we need at present" because of its ability to provoke resistance. "I hope it will drive them to action," Loguen declared; "I never had a better hearing."[73] No one other than a fugitive slave could excite the country to such extremes. Loguen wished abolitionists and their allies would not only defend their lives but also prepare to combat the Slave Power. By holding as many conventions as possible, he proclaimed, "I would that we could have force sufficient to commence a war upon this State . . . this fall. . . . I, under God, am determined to stand my ground and fight until the war shall end."[74] Whether Loguen was being rhetorical or literal in his call to action, one thing was certain: recent events had prepared the ground for violent response. As opposition to the Fugitive Slave Law grew, confrontations extended beyond the proximity of contested borders and into the heart of the nation's abolitionist center, Boston.

The Fugitive Slave Law in Massachusetts

If Christiana had Parker and Syracuse had Loguen, then Boston had Lewis Hayden. Hayden was one of the greatest and most radical leaders the black community had in Boston. He was born a slave in Lexington, Kentucky, where his personal story of loss and survival fueled his abolitionist activities. While enslaved in Kentucky, Lewis married (albeit not legally, for slaves were not allowed to marry) Esther Harvey and together they had a son. However, in 1836, Lewis and Esther were separated when Esther's master, Joseph Harvey, fell on hard economic times and sold Esther and their child to the famed lawyer and politician Henry Clay. Tragically, Esther bore a second child, who died in infancy. About a month after the infant's death, Clay decided to sell Esther and her only son again. Esther was devastated and informed Hayden,

LEWIS HAYDEN,
Eighteenth Grand Master of Prince Hall Grand Lodge, Boston, Mass.

Figure 4. "Lewis Hayden; Eighteenth Grand Master of Prince Hall Grand Lodge, Boston, Mass." Courtesy of the Jean Blackwell Hutson Research and Reference Division, Schomburg Center for Research in Black Culture, New York Public Library.

though there was little he could do about it. Regardless, Hayden approached Clay and asked him to tell him why he had sold his wife and son. Clay smugly responded that it was his prerogative, "he had bought them and sold them."[75] Hayden never saw or heard from them again. Later, he remarried, to a woman named Harriet, and escaped from Kentucky to Ohio, but the loss of Hayden's first wife and son was a wound that never fully healed.

Hayden and his wife Harriet moved again from Ohio to Michigan and eventually settled in Boston to become a part of the abolitionist movement. Hayden (much like David Walker) opened a clothing store on Cambridge Street in Boston and operated a boardinghouse with his wife on Southac Street (now known as Phillips Street). He and his wife used their businesses to aid fugitive slaves with food, clothing, shelter, and other essentials so that they could travel further north or establish themselves in Boston.

William and Ellen Craft's first home was with the Haydens in Boston. The Crafts were runaway slaves from Macon, Georgia, who famously disguised themselves to escape. Ellen's fair skin allowed her to pose as a disabled white man, while her husband William posed as her slave valet. They were close friends with the Haydens and even had their marriage formalized in the Hayden home, where the white abolitionist Theodore Parker officiated. After the ceremony, Parker presented the couple with a bible and a large bowie knife, one to protect their soul and the other to protect their lives. For them and many others, the Haydens were the salt of the earth and subsequently became stationmasters on the Underground Railroad.

When the Fugitive Slave Law came to Boston, a meeting of the Colored Citizens of Boston was held and Hayden was quickly chosen as the chairman of the group. Though Garrison spoke at the meeting, it was expressly led by black leaders, such as Josiah Henson, William Nell, and John T. Holten, who desired a more radical stance. The meeting was frequently interrupted with chants of "Liberty or death," and a resolution was passed, which included the statement "They who would be free, must themselves strike the blow."[76] Black leaders such as Joshua B. Smith, a caterer with a successful business, urged all runaways to arm themselves with revolvers and announced, "If liberty is not worth fighting for, it is not worth having."[77] Robert Johnson advised black women working in Boston's hotels to be on the lookout for Southern slave catchers and to warn others as soon as possible. He also advised black men to refrain from being aggressive, but if they were attacked by a slave catcher, his instructions were simple: "kill him."[78] Nonresistance would have no place among black leaders.

On October 14, 1850, a group against the Fugitive Slave Law called Fugitives and Their Friends held a rally at Boston's historic Faneuil Hall. Frederick Douglass was in attendance. The new law had compelled him to abandon the moral suasion camp completely. Douglass now openly encouraged resistance to the law and the "shooting down" of any "creature" who would try to steal the life and liberty of a human being. Douglass was at last facing the full impact of his own arguments concerning natural rights. He declared that life and liberty were the most sacred of all human rights and that nothing could be more important than self-defense. Douglass contended that anyone who attacked an enslaved person "be shot down, his punishment is just."[79] Self-defense underpinned all other virtues for Douglass. During his speech in

Faneuil Hall before black and white abolitionists, he predicted how black Americans would respond to the Fugitive Slave Law in Boston: "We must be prepared should this law be put into operation to see the streets of Boston running with blood." Because members of the meeting had committed themselves to resisting the law to the point of death, Douglass believed any altercation over the infringement of liberties would end in violence. Furthermore, Douglass added that he had heard rumors of slave catchers who were preparing to seize him at his home in Rochester, New York. In a tongue-in-cheek manner, he declared that a trapdoor existed inside his attic where he could wait, and because his home was very small and his enemies rather large, he would receive each hunter one at a time.[80] The audience applauded Douglass' desire to face slave catchers.

Overwhelmingly, black abolitionist numbers grew. The vigilance committee over which Hayden presided had grown to more than a hundred members. Hayden's home essentially became a fort. Runaway after runaway fled to the Hayden home for support, supplies, and protection. He could be trusted to the point of death. Allegedly, he made sure to have two kegs of gunpowder under his front porch. If slave catchers approached his door, he would answer with a candlestick in his hand and threaten to blow up his home before giving fugitives over to them. No one was willing to call his bluff.

In 1851, when a runaway slave named Fred Wilkins, also known as Shadrach, from Norfolk, Virginia, was captured in Boston by deputy marshals, Hayden was first on the scene. Men from the vigilance committee gathered around the courtroom in which Shadrach was being held and caused a commotion. The men conspired and collectively bum-rushed the court, seized Shadrach, and took him outside the city to safety along the Underground Railroad. When federal officials heard what happened, they were furious. Henry Clay, the architect of the Fugitive Slave Law and former owner of Hayden's wife Esther, asked on the floor of the Senate, "By whom was this mob impelled onward? By our own race? No, sir, but by negroes [sic]; by African descendants; by people who possess no part, as I contend, in our political system."[81] Clay was furious, but in many ways his anger was of his own doing. In a twist of fate, the enslaved man Clay had rebuffed just fifteen years prior was now leading orchestrated strikes against his laws, and he was not alone.

The government was quick to arrest suspected conspirators, including Hayden and the famed black lawyer Robert Morris, along with two other black men, James Scott and John Foyce, for the Shadrach rescue. The American Antislavery Society posted $3,000 as bail for Hayden, while the vigilance committee collected contributions for lawyers. Though the federal prosecutors did everything in their power to select jury members who favored the Fugitive Slave Law, the case was declared a mistrial because of one juror who held out for a not guilty verdict. Everyone was dismissed and free to go. About a year after the trial, Richard Henry Dana, a lawyer for the accused men, happened to meet a former juror who explained to him why it would have been impossible for the prosecution to win a conviction: "I was the twelfth juror in the case," he declared, "and I was the man who drove Shadrach over the [state] line."[82]

Not only had fugitive slaves become political, but fugitive slave cases made political careers, the best example being Senator Charles Sumner. He was one of the few abolitionists who possessed a desire for political influence and position. Sumner strongly opposed the Compromise of 1850, and the Fugitive Slave Law effectively launched his political career. When Sumner was in the Senate, he led a "one-man crusade in Congress" for the repeal of the act. The historian Manisha Sinha explains that Sumner had a prominent role in the escape of the Crafts, advised the lawyers of the fugitive slave Fred "Shadrach" Wilkins, and served as counsel in another famous case, the Thomas Sims fugitive case of 1851. While Sims was returned to slavery in Georgia, his case compelled abolitionists to protest and impassioned many of the people living in Boston. As senator, Sumner was able to obtain presidential pardons for two men accused of assisting runaway slaves, as well as freedom for the wife and children of another fugitive slave. Sumner, among a select few, represented the kind of collective political commitment necessary to produce change.[83] Indeed, by the middle of the decade, Sumner was involved in almost every high-profile fugitive slave case, including the trial of the most controversial fugitive slave case yet, Anthony Burns.

In the spring of 1854, no one expected how the capture and return of one fugitive slave could catapult the city of Boston into chaos. While living in Boston, a runaway slave, Anthony Burns, was arrested by slave catchers. As a slave, Burns had lived in Alexandria, Virginia, and fled to Boston by ship to pursue his own freedom. He, too, obtained a job in the clothing store owned and operated by Hayden. When Burns attempted to send for his brother, his master, Charles Suttle, was alerted of his whereabouts and traveled to Boston to retrieve him. While walking home from work, Burns was captured by authorities and jailed. When it appeared that Burns was likely to be reenslaved, a small group of black and white Bostonians met in the basement of Tremont

Temple to plot his release. Led by Hayden and Thomas Wentworth Higginson, a minister and white abolitionist known for his militancy, the group decided they would rescue Burns by force if necessary. As they proceeded to storm the courthouse, word of their intention spread, and soon thousands of abolitionists and supporters from all over the city descended upon the courthouse to protest Burns's arrest and seek his release. As the mob began to riot outside the courthouse, Hayden used a battering ram to open the courthouse door. Fighting ensued on both sides and in the middle of the commotion US marshal James Batchelder, cried out that he had been stabbed. He died within minutes because an object probably hit his femoral artery.[84] Only recently have scholars discovered that Hayden was Batchelder's murderer. In a letter to Higginson, William F. Channing acknowledged Hayden as the man who put an end to the marshal's life:

That he [Hayden] believes he fired the fatal shot there is no question. He told me that he saw you in a corner, with the deputy marshals hammering your head with their clubs. He said "They would have killed him, then I fired and they fired back. I did not pursue the inquiry into details from them. But, after the coroner's request on two or three days later (Monday or Saturday he believes) I interviewed my friend, D. Charles T. Jackson, who helped to examine Batchelder's wound. He said it was not a pistol shot the wound of a ball, but of a cutting instrument, sharp at both edges. The entrance of the instrument was a straight line, something more than an inch long. When I saw Hayden I asked him how this could have been. He said he had no ball to fit his pistol and loaded it with a chig—(a slug if it strikes sidewise, as it may, would make such a wound as Jackson describes). The skin contracts upon a gun shot wound. I give you this as the only piece of corroborating circumstantial evidence that I have. I do not remember how complete or in what shape my recollections were written which group sent you or extract I therefore should prefer not to have them printed—But you are very welcome to quote their substance. I drove Hayden out of town to Wm. J. Bowditch's House, the Sunday evening, following the attack on the Court House, after conferring with Theodore Parker. Perhaps Wm. J. Bowditch conversed fully with Hayden and may remember some incidents which I have not given.[85]

William J. Watkins, a fellow black abolitionist and coeditor of *Frederick Douglass' Paper*, was, as usual, outspoken. Defending the person who shot the marshal (we now know it was Hayden), Watkins contended that if he was a murderer, then so were George Washington and all the men who served under him in the defense of liberty. Watkins argued that black leaders believed in peaceably rescuing fugitive slaves if it could be so managed. But if there was no other alternative, Watkins attested, "we believe in rescuing them forcibly." Deadly force was on the table and black leaders felt no "compunction of conscience" for employing it.[86] Watkins' stance regarding self-defense was both practical and political. It was clear that black abolitionists wanted a response that met proslavery violence and aggression with equal fervor. For Watkins, black activists needed to "maintain a consistent warfare with the Slave Power" and no other tool but violence was proving its utility.[87]

Citizens were outraged, not so much over the marshal's death, but over the notion that a black man living in freedom could be seized and sent back to slavery in the city of Boston, a bastion of the antislavery movement. Nonetheless, President Franklin Peirce was bent on enforcing the Fugitive Slave Law. He provided the largest "show of force" to ever take place during peacetime, sending two thousand soldiers and marines equipped with artillery to assist in guarding Burns, and ordering a federal ship to return Burns to Virginia immediately after the trial. Peirce intended to set a precedent, and he did: it cost the federal government over $40,000 to return Burns to slavery, effectively making him one of the most expensive slaves in US history. On June 2, 1854, more than fifty thousand people lined the streets of Boston, as though they were witnessing the funeral procession of a head of state. They wore black and hung flags upside down. They even placed a mock coffin on State Street with a sign labeled "Liberty."[88] In response to Burns's return to slavery, Amos Adams Lawrence was moved from empathy to advocacy. He declared, "We went to bed one night old-fashioned, conservative, compromise Union Whigs & waked up stark mad Abolitionists."[89] While proslavery constituents had won the battle, abolitionists were preparing for war.

The return of Burns served only to exacerbate antislavery sentiment across the North. Abolitionists both black and white began to speak out more forcefully. In contempt, William Lloyd Garrison set fire to copies of the Fugitive Slave Law, the Burns court decision, and the US Constitution. *Frederick Douglass' Paper* announced that it was time for Northern policy to be

Figure 5. Anthony Burns. Courtesy of the Library of Congress.

recognized and respected. The newspaper warned that should the Slave Power agenda continue unbridled, then the showing in Boston would be more of a beginning than an end.[90] Charles Remond professed the same unapologetic attitude toward political violence and the Fugitive Slave Law. In 1854, Remond spoke before the New England Anti-Slavery Convention, largely about the recent Anthony Burns controversy. Remond admitted, "I know, Mr. Chairman, that I am not, as a general thing, a peacemaker. I am irritable, excitable, quarrelsome—I confess it." However, Remond added, "My prayer to God is, that I may never cease to be irritable, that I may never cease to be excitable, that I may never cease to be quarrelsome, until the last slave shall be made free in our country, and the colored man's manhood acknowledged."[91] His audience erupted with loud applause, affirming the speaker's righteous frustration. This was a dramatic change from the Remond who had started his career as a Garrisonian.

The Flight and Fight of Fugitive Slaves

Recording the heroic stories of fugitive slaves who had successfully resisted a return to slavery could not be circulated fast enough. William Still, known as the father of the Underground Railroad and responsible for the successful escape of over eight hundred slaves, made a point of recording the stories of his encounters with runaways. During one particular incident, four runaway slaves—Barnaby Grigby, his wife Mary Elizabeth, Frank Wanzer, and Emily Foster—escaped from Loudon County, Virginia, and journeyed over a hundred miles on horseback and in a carriage stolen from their master on Christmas Eve of 1855.[92] With Frank Wanzer leading them, the group suffered from hunger, freezing temperatures, and exhaustion as they traveled to their eventual destination of Canada. When they had made it as far as Cheat River, Maryland, "six white men, and a boy," who suspected they were fugitives, confronted them. They planned to attack the group and return them to their rightful owners. When asked to account for themselves, Wanzer declared that riding along civilly was not cause for interruption. But the white men were convinced that the group was composed of fugitives and refused to leave until they surrendered. Feeling cornered and without alternatives, the runaways pulled out their concealed pistols and dirks. Both men and women declared they would not be taken! One of the white men raised his gun and pointed it directly at one of the women, threatening to shoot, perhaps thinking she

Figure 6. "A Bold Stroke for Freedom," Maryland, December 25, 1855. Engraving by Charles
Reed depicting Barnaby Grigby's Escape. From William Still, *The Underground Railroad*
(Philadelphia: Porter & Coats, 1872). Courtesy of the Library Company of Philadelphia.

would surrender out of fear. With a double-barreled pistol in one hand and a
long dirk knife in the other, the woman shouted back, "Shoot! Shoot!! Shoot!!!"
Undeterred, she egged him on. Once again, black women refused to play the
role of a damsel in distress. In the face of such unflinching determination to
"spill blood, kill, or die," the group of white men left the travelers to continue
on their way. It appeared that slave catchers were only keen to return slaves so
long as their own lives were not at risk. Returning unarmed or outnumbered
men and women was easy; confronting armed men and women with nothing
to lose was an act of foolishness.[93]

The *Frederick Examiner*, a local newspaper in Maryland, received word
of the events that had taken place. Rather than report the true facts of the
story, they informed readers that most of the group succeeded in escaping
while one black man was shot in the back as he tried to flee on a horse. William Still surmised that the reporter misinformed his readers because they
did not wish to reveal the bold stances fugitives, and in particular black

women, were willing to take. Nor did they wish to undermine the prevailing myth of the docile, loyal slave.[94] Eventually, the four made their way to Syracuse, where they met up with the vigilance committee headed by Loguen. After they celebrated their freedom with newfound friends, they proceeded to Toronto and were there "gladly received by the Ladies' Society for aiding colored refugees."[95]

Times were changing. When John Anderson, an escaped slave who had fled to Canada, gave his testimony before an audience, he received great and prolonged cheering. As Anderson approached the crowd, he modestly declared that he was not used to public speaking and only wanted to say a few words about his experiences and escape from slavery. He reported that in order to escape bondage he had to cut and run and fight and shed blood. "I don't like to shed blood," he added. "That is what is called fighting in war, I believe." The audience then erupted with cries of "You did right" and "Hear, hear!" Anderson, heavy with regret, told the audience he had tried everything in his ability to evade his pursuer and to avoid killing him. He had warned the pursuer that if he continued to follow him, he would slay him. Pursued for two or three hours longer, Anderson recounted that the man would not leave him and so he killed him. Again, the audience erupted with affirmation, shouting "Bravo!" and "You did right." He concluded that while he regretted his actions, it was his only alternative to prevent being taking back into bondage. He claimed he was a Christian man and hoped that after the murder he could still be considered a godly man.[96]

The crowd interrupted again by cheering and shouting, "It was a justifiable act." The reverend chairman of the meeting proclaimed that if there was any kind of defense that was right, then one should fully endorse the opinion so loudly expressed in the meeting. Then the chairman added, "John Anderson did perfectly right. . . . Does our fugitive friend look like a murderer?" The response of the audience was a resounding, "Hear, hear and No, no."[97] The days of nonresistance were over. Now, a fugitive slave could kill his pursuer and produce excitement and applause among public audiences. He could even still be considered Christian.

In many ways, the tenets of physical and political violence were nothing more than a recycled strategy derived from four basic principles. First, fugitive slaves believed they were justified in using violence to protect their freedom just as much as the American revolutionaries and Haitians had been in securing theirs.[98] For black abolitionists, the American and Haitian Revolutions were more than a set of principles: they were precedents. In a letter published in the *North Star*, fugitive slaves declared, "If the American revolutionists had excuse for shedding but one drop of blood, then have the American slaves excuse for making blood to flow 'even unto the horse-bridles.'"[99] Second, black abolitionists justified self-defense and collective defense. In response to the Fugitive Slave Law, Douglass appealed to the natural law of self-preservation. He declared that "to act to enslave a fellow man is to declare war against him and to endow him with the right to war—the liberty to kill his aggressor." Vigilance groups and protection societies operated on this premise as well.[100] Third, the fugitive slave had no rights and was not given the opportunity to testify or present evidence, which left men and women with few alternatives. Many black abolitionists who wanted America to be their home believed that physical violence was the only alternative for a suspected fugitive slave. Fourth, abolitionists argued that the principles of the Fugitive Slave Law contradicted the laws of God. Loguen declared, "I owe my freedom to the God who made me, and who stirred me to claim it against all other beings in God's universe. I received my freedom from Heaven, and with it came the command to defend my title to it."[101] Indeed, the Bible validated such commands: "Thou shalt not deliver unto his master the servant which is escaped from his master unto thee."[102] For an enslaved people who survived on biblical principles, such scripture carried significant meaning and may have been their most important tenet.

Just three years after Remond gave his speech on the coming of the Fugitive Slave Law and the inaction of free black people, the social and political climate was constantly changing. For Remond, each forceful episode during the antebellum period appeared to be building up to the eventual demise of slavery. Despite the Fugitive Slave Law, Remond was surprisingly optimistic: "I may speak for the colored people of New England, at least when I say, *We feel encouraged.* We were encouraged by the Jerry Rescue, at Syracuse; by the death of slaveholders at Christiana; and we were encouraged by the deaths of Calhoun, Clay, and Webster, that trio of defenders of slavery." He saw these episodes as small victories for the movement.[103]

The resistance that resulted from the Fugitive Slave Law was an indication of the degree to which black abolitionists were willing to rely on force. At the black Ohio state convention, the leadership argued that white Americans could employ peaceful reform with the ballot, but black Americans could employ reform only through violence.[104] For too long, the black community had turned the other cheek and engaged in the tactic of moral suasion and nonresistance and accomplished little. The Fugitive Slave Law presented them with the impetus and the opportunity to take matters into their own hands. Individual and collective protective defense by African Americans proved their strength and ability to manufacture change. Black leaders would be the most discussed political figures who ran not for office but for freedom. Violence would be the new political tool for the oppressed, the new method of a casting a ballot for progress.

CHAPTER 3

From Prayers to Pistols

The Struggle for Progress

I prayed for twenty years but received no answer until I
prayed with my legs.

—Frederick Douglass

Slave catching persisted well into the 1850s and continued to ignite unyielding defiance until the Civil War. Regardless of the numerous heroic rescues,
the power and persistence of the law prevailed. The expansion of slavery and
the Slave Power's advantages concerning the law caused many abolitionists to
abandon all attempts at moral suasion. Just as Henry Highland Garnet argued for bloodshed a decade prior in his famous speech, now others were in
agreement, including Frederick Douglass. In the summer of 1853, Jermain
Loguen expressed the opinion that slavery would be abolished through either
agitation or bloodshed, admitting, "I sometimes think that I care not which."
A year later, H. Ford Douglas contemplated abandoning not only moral suasion, but the United States as well. He claimed that because the United States
treated him "as a stranger and an alien," he could join a foreign enemy and
fight against the United States without being a traitor.[1] As time passed, the
progress for which abolitionists fought did not seem inevitable. In fact, progress felt stymied.

Well into the 1850s, feelings of angst, hopelessness, and desperation began
to overwhelm the movement. Black abolitionists faced an uphill battle in
their endeavor to combat slavery and inequality when up against the political
strength of the Slave Power. In an antislavery newspaper, black abolitionists
summed up the political will and character of the government regarding the

enslaved, noting that proslavery legislative acts outnumbered those devoted to any other topic, even as senators proclaimed their desire to help the poor and the disenfranchised.[2] The irony of this dynamic was not lost on black abolitionists. Few, if any, black Americans had the patience to wait the untold number of years it might have taken for moral suasion to convince the Slave Power that their cause was just. The 1850s had brought nothing black abolitionists saw as success. Instead, black Americans saw the expansion of slavery into the territories and a series of legal decisions that strengthened their status as property and people without inalienable rights.

In 1854, the Kansas-Nebraska Act established the territories of Kansas and Nebraska and allowed residents of each territory to declare whether they would become a free or a slaveholding state. Aside from the Fugitive Slave Law, nothing brewed a more politically violent response than the issue of whether Kansas would enter the nation as a free or a slave territory. The Kansas-Nebraska Act was, for many, a collection of concessions made to the Slave Power. Popular sovereignty allowed for the free or slave status of the territory to be decided by its inhabitants. Kansas was the perfect site of the contest for power because of its proximity to the slave state Missouri (Nebraska was so far north that few questioned its future as a free territory).

Abolitionists, slave owners, politicians, and pure opportunists sent every person and resource they had to Kansas to secure their agenda, by force if necessary. Between 1854 and 1856, a series of violent events took place over the issue of slavery, perhaps more than at any other time prior to the Civil War. By the fall of 1856, Kansas had experienced unprecedented bloodshed committed by large numbers of proslavery forces that were taking up arms to defend their cause. The persistent violence that accompanied the campaign to determine whether Kansas would become a free or slave territory resulted in the deaths of fifty-five people, giving the territory the sobriquet Bleeding Kansas.

While the Fugitive Slave Law had accelerated ideas about self-defense, Kansas exacerbated a shifting orientation that was well underway for black leaders and served as the final straw for white abolitionists who remained undecided regarding changing tactics. Black leaders were calling for radical change and the equation was simple: the violent institution of slavery required a violent demise. Given this premise, black abolitionists found legitimacy in their claims for a violent destruction of slavery. In their anger and weariness, black leaders developed their own political language, their own political party, and even their own military companies to respond. Throughout the 1850s the greater willingness to countenance violence as not only morally justified but politically necessary was brought about by events such as Bleeding Kansas and a growing Slave Power. The political dismantling of slavery mandated legal actions such as federal legislation that would effectively abolish slavery. Thus, states in contestation over slavery, like Kansas, represented increased political capital among slave states. The contest over slavery was not only verbal but also physical. The more slavery expanded, the more white abolitionists doubted their ability to break its hold without meeting the system tool for tool.

The entire decade of the 1850s witnessed attempts to deprive black Americans of civic and legal rights, both politically and socially. The Fugitive Slave Law was only the beginning. Some Southern states attempted to drive out or enslave free black Americans; some Western states barred black Americans from entering altogether. Farther south, the Slave Power was even pursuing the expansion of slavery into Cuba and Mexico.[3] In 1857, the Supreme Court handed down the *Dred Scott* decision to both the states and US territories. The court declared that black Americans, free or enslaved, had essentially "no rights which white men were bound to respect."[4] It was clear that black Americans had few alternatives.

Throughout the 1850s, each piece of proslavery legislation, each incident of slave-catching violence, served to compound militancy among black Americans and bring about the conversion of white abolitionists as they joined their black partners in the belief that violence was the most effective political tool to produce change regarding abolition. This decade is also known for being a moment of black militancy, particularly during black conventions. From the contest over Kansas and the caning of Charles Sumner to the Dred Scott Decision, each political consequence led to the belief that politics, force, and armed resistance should be the response of black leaders and their white allies. Entry to formal politics for African Americans was about reestablishing the twofold goals of all black Americans: immediate emancipation and equality under the law. Political parties such as the Free Soil Movement or even the Republican Party were more concerned about the containment of slavery than they were its complete abolition. The shift toward greater radicalism and violence impacted the entire spectrum of black and white abolitionists in the North and stemmed from a growing inability to stop slavery's expansion and secure freedom and equality for all black Americans.

Kansas and the Response of Political Parties

Mary Ann Shadd Cary's newspaper, the *Provincial Freeman* was the first and longest lasting in North America edited by an African American woman. Shadd Cary was highly influential in social activism and the Underground Railroad. Born to free parents, she was educated in Quaker schools in Pennsylvania, because it was illegal to educate black people in her home state of Delaware. She taught children in racially integrated schools, and when she settled with her brother in Winsor Ontario, just across the border from Detroit, she used her press to recruit more black Americans to Canada and promote black empowerment. Shadd Cary acknowledged that white Northerners understood the repeal of the Missouri Compromise as an affront to their own liberty but, unfortunately, were not concerned as to how it affected black Americans.[5] Her newspaper reported: "The rights of white men had been invaded; a solemn compact entered into with white Americans had been broken." She lamented that in the fight to combat slavery and its expansion, the struggles of the slave and free black Americans had been left out of the equation and out of the consciousness of white Northerners.

Among black leaders, the contest over the Kansas-Nebraska Act did not go unnoticed. *Frederick Douglass' Paper* explained that the Nebraska Bill "not only permits the existence of Slavery by a vote of the people in Nebraska and Kansas, but it absolutely and for ever annuls the Missouri Compromise." The Compromise of 1820 had declared that there should be no slavery in any new territory north of latitude 36°30′, but now that ruling was overturned. The newspaper contended that if the Missouri Compromise could be so easily rescinded, then "they [Congress] should claim a revocation and abrogation of the latter compromise which contains the obnoxious Fugitive Slave Law!"[6] But it was unlikely that any legislation that favored the enslaved would be enacted. For some radical abolitionists, the Free Soil Party and the Republican Party were too conservative in their stances on ending slavery and too racist when it came to equality among free African Americans. In 1854, William J. Wilson wrote a dispatch denouncing the persistent institution of slavery and calling black men to arms. Wilson proclaimed, "Let the tocsin be sounded, and to arms every man whose skin is not whitened with the curse of God; and let our motto be, 'hands off or death.'"[7]

The Kansas-Nebraska Act inspired violent resistance from both Northerners and Southerners alike. Illinois senator Stephen A. Douglas never intended

Kansas to lead to bloodshed. His initial purpose was to open thousands of acres for new farms and make a Midwestern Transcontinental Railroad possible. But replacing the Missouri Compromise's prohibition on slavery in the new territories with popular sovereignty paved the way for chaos.

In 1855, during the March election of a territorial legislature, Missourians flooded into the territory to vote in their slaveholding interests. All throughout the territory, voter intimidation was rampant at the polls. Armed Missourians threatened voters and election officials who hailed from free states. When proslavery candidates were elected, many understood the result to be fraudulent. How else could a territory of 2,905 eligible voters cast more than 5,000 ballots? Critics referred to the outcome as the Bogus Legislature.[8] Violence escalated during the winter of 1855–56. In a dispute over a land claim, a Missourian killed a Free-State settler. In retaliation, Free-Staters terrorized the neighborhood, calling out proslavery settlers and their burning homes.

Democratic senator David Atchison, from the state of Missouri, proclaimed that Northerners were nothing more than "negro thieves" and called abolitionists "tyrants." In an attempt to ensure that Kansas would enter the nation as a slave territory, Atchison pressed Missourians to defend slavery "with the bayonet and with blood" and, if necessary, "to kill every God-damned abolitionist in the district."[9] As a proslavery activist and Border Ruffian leader (Border Ruffians were militants who flooded Kansas from Missouri in an attempt to institute slavery in the territory), Atchison refused to allow the state of Missouri to be surrounded by three free states (Illinois, Iowa, and potentially Kansas), because that formation would only encourage more slaves to run away.

At the same time, the Republican Party and the Free Soilers, a third party whose primary goal was to prevent slavery from expanding into the Western territories, were working directly in opposition to the Slave Power and the Border Ruffians. Indeed, the newly formed Republican Party was largely formed because of the Kansas-Nebraska Act. Political parties such as Free Soilers, Whigs, anti-immigrant Know Nothings (of the nativist American Party), and anti-Nebraskan Democrats found solidarity in their desire to keep both territories free. However, it would be incorrect to assume that all Northerners who opposed slavery were abolitionists.

During the eighteenth century, slavery was commonly practiced in the North, and after abolition many Northerners held on to antiblack sentiments. Free Soil was about the protection of wage laborers from slave economies, which undermined those efforts. Most Americans were bent on preserving their own economic interests at the expense of others' (i.e., the enslaved) or the exclusion of others (i.e., free black people, Native Americans, the Irish). One could easily be antislavery without claiming abolitionism. In fact, despite Atchison's claim, abolitionists were always in the minority. The intention of the Republican and Free Soil movements was to obtain and maintain land for the white worker. For the Free Soilers, slavery had nothing to do with oppression and everything to do with the disadvantageous economic position of white workers competing for labor. Furthermore, plantations took up large amounts of land that could be used for homesteads by white working people. Slavery not only monopolized the soil but also brought large amounts of black people wherever it existed. Free Soilers hated the presence of slavery and the presence of black Americans—so much so, that on December 15, 1855, they voted 1,287 to 453 to outlaw black people, slave or free, from entering Kansas. As far as the Free Soilers and the Republicans were concerned, Kansas should be free of black people altogether. Politically, the Kansas-Nebraska Act solidified two major parties as oppositional foes: the Democratic South and the Republican North.

Harkening back to the early colonization schemes of the ACS (American Colonization Society), reportedly the *New York Tribune's* editor Horace Greeley, had announced a desire to export black Americans out of the United States. Prominent African American leaders recognized that many who touted free labor simultaneously claimed that they "didn't want the niggers about them" and that this was a problematic and primary cause of black leaders' political ineffectiveness.[10] Much of the frustration black abolitionists felt stemmed from belief that the apparent struggle for "white liberty" had significantly undercut the struggle of those in deepest need.[11] During the antebellum years, and in particular during the period of Bleeding Kansas, it was entirely possible to hold both antislavery and antiblack sentiments. Even Douglass commented, "Opposing slavery and hating its victims has become a very common form of abolitionism." As one scholar has put it, "To proclaim both free soil and white supremacy" was the Republican way.[12]

Expansion and Expense

Black abolitionists used the Kansas-Nebraska Act as a platform for discussing injustice in general. They wanted to make sure antislavery readers and their audiences understood what the underlying issues were and the deep

concerns over the expansion of slavery. At the Twenty-First Annual Massachusetts Antislavery Society meeting, leaders stated that previously slavery as
an institution had been "safe and strong." They contended that all parties,
both church and state, had quietly acquiesced to slavery's existence. However,
the Slave Power had taken a more aggressive position in recent years. The
Liberator proclaimed, "When men bestir themselves, wage war, and strive to
strengthen their position, it shows that they feel they are weak and in danger."[13] The fierce contest over the territory of Kansas was a major sign of vul-
nerability on behalf of the slaveholding political powers. The activist William
J. Watkins was an orator leader in the black Canadian community who
moved to Canada from Baltimore. His cousin, Frances Ellen Watkins Harper,
was also a leading voice on the antislavery circuit. As editor of the *Frederick
Douglass' Paper*, William Watkins was concerned that observers need not
foolishly think the Kansas issue was innocent. Watkins argued that the exten-
sion of slavery had nothing to do with new land suitable for farming but was
based on greed from slaveholders who sought to expand their territories. He
exclaimed, "The cupidity of slavery has not respect for climate, or soil, or
geographical position."[14]

Paradoxically, the more the Slave Power worked to push its political agenda,
the more it indirectly bolstered the enthusiasm of the antislavery movement
and Slave Power opponents. Watkins wrote, "Slaveholders and their apolo-
gists are unconsciously erecting a gallows upon which to hang themselves."[15]
He claimed that slaveholders were only accelerating their own demise and
that of the foul system of slavery. Watkins believed that the Slave Power's agitation, particularly in the areas of the Fugitive Slave Law and the Kansas-
Nebraska Act, would not succeed because their desire to expand slavery
would lead to unintended consequences in the North. The Fugitive Slave Law
had continuously disrupted Northerners' way of life. The controversy over
Kansas would become even more dominant in the public consciousness than
fugitive slave cases.

Furthermore, the battles in Kansas left Americans wanting to know more
not only about these controversial topics but also about their consequences.
If Southerners could claim Kansas, then their representation in Congress
could grow, for the three-fifths clause (which stated that the enslaved represented three-fifths of a person) allowed for the enslaved to be counted regarding both the distribution of taxes and the apportionment of the members
of the United States House of Representatives. Most Northerners were not
willing to see slavery spread throughout the United States at the expense of

their own economic and political power and consequently would vote Democrats out.[16]

Thus, the controversy over Kansas had the greatest impact in the struggle for political power. Northerners, Southerners, and black Americans both free and enslaved could sense the unavoidable clash that was coming and that slavery as an institution existed on borrowed time. Watkins described the contentious climate aptly, speaking on the anniversary of the emancipation of the British West Indies to both honor the occasion and encourage a similar result in his own country. He noted that the dark crisis over slavery transcended all of the nation's previous crises, was omnipresent, and would be resolved only through the initiating actions of the enslaved.[17] He predicted that liberty and slavery were "marshalling their respective armies for a mighty conflict," a conflict that was inevitable because freedom and slavery were in direct opposition. For Watkins, it was impossible for free labor and slavery to live side by side in the United States of America. He claimed, "The living and the dead, chained together in one habitation, is the most repugnant and hideous anomaly ever revealed to the gaze of angels or of men."[18] Kansas was merely a sign of things to come. Kansas was also the greatest instance in which abolitionists recognized the need for more than the printing press and financial resources: as in Christiana, Boston, and Ohio, actual arms were required.

Radical Political Abolitionists

Strategy for social and political advancement was not left up to the electoral process alone. Black and white abolitionists came together to form the Radical Political Abolition Party in response to the Kansas-Nebraska Act. In 1855, the Radical Political Abolition Party was a descendent of Gerrit Smith's Liberty Party, which was a minor and short-lived party that had moderate success during the 1840s. The Liberty Party believed the US Constitution was an antislavery document. It directly opposed the view of Garrison's American Antislavery Society, which saw the Constitution as a proslavery document and the political arena as an ineffective means to abolish slavery. The Liberty Party also believed that political tools were the best equipment with which to abolish slavery immediately. It was a legitimate political party and was composed of America's leading black abolitionists—Frederick Douglass, Jermain Loguen, James McCune Smith—and white abolitionists—Gerrit Smith, John Brown, and Lewis Tappan.

In their revamped version of the Liberty Party, Radical Political Abolitionists wanted to do more than prevent the spread of slavery they wanted to
eradicate it altogether. While Free Soilers and Republicans were playing defense in terms of slavery's expansion, Radical Abolitionists were taking up an
offensive stance. They refused to compromise with the Slave Power or with
anyone who wanted to navigate around the issue of slavery. Furthermore,
they firmly advocated for African American rights, including citizenship.
They had big plans. The Radical Political Abolition Party was the first to have
its national convention and name a black man to chair. In fact, McCune
Smith was nominated for secretary of state. The party was not only concerned
with black liberation but also with addressing the needs of oppressed peoples
everywhere. They petitioned for an end to women's status as second-class citizens, wanted to end the genocide of Native Americans, and even believed in
the redistribution of political power and resources. Radical Political Abolitionists did not just break from moral suasion, they openly embraced the
idea of insurrection and the efforts of John Brown.

Radical Political Abolitionists saw themselves as part of a crusade, in
which they were called to eradicate evil. According to one historian, Radical
Political Abolitionists believed in "sacred self-sovereignty." Along these lines
violence was justified and even sanctioned from a biblical standpoint.[19]
Should their political means fail, violence was available. In fact, at their June
meeting they acknowledged that armed resistance was the only viable option
to combat slavery in places such as the Kansas and Nebraska territories. Mc-
Cune Smith, one of the founders of the Radical Political Abolitionist Party,
stated that they intended to abolish slavery "by means of the Constitution; or
otherwise." He clarified: "Should there be any quarrel in the future as to the
meaning of [or otherwise]," he told Gerrit Smith, "I mean fight."[20] McCune
Smith was an avid supporter of using physical force. It was during 1856, when
Kansas was erupting in violence, that he declared, "Our white brethren cannot understand us unless we speak to them in their own language; they recognize only the philosophy of force." He claimed that the idea of equal
humanity could not get through the "thick skulls of the Caucasians, unless
beaten into them."[21]

Furthermore, Radical Political Abolitionists saw themselves as the sole
solution to immediate abolition. They collected funds on behalf of John
Brown for his missions both in Kansas and eventually his raid on Harpers
Ferry. Garrison called the Radical Abolitionists "Madmen."[22] But by the
1850s, most black abolitionists who may not have joined the Radical Political

Abolitionist Party firmly believed that politics, not moral suasion, was the most effective way to overthrow slavery.

In June 1855, the newly formed party held one of its conventions, in Syracuse, New York. Their goal was to remove slavery from the national territories and the states "by means of our national political power."[23] They claimed that politically the Whigs, Democrats, and Know-Nothing Parties were all complicit in maintaining the institution of slavery. They argued that Free Soilers were antislavery but did not believe that the federal government should interfere with the laws of states. Finally, they acknowledged the American Anti-Slavery Society, or Garrison Party, labored only within the limits of moral suasion to abolish slavery and it employed no political power to this end. Accordingly, the party saw itself as "the only political party in the land, that insists on the right and duty to wield the political power of the nation for the overthrow of every part and parcel of American Slavery."[24] For the members, the Constitution demanded and required the abolition of all American slavery.

Black abolitionists and their allies began to use political power as a weapon. They compelled moderate leaders to move away from the center and consider a more radical approach. Just as gag orders in Congress and the Fugitive Slave Act served as a response to abolitionists' efforts through the Underground Railroad and antislavery newspapers, so too Kansas reflected a dialectic between antislavery and proslavery factions. The activism of the Radical Political Abolition Party forced a conservative Republican Party further from the center in advocating for the enslaved. Formal politics were the only way that free black Americans could exercise any rights or freedom in the North. Martin Delany exclaimed that free black Americans were just as oppressed as enslaved black Americans. Just as the enslaved were denied all civil, religious, and social privileges, except for what they got by mere sufferance, he claimed, "so are we." He continued, "They [the enslaved] have no part nor lot in the government of the country, neither have we. They are ruled and governed without representation, existing as mere nonentities among the citizens, and excrescences on the body politics—a mere dreg in the community, and so are we." If free black Americans were truly free men, Delany asked, then where was their political superiority to the enslaved?[25] Black abolitionists required more than emancipation; they desired economic, social, and political power. While helping runaway slaves make their way to freedom was satisfying to white abolitionists, most black leaders understood that there was a dual task at hand: eradicating slavery

and simultaneously elevating free black Americans. Therein lay the importance of political power, securing the ballot, and putting it to use.[26]

Matching formal politics with abolitionism courted violence because it
was the only strategy that could legally eradicate slavery. It threatened the
economic livelihood of the slaveholding South and white supremacy altogether. Slaveholders and those invested in slavery made it clear they were
willing to risk their lives and the lives of those in opposition to them to preserve both oppression of African Americans and the sovereignty of slavery.
Southern politicians and slaveholding states had long espoused violence to
combat abolitionists. Even the slightest infractions involving antislavery positions invoked harsh prison sentences or courted violent reprisal. This was
best illustrated in the caning of Charles Sumner.

A champion of civil rights and a Harvard-educated lawyer, Sumner understood the utility of politics as the best tool to bring about reform. In 1843,
he opposed the Massachusetts state law that prohibited interracial marriage.
In 1845, he refused to speak before segregated audiences at the New Bedford
Lyceum. In 1848, he helped to form the Free Soil party and protested the annexation of Texas and the Mexican War. In 1849, he worked to integrate public schools and represented Sarah Roberts, a young black child whose
landmark case inspired the fight to open up Boston schools for all children.
In 1851, he was elected as a Free Soiler to the US Senate, where he continued
his antislavery efforts. By the mid-1850s, he was endorsing the Republican
Party and speaking out against the Kansas-Nebraska Act. He was adamant
about thwarting the Slave Power and its expanding influence on American
politics. Senator Stephen A. Douglas blamed Sumner for promoting "the
cause of niggerism," and Senator Andrew P. Butler continually let it be known
with derogatory language how little he thought of Sumner and those who
endorsed abolitionism. In short, Sumner was hated by defenders of slavery
long before his gave one of his more famous speeches on the Senate floor regarding Kansas.[27]

On May 19 and 20, 1856, Sumner spoke out against the Kansas-Nebraska
Act during a speech in which he ridiculed its authors, Douglas and Butler,
using sexual imagery. He claimed Southerners' "crime against Kansas" was
akin to the rape of a virgin and that Senator Butler was in love with a harlot—
known as slavery. His three-hour speech was so controversial that Stephen
Douglas remarked to a colleague during the speech, "This damn fool Sumner
is going to get himself shot by some other damn fool."[28]

Sure enough, Preston Brooks, a congressman from South Carolina and nephew to Senator Andrew Butler, intended to make a lesson out of Sumner. Political violence took place not only in the remote and growing territories of the West but also in the Senate chamber of the nation's capital. On May 22, just two days later, while sitting at his chamber desk, Brooks approached Sumner and stated, "I have read your speech twice over carefully. It is a libel on South Carolina, and Mr. Butler, who is a relative of mine." At that moment, he began to strike Sumner over the head using a thick gutta-percha cane with a gold head. Sumner was repeatedly bludgeoned over his entire body. He tried to crawl under his desk for refuge, but given that his desk was bolted to the floor, it only served has a holding pin while Brooks continued to take aim at him. Brooks beat him so fearlessly that the desk eventually released from the floor. As Sumner lay bloodied and unconscious, Brooks stopped only when his cane broke.[29] All attempts to come to Sumner's rescue were thwarted while a fellow South Carolinian, Representative Laurence M. Keitt, a proslavery Democrat, stood at the door of the chamber with his pistol until Brooks was satisfied. In the end, Sumner miraculously survived. It took him more than three years to recover from his injuries. Some might argue he never fully recovered.

Letters of support poured in from the black community to Sumner. Black abolitionists and leaders such as Robert Morris, William C. Nell, John S. Rock, and the Reverend Leonard Grimes came together at Boston's Twelfth Baptist Church to organize a public meeting in honor of "our Senator." Black people undoubtedly connected Sumner's attack to their own violence experienced in slavery. However, in the *Liberator*, one abolitionist acknowledged, "I would not love him [Sumner] the less; but I think we would all do well to love Brooks's slaves a little more . . . and not forget altogether the millions of victims, who, unlike Mr. Sumner, are not loaded with sympathy and honors."[30] While free black Americans saw what Sumner experienced as tragic, it also proved that if Sumner attempted to morally convict Butler of wrongdoing, then moral suasion was not only useless, but deadly. In an editorial for the *Provincial Freeman*, Mary Ann Shadd Cary contended that the show of "Ruffianism in the Halls of Legislature" indicated that the inherent violence of slavery had spread "from the black man to the white."[31] The beating of Sumner marked a turning point in which not only abolitionists but also white political leaders could be targets of violence.

Sumner's attack validated African Americans' desire to intervene in politics at the national level and have their voices heard. One of the most remarkable responses to Sumner's beating came from an editorial in the *New Orleans*

Daily Creole, a black newspaper that debuted about a month after the attack. The op-ed was titled "A Challenge to Mr. Brooks." Mrs. Amelia R. M. Robinson called the attacks cowardly—to beat a man unarmed and down. She referred to Brooks as a "cringing puppy" whom she would gladly challenge to meet her any place with "pistols, rifles, or cowhides." The outrage Robinson felt had no bearing on her sex. She, like other black male leaders, was exasperated by sacrifices that had cost her dearly. She was fifty years old and a widow. She has lost two of her sons in the Mexican War. Brooks's actions represented a direct affront to her own liberty, a liberty that she believed her country should protect. "Now, then, Mr. Brooks," Robinson challenged, "Let us see some of your boasted courage!" You are afraid to meet a man! Dare you meet a woman?" Robinson declared that she was anxious to do her country some service either by "whipping or choking the cowardly ruffian," who threatened what she perceived as America's most precious right—freedom of speech. Robinson was willing to put her strong words into print to expose her distain regarding the attack of Sumner. And more than any man, she was willing to publicly retaliate.[32] While many were praying for Sumner, Robinson illustrates what she was willing to do with a pistol.

Radical White Abolitionists and Kansas

Many white abolitionists were finally responding to the pressure from black abolitionists to consider political means in addition to armed resistance. The 1850s made it clear for white leadership in the movement that political reform and violence went hand in hand. Frederick Douglass stressed that although in Kansas every advantage was on the side of the Slave Power (the repeal of the Missouri Compromise, the strength of the Democratic Party, the power and patronage of the federal government), the battle over Kansas's status rekindled the zeal of the abolitionist movement. Kansas presented African Americans with the violence and threat of violence that followed them every day. The times were calling for deeper investments from white allies, either from their pocketbooks or their willingness to risk physical confrontation. Douglass noted that men of both great and meager means lent their resources to ensure that Kansas would be a free territory. Gerrit Smith, a white abolitionist, social reformer, and philanthropist from New York, promised to donate money to the cause of bringing Kansas in as a free territory. He declared, "Draw on me $1000 per month while the conflict lasts." Such financial support was important, but Douglass acknowledged that the greatest sacrifices were made by the men who traveled to Kansas and became heroes and martyrs.[33] Among white abolitionists, perhaps the greatest of these was John Brown.

Brown found himself on the side of violence when, in 1856, he and his sons killed five proslavery settlers at Pottawatomie. That same year, Brown was nicknamed Osawatomie Brown for his use of guerilla warfare when he fought valiantly with two dozen men against Major General John W. Reid and his troops of over three hundred Missourians in Osawatomie, Kansas. Brown and Bleeding Kansas became national news, and the territories remained contested until January 1861, when Kansas was admitted to the Union as a free state, and 1867, when Nebraska was admitted to the Union as a state after the Civil War.

Brown made it his personal task to travel to Kansas to help keep the Kansas and Nebraska territories from falling into the hands of slaveholders. Brown was outraged by the caning of Charles Sumner and by the violence that was taking place at the hands of Border Ruffians against abolitionists and their families who desired these lands to be free from slavery. Brown was infuriated by what he considered to be a lack of courage among the antislavery partisans and sought out donors to obtain supplies and guns for defense.[34] Brown went so far as to petition abolitionists at a convention in Syracuse, New York, for money to buy guns for his work in Kansas. His request brought about intense division among the group, with some offering to help and others objecting to the plan. Nevertheless, Brown found plenty of support when he traveled to Akron, Ohio. There, he received an outpouring of money, weapons, ammunition, and clothing.[35]

One affirmative response came from Henry Ward Beecher, a white abolitionist and the brother of Harriet Beecher Stowe, who pledged that his own Plymouth Church would donate twenty-five Sharp rifles to aid in the work of antislavery men.[36] The firearms became known as Beecher Bibles because they were often shipped in wooden crates marked "Bibles" or "books."[37] An article in the New York Tribune reported that as far as Beecher was concerned, the rifles would do more good than a hundred Bibles in persuading proslavery individuals to change their course.[38] Beecher, his congregation, and many other white abolitionists were making it clear that it was neither moral suasion nor votes that would result in freedom, but force. Brown used all the resources he could muster for arms and supplies necessary to confront proslavery forces.

In retrospect, Gerrit Smith acknowledged that regarding Bleeding Kansas, it was not "mere words [that] have kept slavery out of Kansas; or that mere words will suffice to resist its aggressions elsewhere. These aggressions can be successfully resisted only by such men as have consecrated to the mighty work [of the] head and heart and arm and purse."[39] Smith also became the single largest financier of John Brown in Kansas during his famous Pottawatomie Massacre. Smith, along with black abolitionists, understood that effective antislavery necessitated a conviction, resources (financial or otherwise), and force to accomplish the task and that the greatest of these was force.

In 1854, Smith lamented that the Republican Party was truly "the white man's party" because it did not fight to repeal the Fugitive Slave Act or abolish slavery in the District of Columbia. Smith wrote to Douglass, "As you are aware, I went to Congress with very little hope of the peaceful termination of American slavery. I have returned with less."[40] He added that before the men who would be capable of bringing slavery to a voluntary termination could arise, "American slavery will have expired in blood."[41]

Kansas and black abolitionists had a strong effect upon antislavery whites. A black political abolitionist and merchant from Portland, Oregon, Abner H. Francis, claimed in *Frederick Douglass' Paper* that black Americans' hope for political change rested in the hands of sympathetic antislavery white Americans.[42] White support could not have been strong had it not been for the willingness of black leaders to effectively persuade and pressure followers. One by one, white abolitionists who touted moral suasion began to see the efficacy of force and the futility of nonviolence. It is important to note that the white abolitionists who began to make ideological shifts were prominent leaders within their organizations. The famed author and abolitionist Lydia Marie Child explained how the outbreaks of violence in Kansas convinced her that her stance on nonresistance was ineffective. Child wrote a letter to then-recovering Senator Charles Sumner expressing her doubts about the abolition of slavery via peaceful measures. In addition, Child's poem "The Kansas Emigrants" was intended to unify antislavery forces and explain the possible need for violence to combat slavery. Her poem was widely circulated in the *New York Tribune* in the fall of 1856 and served to reveal Child's changing ideology.[43] In an 1857 letter to a friend, the abolitionist, political activist, and former Quaker Angelina Grimké Weld professed herself "amazed" by the conversion in her personal beliefs regarding the abolition of slavery. Grimké concluded that "slavery is more abhorrent . . . to Christianity than murder. . . .

We are compelled to choose between two evils, and all that we can do is take the *least*, and baptize liberty in blood, if it must be so."[44] Although she had been a staunch Garrisonian, Grimké renounced her pacifism for the sake of Kansas and progress. In 1857, a white Quaker, abolitionist, and close friend of Garrison and Grimké, Abby Kelley, made it clear that she stood not only for the abolition of slavery but also for full civil rights and equality for black Americans. She even took bold steps to share in the persecution with them, declaring, "I rejoice to be identified with the despised people of color. If they are to be despised, so ought their advocates to be." Kelley declared that slavery itself was warfare. She argued, "Since slavery was maintained by force, it might justly be opposed in the same way,"[45] and added, "The question is not whether we shall counsel the slaves to forsake peace, and commence war; the *war exists already*, and has been waged unremittingly ever since the slave has been in bondage." Quakers were known for their staunch pacifism and antislavery views, and when one of their group openly discussed "unremitting war," there could be little doubt about the increased frustration and disgust regarding the institution of slavery.[46] The shift from nonresistance to political violence and radical abolitionism in the 1850s was remarkable primarily for how it manifested in those members of society who would least be expected to be won over by the philosophy: women and Quakers.

Another white abolitionist and distant cousin to Childs, Charles Stearns, proclaimed his frustrations when he lived in Bleeding Kansas in 1854. Living a life committed to nonresistance, Stearns experienced attacks and beatings as a result. In a letter to Garrison, he explained why he had abandoned his peace principles and claimed that after much prolonged soul searching he had endured enough. Stearns wrote that he had "when smitten, literally turned the other cheek, and had been smitten on that also." He concluded that "if non-resistance is not a safe principle . . . it cannot be a true one."[47] Stearns wrote in the *Liberator* that because of the "epidemic of cold-blooded murders in the vicinity of the free-state capital," he now worked on the town's security and shouldered "arms in round-the-clock guard duty."[48] He added that Garrison would have understood his change of heart if he himself had "come to Kansas and gone fighting the Missouri wild beasts."[49] In the midst of crisis, Stearns' actions still stood in direct opposition to Garrison's practices. In response, Garrison placed his comments below one of Stearns's letters in the *Liberator*: "It is evident that our impulsive friend Stearns has been thoroughly frightened out of his peace principles, as Peter denied his Lord to save himself from impending danger. We compassionate his weakness."[50]

Garrison refused to fold under pressure, and his continued adherence to nonviolence earned him critics. Kelley contended that Garrison had become "complacent and out of touch." She charged Garrison with sitting behind a desk while field agents (many of them black) were on the front lines.[51] The abolitionist movement was at a turning point. The prevention of slave expansion was not the same as its abolition. If violence was required to stop slave expansion in Kansas, how much more would be required to abolish slavery completely? This was a question Garrison was still willing to answer only with the pen and podium rather than by testing his beliefs in the field.

Paradoxically, Garrison's peers labeled him a radical not because of his belief that slavery was wrong, but because he refused to recognize violence as a necessary force in accomplishing the abolition of slavery. By the late 1850s, Garrison had lost nearly all of his following. In a matter of a few short but eventful years, Garrisonian nonresistance had lost orators, ministers, women, Quakers, and, especially, black abolitionists. The political atmosphere changed people. The pervasiveness of the Slave Power increased the militancy of black Americans, which in turn influenced white Northerners.

According to the *Liberator*, the prominent abolitionist and orator Wendell Phillips told the Massachusetts Anti-Slavery Society in 1859 that he was "glad that every five minutes gave birth to a black baby, for in its infant wail he recognized the voice which should yet shout the war cry of insurrection; its baby hand would one day hold the dagger which should reach the master's heart."[52] That same year, Henry Clarke Wright, a white abolitionist and Garrisonian pacifist from Massachusetts, charged at an antislavery meeting that "resistance to slaveholders and slavehunters is obedience to God, and a sacred duty to man." Wright insisted that it was "the right and duty of the North . . . to instigate the slaves to insurrection."[53] Calls for slave rebellions, self-defense, and political dissent became mainstream within the abolitionist movement. Although black abolitionists were the first to acknowledge the utility of political violence two decades prior, the belated commitment of ordinary Americans to antislavery was enough to send an overflow of supporters in favor of force. Ultimately, the "right of revolution," birthed in the movement for American independence, was revived. In the face of inadequate alternatives and closed doors, the belief that political violence was justified was still held by many Americans.[54]

Heightened Militancy and Military Companies

While black abolitionists expressed hostility toward the Slave Power, slave expansion, and political disenfranchisement, their increasingly violent language rarely manifested in destructive activity.[55] What they achieved through airing their grievances was a heightened level of militancy that fueled the black community during the 1850s. This militancy manifested itself largely in language: threats, taunting, the encouragement of slave rebellions, and fierce forms of self-defense. Prominent black abolitionists such as Wells Brown openly encouraged slave uprisings; John S. Rock hailed the accomplishments of rebellion; Frederick Douglass argued for the utility of insurrection; and Charles Remond predicted their inevitability.[56] Threatening language was a powerful tool because regardless of how black leaders responded, their speeches and threats never fell on deaf ears. What was felt by many black Americans during the 1830s and '40s could now be expressed without reservation in the 1850s.

At a state convention in Ohio, discontented black leaders proclaimed that they would be "ready to welcome any revolution or invasion as a relief."[57] Moderate agitation felt inadequate to black leaders who needed more than a change of heart. The black abolitionist and educator Peter H. Clark explained that he was "ready to start grabbing for his rights instead of following the old pattern of petitioning."[58] In addition, Ohio leaders such as Watkins, along with John M. Langston and William H. Day, jointly proclaimed they were prepared to "resort to arms" in defiance of proslavery legislation. At such times, black abolitionists and leaders were speaking not only for themselves, but for a community whose sentiments were not far behind them.[59] The political climate had produced a cumulative effect among black Americans, who understood increasingly that threats and protective violence were the only effective tools for generating an acceptable response. The scholar Howard Holman Bell, who surveyed black convention movements over the course of thirty years, from 1830 to 1861, explained that although many expressions of black militancy between 1848 and 1859 were concentrated in the Ohio area, black Americans in states from Maine to Illinois and as far as California expressed sentiments of strong hostility toward the United States government.[60]

While some saw the value of staying on the offense with threats of rebellion, others considered fortifying their defenses. Early vigilance committees working for the Underground Railroad and against the Fugitive Slave Law prepared the way for military companies. In 1853 in Boston, William J. Watkins, along with sixty-five other African American petitioners, appealed to the legislative committee for a charter to form an independent military company among them.[61] Watkins asked rhetorically, "WHY SHOULD THIS PETITION BE GRANTED?" He answered his own question: "It should be granted because the request is a reasonable one, and one emanating from a body of men who have an absolute right to demand it." If anyone needed protection it was the black community. Watkins's rationale was utterly practical: that black Americans had the right to breathe, unhindered, the pure air of heaven. He insisted that the only way black people could be elevated as a race was if they were given rights. "Give us our rights, we ask no more. Treat us like men," Watkins demanded. He declared that if black men were placed in a position to command respect, no one would need to fear the consequences.[62] Although Watkins's petition was an attempt to persuade the legislative committee, time proved that black abolitionists would no longer be willing to ask permission. Instead of petitioning, they simply created their own militias, unapologetically and quite successfully.

During the 1850s, many black leaders effectively established military companies in their hometowns without the aid of white counterparts. Samuel Ward acknowledged that "the young blacks of the Republic are everywhere acquiring a love for martial pastimes. . . . Their independent Companies of military . . . are becoming common in many of the large towns."[63] These particular black companies sprang up all over New England and the Midwest. In 1854, New Bedford, Massachusetts, hailed the Union Cadets. In 1855, Boston boasted of its Massasoit Guards, and Providence, Rhode Island, of its National Guards. Black troops in New York City were named the MacFarian Guard and the Independent Attee Guard in Brooklyn. In 1857, black troops in Cincinnati, Ohio, were named the Attucks Blues. By 1859, there were several black companies in Pennsylvania: the Douglass Guards in Reading and the Henry Highland Garnet Guards in Harrisburg, and Pittsburgh had the benefit of two military units.[64] The Henry Highland Garnet Guards made quite an impression when both white and black crowds lined the streets to see the remarkable procession of men marching throughout town.[65] Marching to celebrate Emancipation Day in the West Indies, the Garnet Guards were handsomely dressed from head to toe with fatigue caps, charcoal-colored coats, and matching trousers with black stripes along the side. The coat was completed with a crisp white belt as they carried brand new muskets.[66] By the end of the 1850s, black military companies could be found in almost every state throughout the West and North. Altogether they boasted an enrollment of more than eighty-five hundred men.[67] Even though some marched with broomsticks and others with farm equipment or rifles, the image was symbolic and powerful. The development and presence of such companies represented resistance, self-determination, self-defense, collective defense, and pride.

Frederick Douglass offered a powerful illustration of what it meant to see black military companies march at an 1855 commemoration of West India Day in New Bedford, Massachusetts. He wrote one of the few existing comments about black militias, in which he expressed his apprehension that black soldiers would appear ridiculous and described his relief and admiration at finding them to be well ordered and competent. "They marched, halted, wheeled, and handled their arms just as you have seen well drilled white soldiers do," exclaimed Douglass. Few were unimpressed. The soldiers compelled admiration. He added that he would not debate whether such companies should exist at all, explaining, "If a knowledge of the use of arms is desirable in any people, it is desirable in us.[68]

Most important, these black military companies reminded their audiences of the reasons for their existence. The pervasiveness of the Fugitive Slave Law and the pervasive racism of white people, even those who supported abolition, left all black Americans vulnerable to violence. Many were snatched from their homes or jobs by slave catchers, and all black people were susceptible to random attacks. It only made sense that in a decade full of violent assaults on African Americans, black military companies would arise. Much like the battles in Bleeding Kansas, these black formations represented perhaps the ultimate rehearsal for war. The militancy not only of black speakers and gatherings but also, most visibly, of these militias served as a deterrent to any potential aggressor. As one historian rightly contends, the "performative politics of the street" was intended to demonstrate resistance, militancy, and power. The images of radical black men marching as soldiers made obsolete the older images of the "prostrate slave with outstretched hands pleading" for emancipation or the "grateful slave thankful for his freedom."[69] Black Americans had already carried the beginnings of war into the Northern States. As seen in Christiana, they had been active in martial activities, formally and informally, prior to the Civil War and throughout the 1850s. Indeed, black militias were the epitome of antislavery mobilization, the remedy for ridicule, and the proper response of collective defense.

The Dred Scott Decision

Toward the end of the 1850s, black abolitionists faced another blow. In addition to Kansas and Charles Sumner, perhaps the strongest and final setback came in 1857 with the Supreme Court decision in the case of Dred Scott. Born a slave in Virginia in 1795, Dred Scott had been relocated by his master several times from Alabama to Missouri. Scott was living in Saint Louis, Missouri, when his master, Peter Blow, sold Scott to the US army surgeon Dr. John Emerson. In 1836, Emerson relocated again to the free state of Illinois. After he spent considerable time in Illinois and the free territory of Wisconsin, he was eventually returned to Saint Louis. By then, Scott was married with a child. When Scott attempted to purchase his freedom from Emerson's widow, Irene, she refused. So, in 1846, Scott took legal action with the help of abolitionist lawyers and sued for his freedom on the grounds that it was illegal to be enslaved in free territories and therefore his emancipation was required. By 1857, his case made its way to the Supreme Court, where it was decided by a six-to-three vote that Scott was not a citizen given his enslaved status and therefore he had no rights, including the capacity to sue. Furthermore, the court ruled that the Missouri Compromise of 1820 (which prohibited slavery in certain territories) was thereby unconstitutional. Chief Justice Roger B. Taney, a proslavery sympathizer, wrote what he feared would result from granting Scott his petition. He claimed ruling in favor of Scott would give black Americans the right to enter every other state whenever they pleased; it would allow full liberty of speech in public and private. He cringed at the thought of allowing black Americans to hold meetings on political affairs or, worse, to "keep and carry arms wherever they went."[70] For many—even those who opposed slavery—the prospect of black people asserting their rights, or indeed them having rights at all, was unthinkable.

Long before Taney wrote his infamous opinion, black abolitionists rejected it. Remond was furious. At an antislavery convention, he expressed his hope that the participants had come to the gathering for more than a "parade and show." He called on the convention to take on a "defiant attitude regarding all laws which oppressed the colored man, whether they emanated from that scoundrel Judge Taney, or any other source." Remond believed that nothing would ever be accomplished by a "miserable temporizing and qualifying policy" and that by now, abolitionists and the opponents of slavery were "large enough and old enough to defy American slavery in this country." Remond made it clear that as far as he was concerned, Justice Taney's decision had no validity.[71]

These sentiments rang true to Robert Morris, the second black man admitted to practice law in Massachusetts, who often used his skills to provide justice to other black Americans. He was in full agreement with the comments made by Remond and took his statements even further. Morris believed that there was not a black lawyer in Boston who was not of the same opinion. Furthermore, Morris claimed that not one of the Massachusetts judges, from Judge Russell to Judge Shaw, approved of the Dred Scott decision. Judge Shaw went so far as to renounce the Dred Scott decision so it would have no effect in the state of Massachusetts. Morris declared, "Slavery will not peaceably go out, but must be removed by a strong arm." By "strong arm," Morris meant physical force or, at the very least, protective violence. He was unwilling to see black people politically or physically vulnerable before their local or state governments.

He then readdressed the notion of black military companies. For some time, Morris had been petitioning the state to allow black men to form their own official military companies to ensure the protection of black communities. He claimed, "The respectable and intelligent young colored men of Boston were not represented here to-day by a military company. It was high time they left off playing and went down into seriousness." He added that when the state granted black men the right to form military companies, black soldiers would prove to be exemplary as well.[72] For Morris, the true secret of the advancement of black Americans was their insisting on their rights and the protection of those rights under the law.[73] Some black men at a colored convention had dressed up that day in soldiers' uniforms to demonstrate their lack of formal commission by the state and their legal right to form military companies, as well as to show the beneficial force they could wield if granted the right. Morris hoped that the convention would constitute as a show of force and prove that African Americans living in the state of Massachusetts would trample underfoot the doctrines of the Dred Scott decision. He advised people that if a fugitive slave came to New Bedford and anyone tried to capture him, the residents should send a telegraph to Bostonian friends, who would come in great numbers and offer support until the fugitive was safe.[74] Along similar lines, William Wells Brown called on black Americans and allies to have a defiant attitude not only toward the oppression of slavery but also toward the decision of Judge Taney. He encouraged the movement to "make the Old Bay State too hot for the foot of a slaveholder." Brown maintained that, by their example, they would "make the country acknowledge their rights as men and women."[75]

Watkins, on the other hand, held everyone responsible for the current state of American political turmoil. He claimed, "The people of 1857, are responsible for the slavery of 1857." Watkins believed that those who attempted to shrug off the responsibilities of abolition and freedom were "cowardly" and "unfaithful to freedom." Indeed, freedom did require responsibility. No one could deny the principles and creed upon which the country had been built. Watkins added that there was no legitimate reason for interpreting the United States Constitution as a document that was against the sole purpose of securing and protecting the liberty of its people.[76] For Watkins, the ruling of the Supreme Court reflected an abandonment of responsibility.

Frederick Douglass, too, had strong opinions regarding the Dred Scott decision. He acknowledged his own shift in ideology concerning self-determination and militancy shortly after the Taney decision, which prompted him to announce that he now saw himself primarily as a black leader, as opposed to an antislavery leader. The Dred Scott decision provoked a separatist sentiment in African Americans. The impossibility of obtaining basic American rights had caused black Americans to look inward for fulfillment, affirmation, and protection. By 1857, loyal Garrisonians such as Remond, Brown, and Nell had all begun to reconsider their position within the movement, as well as the separatist activities of which they had previously disapproved.[77] With the court's decision, Remond began to advocate for slave rebellions and violence against the South. He no longer cared about the niceties of moral suasion or the potential fallout. The failings of the abolitionist movement and of the justice system had left him enraged.

A relentless advocate for women's rights, Mary Ann Shadd Cary had her own solution to the Dred Scott decision: leave. In a meeting held in Philadelphia, many women who were wives of prominent abolitionists met to discuss their feelings regarding the court's decision. In attendance was Lucretia Mott, Letitia George Still (wife of William Still), Sarah Parker Remond (sister of Charles Remond), and Harriet Forten Purvis (daughter of the wealthy sailmaker James Forten and wife of Robert Purvis). Shadd Cary wrote, "The resolutions were strong and pointed, but why not go further?" She claimed this was not the time for strong words only, action was needed. She asked if the Purvises, Remonds, and others who took part in the meeting intend to stay in the United States? "If so, the resolutions amount to nothing," and she added, "Your national ship is rotten sinking, why not leave it, and why not say so boldly, manfully?" Shadd Cary had taken up residence in Canada since 1853. After the Fugitive Slave Law, the solution for Shadd Cary was clear. In her view, America was never going to grant black people anything near the kind of rights and privileges that could be experienced in Canada. She argued it would be better for black leadership to consider the reality in Canada and emigrate than continue to hope and theorize for a better life in America.[78]

While Shadd Cary pushed flight over fighting, the prevailing notion was to stay and make a good stand. Many came see the power of fighting back. In response to the Dred Scott decision, Henry Highland Garnet claimed, "Our people will not always consent to be trodden under foot; they will arm themselves some day, if need be, to secure their rights . . . armed with a box of lucifer matches, the black man will have the power in his hands."[79] The historian Catherine Clinton argues that the Dred Scott decision may have been part of the reason Harriet Tubman chose to return to the United States from Canada. The political climate suggested now was not the time to retreat. Before the start of the Civil War, even Shadd Cary changed her views. She returned to the United States in 1860 after the death of her husband. When the Civil War broke out, Martin Delany, a proponent of emigration as well, convinced Shadd Cary to help enlist black volunteers to fight for the Union. Fleeing was practical, but fighting was powerful.

A Movement with Momentum

By the late 1850s, black abolitionists had reached their breaking point. Leaders who had spent most of their lives working for the movement could chart its evolution from the failed tactics of moral suasion and Garrison's policy of nonresistance to the limited and weak cooperation of political parties dominated by white men in the 1840s.[80] What made the decade preceding the Civil War so different was the way black leaders sought to determine their own destiny, by means of force if necessary, in the face of constant political defeats. The 1830s and '40s were made up of black leaders seeking and securing white allies. By the 1850s, black leaders took up a position of armed resistance regardless of white support.

On August 3, 1857, Douglass delivered his "West India Emancipation" speech in Canandaigua, New York. There, he expounded upon the heroic leadership of black Americans who relied on force and self-determination, lauding the efforts of those who had died or used violence rather than submit.

He believed their efforts helped to keep the slave catchers at bay. One by one, he described some of the most controversial episodes of the antebellum period for black Americans. He discussed the famous tragedy of Margaret Garner, who ran away from a plantation in Kentucky with seven of her family members, four of them her own children no older than six years old. The Garners had experienced only hours in freedom in the free state of Ohio when US Marshals and their master surrounded their safe house and demanded their return. Garner made national headlines when she plunged a knife into the throat of her infant to save her from the hell of slavery. Douglass believed Garner should be honored. "Every fugitive from slavery," Douglass proclaimed, "who, like the noble William Thomas at Wilkes Barre, prefers to perish in a river made red by his own blood to submission to the hell hounds who were hunting and shooting him should be esteemed as a glorious martyr, worthy to be held in grateful memory by our people." He referenced the fugitive Horace of Mechanicsburg, Ohio, who taught slave catchers in Kentucky that arresting him was a deadly proposition. He also recalled William Parker and his allies who defended themselves at Christiana with both "prayers and pistols."[81]

Douglass credited black resistance with having turned the political tides. As the political landscape became increasingly resistant to ensuring the rights of African Americans, black Americans became more radical, independent, and self-determined. Even issues such as emigration, which met fierce resistance from the black community, slowly became more appealing.[82] The more legislation attempted to constrict black Americans' livelihoods, the more black Americans sought to demonstrate their capacity to determine their own lives, here or elsewhere.

Although no single issue pulled black abolitionists into militancy, the compounded issues and concerns that arose in the 1850s as a result of the Fugitive Slave Law—the violence surrounding the Kansas-Nebraska Act, the beating of Charles Sumner, and the Dred Scott decision—collectively accelerated black militancy. Each altercation and episode during the antebellum period made it clear that abolition was just a beginning. The real battle was American's need to confront equality for all its peoples, and ensuring equality necessitated political power and force, if necessary. In a speech delivered at Mozart Hall in New York, Charles Remond declared, "This, Mr. Chairman, leads me to remark that the question of anti-slavery and pro-slavery in the United States is not the black man's question; that the question of slavery and anti-slavery is practically an American question—all the way American, from beginning to end—and especially with every *decent* American."[83]

Throughout the 1850s, the United States continued to be bitterly divided. On August 15, 1855, a disheartened Abraham Lincoln wrote to George Robertson, a Kentucky lawyer and professor who had once served as legal counsel for him, "That spirit which desired the peaceful extinction of slavery has itself become extinct. . . . Experience has demonstrated, I think, that there is no peaceful extinction of slavery in prospect for us."[84] The period of the 1830s and '40s was not just a moment within the movement, it was a chance for a slaveholding South to hear from black leaders who wanted to end slavery peacefully. By 1850, the call for prayers and petitions changed to politics and pistols.

Ultimately, black abolitionists and the enslaved were not only leading the cause of political violence but also giving the abolitionist movement the momentum it would need to force the issue of slavery into the hearts and minds of white Northerners and politicians. From the Fugitive Slave Law to the Kansas-Nebraska Act, from Jerry to Anthony, from Garner to Grimké, and from Sumner to Scott, antislavery tension grew for both the enslaved and the slave-owning class. During the turbulent 1850s, black Americans' contributions to the violent atmosphere presented the nation with a countdown to the demise of slavery. More than ever, black Americans came to the same conclusion: immediate abolition was the only option and violence was surest accelerator. However, more than a decade prior, McCune Smith made it clear that insurrection was not the fruit of emancipation but the fruit of slavery. Violence was the inevitable consequence of withholding men and women from their liberty.[85]

In August 1859, Gerrit Smith acknowledged that it was no wonder black people concluded there was no resource left to them but God and insurrections. He called it "a terrible remedy for a terrible wrong" and one that was unavoidable if the slaveholding South did not end its institutions.[86] Smith added that many would proclaim slave insurrections to be failures and futile attempts to bring about freedom. "Yes," was Smith's response, "but will not slavery nevertheless be put down by them? For what portions are there of the South that will cling to slavery after two or three considerable insurrections shall have filled the whole South with horror?"[87] Just two months later, John Brown gave one considerable reason for the entire country to lose faith in the peaceful extinction of slavery.[88]

CHAPTER 4

Black Leadership

The Silenced Partners of Harpers Ferry

> [Brown] has struck the bottom line of the philosophy which
> underlies the abolition movement. . . . Slavery is a system of
> brute force. . . . It must be met with its own weapons.
> —Frederick Douglass

John Brown's raid on Harpers Ferry is a familiar story in antebellum history.[1] In 1859, Brown led a small group of men into Virginia with the goal of igniting a slave rebellion. The hope was to capture the federal armory located in Harpers Ferry, transport as many enslaved people to freedom as possible, and ultimately overthrow the institution of slavery. But the raid was quickly defeated by state militia, and Brown and his captured comrades were charged with treason and sentenced to the gallows. Many historians see Brown's raid as the final forerunner to the Civil War. Missing is the pivotal influence of black leadership on Brown's thought and actions.[2] For Brown would not have become the fearsome abolitionist he is known as had he not chosen to take inspiration from the pantheon of defiant and militant black figures such as Toussaint Louverture, Gabriel (Prosser), David Walker, Nat Turner, and others. No other episode in antebellum history centralizes black thought on the use of force to overthrow slavery better than Harpers Ferry. The best way to understand black activism and contributions to dismantling slavery in this moment is to decenter Brown from the narrative of Harpers Ferry, which is quite often conveyed as a fanatical white man's bleeding and foolish heart. Thus, this chapter is not so much about Brown as it is about the silent and silenced influences that relegated black leaders to the periphery and propelled Brown to the center of a radical movement to end slavery. What might it do to envision Brown not as a leader of a single, anomalous event but as a follower of black revolutionary violence who put this tradition into practice? By examining the inspiration Brown drew from black leadership and what Harpers Ferry did to exacerbate the perception of black violence, we can pivot our understanding of radical abolitionism from white leaders who have been placed at the heart of heroism to a perspective that seats black leadership at the center of change.

Too often within scholarship historians have focused on the white philanthropists and Brown's "secret six" partners as those who made Harpers Ferry possible.[3] In fact, there are several books that focus solely on this half dozen group of white men connected to Brown's plan, but there is not a single book devoted to the five African Americans who joined Brown or to the black leaders who helped to fund him.[4] In addition, scholars have a tendency to focus on Brown's actions at Harpers Ferry alone, marginalizing African American contributions. By uncovering the numerous ways in which black leaders inspired Brown's ideology of political violence, we can see how abolitionists such as Frederick Douglass, Jermain Loguen, Henry Highland Garnet, and especially black women such as Mary Ellen Pleasant and Harriet Tubman, were central agents in this episode.

Though Brown's raid included minimal black participation, his actions still symbolized both the promise and the peril of black political violence. For many white Americans, Brown represented the black political violence that they understood in Haiti and feared in America. One livid Southerner claimed the raid was "nothing more nor nothing less than an attempt to do on a vast scale what was done in St. Domingo in 1791."[5] As an ally to black Americans who used violence to combat oppression, Brown was part of the tradition Toussaint Louverture invoked in his famous last words: "In overthrowing me, you have done no more than cut down the trunk of the tree of the black liberty in St-Domingue—it will spring back from the roots, for they are numerous and deep." In the same vein, nothing reads truer than George William Curtis's summation of Brown. Curtis, a white abolitionist and well-known writer and public speaker, claimed just days after Brown's execution that Brown was "not buried but planted." Much like a dandelion, Curtis professed that "he [Brown] will spring up a hundred-fold."[6] Brown and the black men and women who aided and joined him are part of this prophecy and the legacy of black people working to end oppression through forceful or violent means.

Black Leaders Inspire and Influence

Brown was tremendously affected by the Haitian Revolution and Nat Turner's rebellion. Such events changed the way he perceived slavery's probable demise. As a result, he studied insurrectionary warfare and became well versed about the island of Saint-Domingue and its inhabitants' success in defeating the French. Haiti's influence did not end with the early slave rebellions of the nineteenth century. Indeed, well into the 1850s Haiti's history played a formidable role in the development of black political violence to abolish slavery. For Brown, the memory of Louverture fed his faith in revolutionary black violence. The many writings, articles, and books that centered on the history and impact of the Haitian Revolution inspired him.[7] And Brown was not alone. The white abolitionist Wendell Phillips traveled around the country giving his famous speech, "Toussaint L'Ouverture: The Hero of St. Domingo," while carrying a copy of Harriet Martineau's biography of Toussaint Louverture.[8] Phillips' speech was immensely popular, and copies of it could be found in several newspapers, such as *Vanity Fair*, the *Chicago Tribune*, and the *New York Tribune*.[9] While scholars do not know whether Brown was in attendance at any of the speeches Phillips and others presented on Toussaint, he was certainly aware of them.

Furthermore, Francis Jackson Meriam, a white abolitionist from Massachusetts who participated in the raid, had just returned from a trip to Haiti prior to it. This trip, along with Lewis Hayden's persuasion, convinced Meriam to join in Brown's efforts. Meriam, together with James Redpath, intended to write a report on the Haitian people and their nation.[10] Redpath and Brown discussed the influence of the Haitian Revolution frequently, and both came to advocate slave rebellions. They saw black people as being fully capable of determining their freedom and future.

Brown was also aware of the major fugitive slave cases such as the Christiana Resistance, the Jerry Rescue, and the capture and case of Anthony Burns. Hayden's by-any-means-necessary approach to self-defense and efforts in Boston had become legendary. Brown became acquainted with Jermain Loguen because of his reputation and leadership during the Jerry Rescue in Syracuse, New York. Together, Brown, Loguen, and Hayden forged strong friendships. In Ohio, Brown met with the Langston brothers, John Mercer and Charles H. They were extremely active in the movement, assisting runaway slaves to freedom and founding the Ohio Antislavery Society.

John Brown Jr. and the Langston brothers were graduates of Oberlin College as well. Brown Sr. was enamored with these men. He even attended the trial of Charles H. Langston, who served a twenty-day jail sentence in the spring of 1859 for assisting the fugitive slave John Price, also known as the Oberlin-Wellington rescue. When Brown heard Langston's passionate plea before the court, he immediately sought to enlist his help for Harpers Ferry. John Langston, too, believed in armed resistance and initially worked with Brown to plan the raid but did not participate. All over the country, Brown saw black Americans were taking the lead on political violence and self-defense and it was clear he wanted to be a part of it. When black men told Brown of their changing attitudes and methods to combat slavery, Brown encouraged them with a maxim made popular by Oliver Cromwell, "Trust in God, and keep your powder dry."[11]

It is important to note that there were few, if any, degrees of separation among major black leaders in the movement. For one, black conventions took place all over the country. Black leaders were in constant discussion over strategy, need, and the latest fugitive slave cases. They met together, ate together, prayed together, and protected one another. They were family, friends, and fans. As mentioned earlier, Douglass sheltered William Parker in his home and named his son Charles after Charles Remond. Loguen's daughter Amelia married Douglass's son Lewis. Henry Highland Garnet and Samuel Ringgold Ward were cousins. Ward was living in Syracuse during the Jerry Rescue and helped file Jerry's manacles off his body. Lewis Sheridan Leary participated in the raid and died eight days later from his wounds. Charles Langston married Leary's widow, Mary Patterson.[12] It was Loguen who accompanied Brown to meet Harriet Tubman in St. Catherine's, Canada. These leaders vouched for each other. They filled in for each other on the lecture circuits. The list of relationships and connections could go on and on. Suffice it to say, few pivotal actions took place outside of the black network. Undoubtedly, each visit together prompted questions about how others in the movement were doing and what needs could be met, but on a more personal level they teased each other and asked about each other's health, children, and spouses.

Brown, who saw himself as an outsider, valued the collective support and affinity the black community offered. In all of Brown's actions, he worked to validate black people's humanity. In addition, Brown was moved by black radicals and their messages advocating black liberation, empowerment, and violent resistance to oppression. He attempted to publish and circulate the radical speeches and works of Garnet, including *Address to the Slaves of the United States of America,* and Walker's *Appeal.*[13] As a radical abolitionist, Brown always went one step further than most antislavery sympathizers. His vow of support did not end with emancipation but with equality. As Brown famously stated, "You may dispose of me very easily . . . but this question is still to be settled—this Negro question, I mean. The end of that is not yet."[14] He understood that the goal of black leadership was always twofold: emancipation and equality, which were inseparable. In African American memory, it was not just Brown's raid but his lifelong commitment to equality and taking risks by any means necessary that, in turn, cultivated their admiration.

Accordingly, Brown made sure to meet with the most influential leaders. He took his son John Brown Jr. with him to meet with Still, Douglass, Garnet, and Stephen Smith in Philadelphia.[15] Smith was a prominent, wealthy, and outspoken free black man living in the city. He had a successful lumber company and vast real estate holdings. He and William Whipper used their wealth to help fund abolitionist causes and funnel fugitive slaves further north. In addition, Robert Purvis was also among the black elite. Educated at Amherst College, his used his father's inheritance to support the abolitionist movement in Philadelphia. From 1831 to 1861, Purvis used his own large home as a station on the Underground Railroad, and he estimated that he helped more than nine thousand slaves (roughly one enslaved person a day) to escape freedom. It is largely believed that Brown carried Purvis's musket on his person during the raid. Brown was not just meeting with black leaders, he was meeting with black people of financial means, resources, and experience with armed resistance.

Likewise, Brown also met with the Gloucesters. Elizabeth and James Newton Gloucester were prominent leaders Brooklyn, New York. James was the founder and minister of Siloam Presbyterian Church. In the winter of 1852, Brown stayed at the Gloucester home for a week and spoke at their church. Elizabeth was a successful business woman and philanthropist. She owned several clothing shops in Manhattan before making her way to Brooklyn. Elizabeth personally donated twenty-five dollars to Brown's cause. The couple charged Brown to "do battle with that ugly foe, slavery." Throughout Brown's extensive travel to cities such as Boston, Rochester, Chicago, Concord, Philadelphia, Oberlin, Providence, New York, and Canada, he sought black guidance and support. And it was during his meetings and visits that Brown was mentored and counseled. Only through these relationships could Brown begin and complete his vision.

Thus, prior to the raid and among the rich network of black leaders, the plan for Brown's raid was widely known. The historian Richard Boyer claims that because "a war psychology" had already pervaded much of the North, by 1859 Brown could publicly announce his purpose of attacking the South's institution of slavery by force. He could also freely ask for and receive contributions to execute his plan at numerous public meetings, several of which were widely attended. It is very likely that entire communities from Iowa to Massachusetts knew of Brown's intentions as a point of general knowledge several months before he and his raiders attacked Harpers Ferry.[16] Altogether, in the planning stages of the raid, Brown was able to build up significant black support and recruit widely.

Brown and Leading Ladies

One of Brown's strongest allies, he believed, was Harriet Tubman. Having made more than a dozen undetected trips back and forth to the South to free the enslaved, Tubman was no stranger to danger. Moving along the Eastern shore, Tubman successfully rescued some three hundred men, women, and children from bondage. She was known to have kept a pistol on her at all times and would not have hesitated to use it. Tubman would threaten to shoot not only any pursing person or dog but also any enslaved runaway who contemplated returning to the plantation to potentially spoil her rescue efforts. Story after story, witnesses testified to Tubman's belief in the utility of force. During one rescue, a man protested among the fleeing group that he was going to return to his plantation when success for their escape looked bleak. Tubman pointed her gun at the man's head and said, "You go on or die." Given these options, the man endured, and just several days later the group arrived in Canada.[17]

For this and so much more, Tubman was just the kind of woman Brown wanted. He eagerly sought out Tubman to enlist her talents to aid his plans. While it is unclear how Tubman and Brown initially met, Brown acknowledged his desire to have her as a possible recruiter and as a guide to help runaway slaves get to freedom in Canada. In April 1858, the two met at least twice while in St. Catherine's to discuss recruiting former slaves for the Harpers Ferry plot. He contended that her crucial knowledge of terrain in Maryland and Pennsylvania would be necessary to conducting a successful attack.[18] Brown admired Tubman's bravery so much that he gave her the

Figure 7. Harriet Tubman. Courtesy of the Library of Congress.

highest compliment he could at the time: he called her General Tubman, sometimes using the pronoun "he" when referring to her.[19] As backhanded as it sounds, equating Tubman to a man was Brown's way of acknowledging her unwavering fearlessness. Tubman agreed to support Brown and his efforts, but fortunately, given the outcome of the raid, she was not in attendance. Some historians speculate that she likely fell ill just prior to the raid.[20] The historian Kate Clifford Larson contends that Tubman might have also been unavailable due to recruiting for the raid; she also ventures that she may have begun to see the plan as unwinnable. Given her head trauma from youth and poor planning, a combination of the two probably held her back. Nevertheless, Larson claims that perhaps the one white person Tubman really admired was Brown, and she was not the only woman to feel this way.[21]

Mary Ellen Pleasant, a black entrepreneur and supporter of the Underground Railroad possibly became the greatest patron Brown ever had. Pleasant built her wealth through her first husband, James Smith, who was a wealthy plantation owner, flour contractor, and abolitionist. When he died, he bequeathed his fortune to Pleasant, and she continued their efforts to emancipate runaway slaves. Pleasant moved about the country but eventually settled in San Francisco with her second husband, John James Pleasant, who thought that California was a prime place for the Underground Railroad. Together, Pleasant and her husband used their resources to sponsor fleeing African Americans and helped them to find employment. She established and owned several restaurants and garnered exceptional wealth when she partnered with Thomas Bell by investing in numerous lucrative businesses. Pleasant is also known for having helped to form the Bank of California.

Between 1857 and 1859, Pleasant used her enormous financial resources to assist Brown as much as she could.[22] When Pleasant traveled back to the East Coast, she spoke about meeting with Brown in Chatham, Canada, during 1858 and donating $30,000 to aid his cause. While much of Pleasant's engagement with Brown remains a mystery, in 1904 Pleasant gave an interview with the *People's Press* on her integral relationship to Brown and Harpers Ferry. Upon Brown's capture, a letter was found on his person, which read: "The axe is laid at the root of the tree and after the first blow is struck there be plenty more money coming. W.E.P." Ill and near death, Pleasant explained the cryptic letter and her involvement:

I have never made this statement in full to anyone, but before I pass away I wish to clear the identity of the party who furnished John

MARY ELLEN ("MAMMY") PLEASANT AT 87 YEARS OF AGE
The first and only photograph taken since she was 13 years old

Figure 8. Mary Ellen Pleasant. Courtesy of the Bancroft Library,
University of California, Berkeley.

Brown with most of his money to start the fight at Harpers Ferry and who signed the letter found on him when he was arrested. I furnished the money and wrote the letter. My initials are M.E.P. For Mary E. Pleasant, but in signing my name I have always made the M so that it looks like a W, and I suppose that little mistake was all that saved me from being captured and hanged alongside of John Brown, and sometimes I wished that I had gone up on the scaffold with him, for I would at least have died in a good cause and in good company.[23]

Thanks to slovenly handwriting, her own initials threw investigators off any potential trail. Because Pleasant knew Brown's raid would involve bloodshed, she elected not to confide in any one about the specific plans she made with Brown or the specific ways in which the money she donated was spent. After meeting with Brown for the last time, Pleasant left Canada and met with a trusted man who took her along the Roanoke River to recruit slaves for the raid. Disguised as a jockey, Pleasant and her companion, bringing along several horses, began meeting with the enslaved at various plantations to help "incite an uprising of the slaves." She stated that the enslaved were ready and willing to engage in a revolt with Brown's help, but her information and troop-gathering efforts were thwarted. She recalled, "We arranged that when Brown made his stand at Harpers Ferry the negroes were to rise in every direction, but our plans were all knocked to pieces by Brown himself."[24] Brown began the raid before the agreed upon time.

It has been speculated that the low turnout was largely due to an unexpected date change of the raid. On October 24, 1859, the *Boston Traveller* indicated that while some black Americans had knowledge of the plot, they found themselves caught off guard when Brown initiated the attack eight days earlier than anticipated. The newspaper claimed rumors of a larger conspiracy spread among free black people living in the area that would encompass uprisings throughout Maryland and Virginia. It was reported that the October 24 was the appointed day for the attempt and "the seizure of the Arsenal was to be the signal to the insurgents."[25] The raid might have had the potential to be an even larger event if Brown had chosen to act on the day supporters expected.

Pleasant declared that she was astounded when she learned the raid had begun and ended swiftly, leaving Brown captured and wounded. "The affair upon which I had staked my money and built so much hope was a fiasco," lamented Pleasant. She never figured out why Brown began the raid without the additional help of those who had pledged to fight. Had Brown waited for the appointed time, it would have been remarkable to see just how effective the raid could have been. When authorities began searching for anyone they suspected of working with Brown, Pleasant disguised herself under a different name (Ellen Smith) and managed to make her way back to her home in San Francisco without detection.

Few have attempted to expound upon Brown's relationship with black women. Tubman and Pleasant were both sought out by Brown. He valued what they could offer regarding strategy, fearlessness, and finances and these women did not hesitate to act. Time and time again we see how black women cannot be separated from the telling and sanctioning of political violence. And while Pleasant could not be the face of rebellion, she could operate as the wallet of rebellion and the eventual usher of freedom.[26] How might the narrative of Brown's raid change to know that it was in large part a black woman who made the entire raid possible? The greatest contribution was not the counsel and contributions of the Secret Six but those of a savvy black woman from California and the potential guidance of America's Moses.

Indeed, the silent and silenced black partners of Harpers Ferry were predominantly black women, including Anna Murray Douglass, the wife of Frederick Douglass, who for over a month hosted Brown while he sought refuge from the authorities regarding his acts in Missouri. In 1858, he used her home to begin planning for his raid. Brown even drafted his provisional constitution in Douglass's home during the three weeks Brown sojourned with them in February.

Furthermore, after Brown's death, black women abolitionists raised money to send to Brown's widow along with letters of condolences and expressions of admiration for her fallen husband. Frances Ellen Watkins, the famous poet and chairman of the Pennsylvania Abolition Society alongside William Still, also sent gifts and one of her beloved poems, "Bury Me in a Free Land."[27] Watkins wrote:

> I ask no monument, proud and high,
> To arrest the gaze of the passers-by;
> All that my yearning spirit craves,
> Is bury me not in a land of slaves.

Often coupled among the silent partners of Brown was a desire for humility and anonymity. The goal was not to be seen as a hero or a martyr but to eradicate slavery. For these women, no monument was necessary to mark their contributions or their death. Freedom was its own reward.

After Brown's hanging, Pleasant received one final letter from Brown. She destroyed it immediately. "Brown was an earnest, sincere man and as brave a man as ever lived," declared Pleasant, "but he lacked judgment and was sometimes foolhardy and cranky. He wrote too much and talked too much." The author and activist W. E. B. Du Bois later wrote in his biography of Brown that black Americans trusted Brown's heart but not his head. Despite all her wealth, Pleasant understood that no amount of money could shield her from the consequences if captured by the authorities, yet she never regretted her involvement or the large sum of money she invested. She believed that while her investment may have been perceived as a failure, she saw it as paving the way for war and, ultimately, emancipation. She claimed, "I always felt that John Brown started the Civil War and that I helped Brown more than any other person financially." In fact, Pleasant wished she had given more. Her dying request was that her tombstone read "She was a friend of John Brown."[28] It was this friendship that became her legacy.

Douglass and the Chatham Convention

Among men, it is likely that Douglass built the strongest relationship with Brown and had the greatest impact on him. Douglass recalled that Garnet and Loguen had mentioned the name of Brown to him. While speaking of Brown, their voices would drop to whispers. Douglass became intrigued and wanted to meet the man. At their initial meeting, Douglass declared, "Whenever he spoke his words commanded earnest attention. His arguments, which I ventured at some points to oppose, seemed to convince all; his appeals touched all, and his will impressed all. Certainly, I never felt myself in the presence of a stronger religious influence than while in this man's house."[29] For Brown, these relationships with black leaders were important. Black abolitionists' approval of his sentiments validated his own course, even if they chose not to participate in his raid.

At the time of Douglass's meeting with Brown, Douglass had recognized the political and psychological effects of self-defense and self-assertion. In addition, Douglass saw the utility of slave revolts in the South. He praised the slave rebellions in the British West Indies. While Douglass did not agree with the general slaughter of Southern slave owners, he believed that the enslaved

were well within their rights to kill a person who attempted to harm and sub-
jugate them. The violence Douglass and Brown both spoke of was centered
on self-defense, not on retaliation. In his autobiography, Douglass recounted
the message Brown conveyed to him during their first meeting in 1847. Brown
told Douglass that for some time he had hoped to find black men to whom he
could safely reveal his plan, but now he was encouraged, "for he saw heads of
such rising up in all directions." For some time, Brown had been observing
Douglass in his action and writings in the US and abroad. He wanted nothing
more than Douglass's support.[30] Brown claimed that slaveholders had forfeited their right to live and that the enslaved had the right to gain this liberty
by violent force. He also related that he did not believe in moral suasion's
ability to liberate the enslaved nor did he see political action as a viable
alternative.

As a result, Brown believed that combating the institution of slavery left
him with few options to completely ensure its overthrow. Harking back to
the early republican ideology of "he who would be free must strike the first
blow," Brown told Douglass he firmly believed in the practice of carrying
arms as a way of obtaining manhood and respect. According to Brown, no
people could have self-respect or be respected without fighting for their
freedom.[31] Interestingly, Douglass commented many times on how convers-
ing with Brown was like talking to another black man. "Though a white gen-
tleman," Douglass felt that "he is in sympathy a black man, and as deeply
interested in our cause, as though his own soul had been pierced with the
iron of slavery."[32]

Douglass's relationship with Brown spanned a significant length of time,
during which Brown tried his hardest to convince Douglass regarding his
plans and hoped that he would join him at Harpers Ferry. Douglass wrote of
how Brown embraced him and declared, "Come with me, Douglass, I will defend you with my life. I want you for a special purpose. When I strike the bees
will begin to swarm, and I shall want you to help hive them."[33] Their shared
values and congenial relationship was not enough; Douglass refused to join
Brown because he thought his plans would not succeed. He attributed his decision to part discretion, part fear, but overall, Douglass could not bypass the
national attention the raid would arouse. He claimed Brown would "rivet the
fetters more firmly than ever on the limbs of the enslaved."[34] And despite an
invitation, Douglass declined to attend the convention in Chatham at which
Brown would reveal his plans and proposal for a new constitution.

In early 1858, thirty-three black Americans and twelve whites gathered in

Chatham, Canada, to make plans for guerilla operations in Kansas and the South and the setting up of an interim government. After Brown met with Martin Delany, he attended the Chatham convention and stayed at Isaac Holden's home. But many of the most prominent black leaders were not in attendance. Tubman was not there, and while Brown sent letters of invitation to Douglass, Loguen, Wendell Phillips, and Gerrit Smith, their attendance was highly unlikely.

The convention held two sessions on May 8 and another two days later on May 10 at a local schoolhouse and church. During the sessions, Brown put forth his own provisional constitution, complete with a preamble and forty-eight articles that included the abolition of slavery, full black citizenship, the election of black officials, and even the election of a black president. The goal of the convention was for Brown to share his plans and recruit for the raid. The plan was simple: to raise a black army, incite a revolution, and eradicate slavery.[35] Brown was convinced that even small numbers of men could affect radical change. Again, he pointed to the island of Haiti for his precedent. Many believed in Brown's theory, even though the practice and implementation of such an act was unlikely. When word came to Brown that authorities in Virginia might be aware of his plans, he arrested all plans until suspensions subsided and he and other black leaders could reconvene.

However, as the time for the raid drew near, key members of the black leadership began to back out for legitimate reasons. Poor planning and a lack of clear strategic guidelines led to black hesitation and the ultimate failure of the raid. While the initial momentum and spirits of the group were high, over time the energy began to wane. Brown struggled to raise adequate financial support needed for guns, ammunition, and supplies. How was one to provide transport, food, sufficient clothing, and shelter to possibly hundreds of runaway slaves while remaining undetected or at the very least unarmed? Even if Brown were to successfully capture the arsenal, he would be moving not trained soldiers but families, the elderly, and children. In addition, it was October. Winter was coming. Some of the most prominent black abolitionists, such as Douglass, donated financial assistance but considered Brown's plan to be strategically flawed and foolish. Garnet turned Brown down because he did not think the raid would be successful and found his timing to be imprudent. Ironically, Garnet, despite his reputation for "resistance," did not feel confident that the enslaved themselves were ready for such a task. Traditionally more conservative than Garnet, Reverend John Gloucester chose to follow in the footsteps of Douglass and collect funds for the raid but offered nothing more. A year prior to the raid, Jermain Loguen accompanied Brown to Canada. Just two days before Brown had a secret meeting of allies, Loguen wrote a letter on May 6, 1858, to Brown stating that he wished to meet with members of the raid before they marched "into the mountains."[36] But in the summer of 1859, things continued to fall apart. Loguen abandoned Brown's efforts to organize black people there into Liberty Leagues—organizations that were created to be third-party solutions to abolition. While virtually every black leader desired abolition, few could agree on a path to lead to it successfully, which led to a diversity of plans, some less effective than others.

Over the course of seventeen months little was accomplished, and those who initially supported Brown began to lose their enthusiasm. Prominent black abolitionists such as Delany, who aided in putting meetings together, became caught up in their own campaigns for emigration when plans for the raid were starting to mature. By the time Brown was prepared to travel to western Virginia, only one of the thirty-three black conspirators maintained his commitment to joining Brown: Osborne Anderson.[37] Not without regret, a black man from Cleveland who was a member of the Chatham convention revealed in a handwritten note that he was not coming to aid Brown but then added that he was disgusted with himself "and the whole Negro set, God damn 'em."[38] In the end, five black men joined Brown: Osborne Anderson, Lewis Leary, Dangerfield Newby, John Anthony Copeland Jr., and Shields Green.

The Raid

When the raid on Harpers Ferry began, Brown and his twenty-one-man "army of liberators" were determined to seize the one hundred thousand weapons held at the federal arsenal in western Virginia. They planned to rally the enslaved and ensure their safe passage to the Blue Ridge Mountains and then on to freedom in Canada. Brown intended to create a domino effect of slave insurrections in the surrounding areas. He believed that once he and his men had entered the town declaring their purpose, the enslaved would come running for freedom and join in the mass liberation of their fellows.

Osborne Anderson claimed that on the Sunday evening of the outbreak, he and some of Brown's men visited the few surrounding plantations and revealed to the enslaved their purposes. Green was among the men tasked with recruiting slaves from the nearby countryside to join the fighting. Given his own fugitive past, his encouragement could have been appealing. Anderson described the enthusiasm the enslaved felt; he reported that "joy and hilarity beamed from every countenance." Anderson attested, "At the slaves' quarters, there was apparently a general jubilee, and they stepped forward manfully, without impressing or coaxing." Anderson wrote of how conspirators had stopped by the home of an elderly black woman living outside the town of Harpers Ferry to tell her of the anticipated plot. He recalled how "liberating the slaves was the very thing she had longed for, prayed for, and dreamed about, time and time again; and her heart was full of rejoicing over the fulfillment of a prophecy which had been her faith for long years."[39] He found that only one person refused to take up arms, a freeborn black man. Anderson commented, "In fact, so far as I could learn, the free blacks of the South are much less reliable than the slaves, and infinitely more fearful."[40]

On Sunday evening, October 16, 1859, Brown and his twenty-one-man army launched their attack and managed to seize the armory, as well as several other strategic points. Anderson, the only black survivor of the raid, provides one of the few reliable eyewitness accounts. In his published account, *A Voice from Harpers Ferry*, Anderson offered his perspective on the raid, its consequences, and most important, a portrait of black men's contributions during the raid.[41] In his preface he explained, "Much has been given as true that never happened; much has been omitted that should have been made known; many things have been left unsaid." Anderson's account gives details of the personal experiences and encounters he shared at Harpers Ferry. He described in detail the valor of his few black comrades. While retreating to their posts, Dangerfield Newby was shot and immediately returned fire as he fell on his side. Before he could recover, he was shot for a second time, through the head, by someone who took aim at him from a brick store window. He died instantly. When Shields Green, known as the "Zouave of the band" saw Newby fall he quickly returned fire, avenging his death. According to Anderson, "Green raised his rifle in an instant, and brought down the cowardly murderer, before the latter could get his gun back through the sash." One word sufficiently described the acts of Anderson's comrades: brave. Though Newby and Leary met their fates on the field, Green and John Copeland faced death calmly at the gallows.[42] The belief that slaves were cowardly could not have been further from the truth. Green, a runaway from South Carolina, played a more prominent role than one might have guessed, being among the youngest in the group at twenty-three years old. Green's actions were what white Southerners feared the most: an

Figure 9. Osborne Perry Anderson. Courtesy of the Kansas State Historical Society.

armed black man unafraid to retaliate against both the system of slavery and those who fought to defend it.

Douglass described Green as unlikely "to shrink from hardships or dangers." He met with Brown and Green in Chambersburg, Pennsylvania, to discuss plans for the raid. In his memoir, Douglass wrote about Green being a man of few words and broken English but ultimately believed "his courage and self-respect made him quite a dignified character."[43] For example, Jeremiah Anderson, one of Brown's men, managed to escape when the raid took an awful turn. He encouraged Green to run away with him. "I told him to come; that we could do nothing more," explained Anderson, but Green, never willing to leave a man behind, replied, "He must go down to de ole man [Brown]."[44]

Within a day and a half, many of Brown's men had been killed or badly wounded by townspeople and members of the militia. While Brown's men killed four people and wounded nine, ten of Brown's men were killed (including two of his sons, Oliver and Watson). The townspeople spared no one— even raiders who tried to negotiate or surrender or under a white flag were shot and killed. The mob desecrated Newby's corpse by cutting off his genitals and ears and leaving his corpse to be consumed by hogs. Will Thompson and Will Leeman, two other raiders, had their corpses used for target practice. Only five of Brown's men managed to escape.[45] When it was all over, Brown and the remaining men were brought to trial, where they were found guilty of treason, of conspiring with slaves to rebel, and of murder. On December 2, 1859, Brown and his fellow raiders were hanged. Of the five black men who joined Brown, Anderson was the only black survivor who managed to escape. The raid was unsuccessful and tragic. Yet, for black Americans, the aftermath of Brown's endeavors produced a chain of events and a battle song that never lost its significance.

For the African Americans who joined Brown or partnered with him in some way, few had regrets. Copeland made powerful statements while awaiting his verdict in a Charlestown, Virginia, jail. Early in adulthood, Copeland was committed to the utility of violence, particularly against slave catchers. He kept a wooden staff on him at all times before he switched to a rifle to protect himself and others from kidnappers. He once clubbed a deputy US marshal and played a crucial role in the Oberlin rescue of 1858. On December 10, 1859, Copeland wrote a letter to his brother in which he asked, "Could I, brother die in a more noble cause?" He concluded, "I am so soon to stand and suffer death for doing what George Washington, the so-called father of his great but slavery-cursed country, was made a hero for doing, while he lived, and when dead his name was immortalized, and his great and noble deeds in behalf of freedom taught by parents to their children." Copeland explained the contradictions between American freedom and American slavery. He saw the American Revolution as unfinished and cited the example of Crispus Attucks, reputed to be the first casualty of the American Revolution, noting, "The blood of black men flowed as freely as that of white men. Yes, the very first blood of black men flowed as freely as that of white men." Copeland argued that while black men had done an equal share of the fighting for American independence, they were never truly compensated by being allowed to share in equal benefits for having done so.[46] Copeland believed that fighting with Brown was an opportunity to lay claim to his own enfranchisement and redeem sentiments that had been abandoned during the American Revolution. Copeland's blood is just meaningful as Brown's in continuing a legacy of America's unfinished revolution.

On December 2, the day of Brown's execution, the Reverend J. Sella Martin, pastor of Boston's Joy Street church and a former fugitive slave, spoke to an audience of nearly four thousand people at Tremont Temple. He exclaimed, "The black man's record in America's past wars was ample evidence of his capacity and willingness to fight, provided he has something for which to fight."[47] But when it came to Brown's raid, Martin believed that poor strategy was a factor. In addition, Brown had been unsuccessful in communicating the logic of his convictions, leaving the enslaved uncertain about how to act. He insisted that "[slaves] were not cowards, but great diplomats. When they saw their masters in the possession of John Brown, in bonds like themselves, they would have been perfect fools had they demonstrated any willingness to join him. They have got sense enough to know, that until there is a perfect demonstration that the white man is their friend—a demonstration bathed in blood—it is all foolishness to co-operate with them."[48] Martin added that the enslaved had not participated because "they have learned this much from the treachery of white men at the North, and the cruelty of white men at the South, that they cannot trust the white man, even when he comes to deliver them."[49] This was the great challenge of freedoms given versus freedom won: some African Americans saw liberation as theirs to take alone.

Martin addressed the array of opinions the raid had produced, stating, "I know that there is some quibbling, some querulousness, some fear, in reference to an out-and-out endorsement of his [Brown's] course." He acknowledged that pacifists objected to his plan on moral and religious grounds, that Northern politicians objected to Brown for fear of the damage it might bring upon the party, and that Southerners objected because it threatened their "dearest idol." But Martin was clear, he was speaking or rationalizing his comments not from a place of rage but of historical context. He claimed he approved of the means to "approve of the end," to which his audience erupted in applause. Again, Martin reiterated that his was not the language of rage but of revolutionary republican values. He reminded his audience of Concord and Bunker Hill and every historic battle in the fight for independence. "The celebration of those events, all go to approve the means that John has used;

the only difference being, that in our battles, in America, means have been used for white men and that John Brown used his means for black men.[50] His words were once again met with applause. Martin's message was straightforward and unequivocal; the real crime was not the events of Harpers Ferry, but the institution of slavery and the use of the violence rendered upon black people. He was not alone in his sentiments. Brown had not only used his means for black men and women, but his actions reflected the ultimate goals of black men and women.

Almost a year after the raid, abolitionists gathered at North Elba, New York, the home and burial site of Brown, on the Fourth of July to remember him and his comrades. The antislavery advocate Richard J. Hinton hosted the ceremony and began by praising the fallen. "The black man can fight for freedom," declared Hinton, "We have ample evidence, both in the blood of Attucks, and that of Leary, Newby, Copeland and Green at Harpers Ferry and Charlestown." Standing at Brown's tomb, Hinton told the audience that with them today was a courageous man, who fought at Harpers Ferry and wears "the proud mark of manhood." Described by a journalist as a tall, handsome mulatto man, Anderson walked to the podium. Hinton disclosed that while the state of Virginia was offering a $1,500 bounty for Anderson, he trusted that the audience would maintain its discretion. To this statement a member of the audience responded, "There are no Democrats here." Hinton returned, "And if there were, we have good revolvers and strong arms, wherewith to defend our friends."[51]

Anderson spoke with a pensive face, sad but earnest eyes, and an air of intellectual power, which had strong impressions on any observer of him. He told the audience that this moment was the first occasion in his life when he felt that he could stand on a Fourth of July platform. All previous celebrations had felt like an attempt to mask a great deception. Undoubtedly, for many abolitionists the Fourth of July represented hypocrisy when juxtaposed against the backdrop of slavery. Staring down at Brown's grave, Anderson shouted, "Thank God, it [hopelessness] was no longer so!" Reporters at the speech wrote that Anderson had "gone to Virginia not as a mulatto, but as a *man*. Thank God for the struggle!" While followers recognized that the sacrifice made by Brown and his men had been costly, they firmly believed it would be repaid. They reckoned that the "17th of October, the 2d and 16th of December, 1859 . . . and this summer day, would be forever blessed in the memories of men; their golden threads would be woven into the web of the future, irradiating its march, and lighting up the path of Liberty and Justice."[52]

Brown's raid marked a new beginning for the abolitionist movement, particularly when the Fourth of July could now be interpreted by black Americans as a moment of progress.

Responses to the Raid

It did not take Americans long to emphasize the lack of black participation in the raid and to weigh in on the reasons they perceived for it. In Chambersburg, Pennsylvania, the newspaper *Valley Spirit* claimed black people's hesitation obvious, "In regard to our blacks it is believed that a portion of them knew the object of these men, were associated with them, and would have joined them if successful." However, the newspaper claimed that there was "no sympathy in this community" for fugitives and added that "if any of them should come this way they will receive no assistance or protection from any of our citizens."[53] Even Abraham Lincoln joined this discourse. To distance himself politically from the raid, Lincoln declared that Harpers Ferry was nothing more than a white man's effort to incite slave insurrections, in which slaves refused to participate. He claimed, "In fact, it was so absurd that the slaves, with all their ignorance, saw plainly enough that it could not succeed."[54] Lincoln wanted it to be clear that the raid should be seen only as a "peculiar" effort by a fanatic and his delusional followers and not the work of the Republican Party. Furthermore, he rebuked white Southern politicians for using the acts of John Brown to break up the Union, stating, "The demise of party politics would bring far more bloodshed than the failed raid."[55] On this point, Lincoln was more correct than he could know.

Of course, white Southerners had their own interpretation of the black community's lack of response. White Virginians were pleased by the lack of black participation. Many explained it either by "prevailing good will and mutual affection between master and slave" or by "congenital black docility," mythical characteristics of black people that slave owners used to promote slavery's paternalistic nature. Black Americans were described as a "good-humored, good for-nothing, half-monkey race, who could certainly not be expected to fight."[56]

Even eighty years later, on the anniversary of Brown's raid, a newspaper bent on promoting similar sentiments about black Americans' childlike natures claimed that Brown had been mistaken to believe that black Americans would join him: "How sadly he misjudged the Negroes, history was to reveal.

Most of them were completely oblivious to his program. Some were frankly hostile. Few empathized with him but did not dare join him." The article concluded by stating that the few who had made timid efforts to join him were "glad to slip home, hoping their absence had not been noticed."[57] There was a common belief that black people refused to fight with Brown because of fear. For slaveholders, minimizing the efforts of the enslaved was crucial. Fear and passivity had been reported as the dominant attitudes of the slaves in the engine house with the hostages and Brown. Some went so far as to say that slaves were sleeping during the afternoon of the raid. But the response of slaveholders in no way supports these beliefs. In truth, it was slaveholders who were afraid.

Despite how events turned out, Anderson reported that the raid had the support of the enslaved community living in the area who were grateful for Brown and his men's presence. The events that took place directly after the raid offer ample evidence to suggest that the enslaved were indeed engaged in resistance. Just a week after the raid, Harpers Ferry experienced an unprecedented number of fires. Five fires occurred on local plantations. The properties of three of the jurors during the trial were also subject to arson. Numerous slave owners found their wheat, supply yards, stables, and haystacks ablaze. It was never proved, but understood by all, that these fires were being set by the enslaved and free black residents as a response to the aftermath of the raid and the trial.[58] Murat Halstad, a newspaper correspondent, recalled to a companion, "The niggers have burned the stacks of one of the jurors who found John Brown guilty." He added that the home of George Turner, a resident of Harpers Ferry who had not been liked by black people living there, also found himself a victim of arson. In addition, several horses and sheep belonging to his brother, William F. Turner, died suddenly, perhaps because of poison. Two weeks after the raid, Henry Highland Garnet commented that raid might have been successful if only "a box of matches [were placed] in the pocket of every slave, and then slavery would be set right."[59] On December 6, 1859, Robert E. Lee wrote, "Reports of alarm still come in" from Harpers Ferry. Lee remarked in facetious tones that he had been sent "to look after the friends of Mr. John Brown."[60] It was clear that the rebellious mood had not passed.

In western Virginia, the selling of slaves rose substantially. From 1850 to 1860, the counties surrounding Harpers Ferry saw a 10 percent (nearly 1,600) decrease in the number of slaves. Though it cannot be proven, W. E. B. Du Bois suspected that the significant hike in the sale of slaves correlated with the raid.[61] He contended that with such evidence, "there is no doubt that Osborne Anderson knew whereof he spoke, when he said that slaves were ready to cooperate." The selling of slaves was also proof that no white slave owner believed in the innate docility of their property. Additionally, over the course of four months after the raid, Virginians purchased more than ten thousand pistols from Baltimore arms dealers. Despite abolitionists' teaching of nonviolence, slaveholders believed that abolitionists were hell-bent on inciting slave rebellions.[62] The actions of white slave owners in the area was recognition of black men and women as agents and historical actors in the buildup to abolition. Their response was never really about Brown but rather about their fear of black people.

Charles Langston cut to the heart of the matter, writing in a daily newspaper that, in regard to Brown's raid, "the white south saw the dusky ghost of General Nat Turner."[63] While it was primarily white men who conducted Brown's raid, it was black men's actions that white Southerners feared most. White Southerners took up a "for us or against us" approach. There was no neutral ground in face of slavery. Any opinion or deed against the institution of slavery was a political act in favor of the advancement of African Americans. Thus, any aspect of antislavery sentiments stood in direct opposition to white supremacy. For the white South, the numbers and the size of Brown's raiding party were never the issue; their greatest fear lay in the domino effect of rebellion. What may have started as a small army of men could have easily snowballed into a planter's worst fears: open rebellion.

As in all slave rebellions in America, the repercussions were swift and fierce. When reports circulated that the abolitionist Lydia Maria Child had nursed Brown's injuries while he was in prison awaiting execution, she received a letter from the wife of the governor of Virginia. Infuriated, the First Lady wrote: "You would soothe with sisterly and motherly care the hoary-headed monster of Harpers Ferry! A man whose aim and intention was to incite the horrors of servile war—to condemn women of your own race, ere death closed their eyes on their sufferings from violence and outrages, to see their husbands and fathers murdered, their children butchered, the ground strewed with the brains of babies." The tone and terror of the letter conveyed a message that could easily have been written by a St. Domingan refugee during the 1790s.[64] In a *Washington Post* article, a white minister by the name of Dr. Joshua Young spoke out about his fears at that time. Young, also an abolitionist, claimed he had never met Brown but sympathized with his endeavors. At the time of Brown's death, Young was the only minister available to officiate at Brown's funeral. Having done so, Young stated he was shunned for it by the people of his hometown in Vermont and was "informed that some people of the town had expressed the sentiment that I ought to be 'strung up as high as old John Brown.'"[65]

Hate mail and threats were nothing compared to the repercussions black Americans bore because of proslavery violence and angst. After the raid, enslaved men and women suspected of associating with Brown were arrested and even lynched. "What in the tone of southern sentiment had been fierce before became furious and uncontrollable now," wrote Douglass. He exclaimed, "A scream for vengeance came up from all sections of the slave States and from great multitudes in the North."[66] Concerned for his own life, he fled to Europe to escape capture and indictment for his connection with Brown. Douglass was confident that if he were found, he would share Brown's fate, because he met with Brown several times and gave him financial assistance. "The morning papers brought no relief," Douglass wrote, "for they announced that the government would spare no pains in ferreting out and bringing to punishment all who were connected with the Harpers Ferry outrage, and that papers as well as persons would be searched for."[67] Douglass remained in Europe until April 1860, when he was able to return to the United States.

A System Met with Its Own Weapons

Despite fear of retaliation and persecution, black leaders refused to denounce Brown's attempts. As they saw it, Brown was not leading black people into death, he was continuing and enhancing the work of black abolitionists who believed that violence was the only weapon that would overthrow the system of slavery. And these acts were no different from the desires of the country's forefathers. H. Ford Douglas, a prominent speaker and Virginian-born fugitive slave living in Illinois, raised an interesting point regarding condemnation of Brown. He declared, "They condemn John Brown as the vilest of criminals, yet laud the Revolutionary fathers for doing what John did." Ford Douglas reasoned that if George Washington and the fathers of the American Revolution were right, so was Brown. He reprimanded Henry Ward Beecher for a sermon in which he declared that Brown was wrong because "there was no prospect of success." Ford Douglas refused to believe that success was the ultimate test of the matter. He asked, "If John Brown was wrong in defeat, would he have been right in success? If our Revolutionary fathers had failed, would they, therefore, have been the greatest of criminals?"[68] Ford Douglas rejected the notion that political violence was a tool to be used only by white men in power. Political violence was a tool to combat powerlessness. Who was more worthy of such tools than the oppressed? Other leaders began to subscribe to his logic as well.

Even William Lloyd Garrison had to concede that Brown's acts bore a sense of legitimacy. Garrison acknowledged that while he was still staunch in his belief in nonviolence, he sympathized with the path Brown had chosen. At Tremont Temple, on the same day Martin gave his speech concerning Brown's execution, Garrison spoke as well. He claimed that if George Washington was right in his attempt, so was Brown. "If men are justified in striking a blow for freedom, when the question is one of a three penny tax on tea," Garrison argued, "then, I say, they are a thousand times more justified, when it is to save fathers, mothers, wives and children from the slave coffle and the auction-block, and to restore them to their God-given rights." By the end of the 1850s, Garrison had made some concessions to political violence that brought about a greater good. He claimed that while he was a pacifist, he was prepared to wish "success to every slave insurrection at the South, and in every slave country." He added, "And I do not see how I compromise or stain my peace profession in making that declaration." Garrison confessed that in the contest between the oppressed and the oppressor, his heart was always with the oppressed and always against the oppressor. He concluded, "I cannot but wish success to all slave insurrections. . . . Rather than see men wearing their chains in cowardly and servile spirit, I would, as an advocate of peace, much rather see them breaking the head of the tyrant with their chains."[69] Perhaps Garrison had resolved the notions of nonresistance and moral suasion; he finally saw slavery as a system that could be abolished only by violent force.

Several months later Douglass echoed similar sentiments in a letter to James Redpath. He argued, "The only penetrable point of a tyrant is the *fear of death*. The outcry that they make, as to the danger of having their *throats* cut is because they deserve to have them *cut*." Douglass rationalized that the efforts of "John Brown and his brave associates," while unsuccessful, "have done more to upset the logic and shake the security of slavery, than all other efforts in that direction for twenty years."[70] Leading up to Brown's raid, it appeared that the abolitionist movement had experienced setback after setback—from the Fugitive Slave Law, to slavery's expansion, to the Dred Scott decision. Brown's raid constituted a major offensive that could not be ignored because it represented a black-centered framework on revolutionary violence. Harpers Ferry created few choices for going forward. The *Anglo-African Magazine* declared, "So, people of the South, people of the North! Men and brethren, choose ye which method of emancipation you prefer—Nat Turner or John Brown's."[71] Either way, the violent demise of slavery was at hand.

Brown in Black Memory

In 1881, more than three decades later, at the fourteenth anniversary of Storer College, an institution in Harpers Ferry devoted primarily to the education of African American youth, Douglass delivered a powerful and memorable address on Brown and his legacy.[72] The speech was published and put in pamphlet form to be distributed for sale at Harpers Ferry on Decoration Day, May 30, 1881. The proceeds were to be used toward the endowment of the John Brown Professorship at Storer. The mere location of the address was testament to the rapid changes that had taken place during the previous twenty years. Douglass, who had fled the country for his protection, could now travel to the very place where Brown had committed the rebellion and speak of Brown as a martyr and a hero before an audience of Virginians. Furthermore, Douglass spoke without reserve in front of the very person who was responsible for Brown's hanging: the Honorable Andrew Hunter, of Charlestown, the district attorney who prosecuted John Brown and secured his execution. He sat on the platform directly behind Douglass during the delivery of the entire address.[73] At the close of the speech, Hunter shook hands with Douglass, congratulated him, and invited him to Charlestown (where John Brown was hanged), adding that if Robert E. Lee were still alive, he too would shake Douglass's hand.[74] To be clear, this was not a case of good sportsmanship. The fundamental issue of slavery and emancipation was the bloodiest episode in American history. The stakes over history and memory had never been higher than they were following the Civil War to reconcile the tremendous loss of life. Douglass understood that Hunter's handshake was not a confession of wrongdoing but a concession of a war that was lost.

Douglass's purpose was to pay a debt long due and, to some extent, vindicate a great historical figure with whom he was well acquainted. "There is no subject which in its interest and importance will be remembered longer, or will form a more thrilling chapter in American history than this strange, wild, bloody and mournful drama," Douglass claimed. He then went on to summarize what he believed was real issue of the raid: the violent overthrow of slavery. He argued that war began with Virginia and not South Carolina and with Harpers Ferry and not Fort Sumter. For Douglass, the lost cause of the century was not Brown's efforts but the South's failed attempt to gain possession of the federal government. Douglass understood that Brown's while plans may have failed, his purposes succeeded. He believed that the central question was whether Brown drew his sword against slavery and lost his life in vain. "And to this I answer ten thousand times, No!" he announced. For Douglass, no man could fail when they forfeited their life for such a noble cause.[75]

Interestingly, Douglass did not grant President Lincoln the same honor he granted Brown. In 1876, just five years before his speech at Harpers Ferry, Douglass refused to place Lincoln at the center of emancipation and black equality during the unveiling of the Freedmen's Memorial in Lincoln Park, Washington, DC, a statue known for its half-naked bondsman shackled and kneeling at the feet of the Lincoln. The statue portrays the quintessential white savior dominating over an indebted black body.[76] At the unveiling, Douglass proclaimed, "Abraham Lincoln was not, in the fullest sense of the word, either our man or our model. In his interests, in his associations, in his habits of thought, and in his prejudices, he was a white man." He went on to say that not only was Lincoln "preeminently the white man's President, entirely devoted to the welfare of white men," but that during the first years of his administration, Lincoln was willing "to deny, postpone, and sacrifice the rights of humanity in the colored people to promote the welfare of the white people of this country." Douglass claimed that white Americans were the true children of Lincoln, while black Americans were "step-children; children by adoption, children by forces of circumstances and necessity." He recognized that it was of supreme importance for white Americans to sing the praises, preserve the memory, and multiply the statues and portraits of Lincoln.[77] In all of Douglass numerous speeches there was one principle he thoroughly understood: the process of memorialization was political.

If Douglass had to put a white face on the poster of emancipation it would not be Lincoln's, but Brown's. Even though Douglass firmly believed that it was the contributions and force of black Americans that led, fought, and won the war, he also recognized the unspoken need for white Americans to see themselves as the face of liberty. Thus, in front of Hunter and those in attendance at Storer College, Douglass co-opted Brown and his radical vision to stand in for the black men and women who made the most social and political contributions to abolition.

Brown was not Harpers Ferry. Harpers Ferry was collective black liberation. Yet Brown has been dissected from the black struggle to represent violence in its totality. This dissection continually robs black abolitionists of
their contributions and limits them to supporting roles for the sake of enhancing white heroism as the official American narrative. While it could be
read that Douglass was not completely wedded to his speech about Brown,
when given the choice between memorializing whiteness at the expense of
black efforts, Brown would always be his choice over Lincoln.

Indeed, Brown has become one of the strongest symbols black leaders
could highlight to underscore their own radicalism. Acknowledging Brown
was a subtle yet direct form of recognizing black violence as a threat to white
supremacy. Accordingly, it is no wonder that the all-black Massachusetts 55th
regiment marched into Charleston, South Carolina, singing "John Brown's
Body" during the Civil War. The song was not a reminder merely of Brown's
actions but also of black people's capacity to inflict fear and terror against the
myth of black docility. In addition, the Niagara Movement, an association
seen as the radical precursor to the NAACP, held its first public meeting in
1906 at the old fort in Harpers Ferry. Fifty men and women gathered at 6:00
a.m. in the morning to perform a sacred pilgrimage. They marched single file
and barefoot on what they considered "hallowed ground" while singing
"John Brown's Body." During that meeting, inspirational speeches were given
by Henrietta Leary Evans (the sister of Lewis Sheridan Leary and aunt to
John A. Copeland Jr.), then Lewis Douglass, son of Frederick Douglass, and
finally Reverdy C. Ransom, pastor of the Charles Street African Methodist
Episcopal Church in Boston. The historian Benjamin Quarles called it "the
most stirring single episode in the life of the Niagara Movement," and Du
Bois referred to it as "one of the greatest meetings that American Negroes
ever held." Well into the twentieth century, memorials and homages to Brown
were common.[78]

Over time, Brown has held scholars at an arresting intellectual and political standoff. Few have attempted to explain the role of violence in the abolitionist movement, especially the relationship between black Americans and
the politics of violence. In 1909, fifty years after the raid, Du Bois published
John Brown, the first biography written by a black author. He was one of the
first writers to explore Brown's relationships with black Americans as well.
Du Bois immediately directed his reader's attention to the detrimental effects of slavery and how it had made Brown's violent vision necessary.
Among his sources was testimony from Osborne Anderson.[79] The inclusion

of Anderson's perspective was critical. At the time, Du Bois wrote, white scholars were opposed to the use of Anderson's narrative because they regarded it as questionable and biased. Many white scholars did not believe an African American could be considered a reliable source.[80] Today Du Bois's biography of Brown warrants even greater attention.

Contemporary historians can no longer afford to ignore African American oral histories deemed controversial because the voices in these histories threaten to decenter whiteness or place too much significance on the leadership of African Americans. Simply put, one cannot divorce Brown from the contributions of African Americans both during the raid and long before the raid was conceived. Yet, the scholar Steven Lubert, who is the first scholar to dedicate an entire study to the contributions of Copeland argued, "Historians have treated most of John Brown's foot soldiers as loyal spear carriers in the operatic sweep of the events at Harper's Ferry."[81] More accurate is the notion that Brown himself was but a foot solider in the long movement toward black freedom. When the Civil War officially began, the arming of black men turned the tide of victory to the hands of the Union. As black soldiers sang "John Brown's Body," finally and for the first time all of Brown's silenced partners were heard.

CHAPTER 5

A Carbonari Wanted

Violence, Emigration, and the Eve of the Civil War

It [abolition] started to free the slave. . . . It ends by leaving
the slave to free himself.

—Frederick Douglass

George Lawrence Jr., the new editor of the radical *Weekly Anglo-African*
newspaper and the New York City agent for the Haytian Emigration Bureau,
wrote the following editorial that went to press just a day after South Carolina's attack on Fort Sumter. The headline read: "A CARBONARI WANTED."[1]
The Carbonari (which translates into "charcoal-burners" in Italian) was a secret revolutionary society founded in early nineteenth-century Italy and
France whose purpose was to violently overthrow authoritarian rule and establish constitutional government in Italy. The editorial was written in response to the arrest of a black family, a man named Harris, his wife, and their
two children. They were taken by slave catchers and sent from Chicago to
Springfield by train to be claimed by a Mr. Patterson of St. Louis County,
Missouri. As the fugitive family was taken, a large crowd of black people
gathered at the train station, where it was believed the family was onboard.
As the train departed, a member of the crowd fired shots at the train and the
onlookers dispersed without further disturbance. The black community was
angry and in despair. More than ten years after the enactment of the Fugitive
Slave Law and with civil war looming, few anticipated black Americans'
being taken from Chicago or any Northern city by slave catchers.

Lawrence wanted men who would strike back. Reporting on the event, he
declared, "We want a Carbonari, as swift and terrible as that which has been

the terror of European tyrants." His message was simple: "Until the whole pack of panting bloodhounds of Commissioners, Marshals and Deputies *know* that for every unfortunate returned to bondage, some *one* of their number will fall under the pistol, knife, or poison of the Avenger, there will be no peace for the poor; no security for the oppressed."[2] For Lawrence, the issues regarding freedom and slavery were synonymous with the issues of life and death. He suggested that if slave catchers believed their lives were at stake for attempting to return fugitive slaves, all slave catching would cease.

Moreover, Lawrence contended, even if black Americans were not strong enough to resist openly, they were strong enough to conspire. His ultimate hope was that strong blows would instill a fear so intense that it would compel change. "'One or two shots were fired at the train,'" Lawrence scoffed, "What imbecility? Why not have saved the powder and ball and fired them through the corrupt heart of the mansteal, Commissioner Corneau?" The newspaper reiterated its motto that "man must be free, if not within the law, then above the law." In a postscript the newspaper declared, "Only through the Red Sea of civil war and insurrection can the sins of this demonized people be washed away."[3] After the attack on Ft. Sumter, it became obvious to all that violence was going to be the vehicle of change in either dissolving the union or maintaining its preservation.

The rapid pace of events that took place in the 1850s fueled the momentum of political violence. With each event, more members of the abolitionist movement became prepared to accept political violence not only as a tool, but as a reasonable vehicle to abolish slavery. For black Americans, there was little moral obligation to uphold laws that preserved their oppression. "Fight and flight" became the surest options to combat their powerlessness. Rapidly, abolitionist speakers were met with applause and cheers when they used threatening language or retold stories of fugitives who had killed slave catchers. By 1859, it appeared that black abolitionists were just as united in their support for violent means as Garrisonians had been in their support for pacifism in the 1830s.[4] Although it is difficult to quantify the percentage of black abolitionists who agitated for war, their purposes, language, and behavior represented a significant branch of the movement.

Black abolitionist tensions and responses on the eve of the Civil War explain how the buildup of black self-determination and political violence influenced the election of Lincoln, the famous mobbing at Tremont Temple, and the growing impetus for emigration. Their contributions significantly moved the country closer to war and compelled many to consider the crux of the conflict: slavery was warfare against black humanity. Both free and en-slaved black Americans were able to have a powerful impact on the social and political landscape, forever changing the trajectory of American history and American protest movements. Black abolitionists and the free black North in general were ready for and anticipated that war would be necessary for emancipation. They also believed that war should ultimately lead to emancipation. In the minds of black leaders, John Brown led a black assault on slavery in 1859 and by the time of the Civil War, Lincoln was inadvertently presiding over a black war of emancipation.

On the eve of war, no other themes dominated black consciousness more than those of self-determination through political violence and of emigra-tion. Black abolitionists saw themselves as the engines and engineers against slavery. A rising feeling of separatism among African American leaders cul-tivated the belief that Garrison no longer represented the leadership or the solution black Americans needed or wanted. For black leadership, the move-ment was not about Garrison, anyway. The movement was about emancipa-tion and radical reform. White leadership was appreciated but not central. The general atmosphere and the events that engendered self-determination made it increasingly clear that the fate of black Americans rested in their own hands.

Black Political Self Determination

Frustrated over how the abolitionist movement had evolved, the African American physician and abolitionist James McCune Smith lamented the state of abolitionist reform in an article he wrote for the *Frederick Douglass' Paper*. He declared with certitude that no one else could do the work that was the province of black Americans, any more than someone else could breathe for him. He exhorted his fellows to take up a stance in the movement that placed the desires of black leadership and labor at the forefront.[5] As a physi-cian and an activist, he could accurately diagnose the problems of black Americans. He admitted that the overall stagnation of the movement had demoralized him to the point of indifference. Neither public sentiment nor political machinations were moving the cause of abolition forward, only sec-tional divisions among free and slave states. The government was weighing the advisability of passing the Lecompton Constitution, which was the sec-ond of four proposed constitutions for the territory of Kansas.

The Lecompton Constitution permitted slavery in the state for present slaveholders and guaranteed the rights of property holders but prevented future importation of slaves into Kansas. McCune Smith asked, "Is it apathy or what is it that causes me to take up the morning paper, and lay it down, without caring a straw, never even looking to see whether Lecompton triumphed or fell yesterday in the House?"[6] He explained that African American apathy was rooted in problems much deeper than surface political issues. At the root of his sentiments was truly not apathy but despair. For McCune Smith, when the antislavery movement had been formalized more than twenty-five years previously under the leadership of Garrison, "no part of the people were so electrified, so excited, so hopeful as we." He claimed that "our deep craving for the acknowledgment of our brotherhood welled up in holy expectation, in beatific joy." However, he could not help but believe the same craving was now "crushed, withered and disappointed," resulting in an attitude of hopeless indifference.[7]

McCune Smith took his assessment even further and acknowledged that it was not apathy he felt but grief—grief over the fact that while men led the way in making Kansas a free state, the same men urged legislators to keep black Americans out of the territory. He believed that if there was ever the opportunity create progress for the abolitionist movement, the decision to be made about Kansas represented that opportunity. He did not feel as though black Americans possessed sincere political allies. Although abolitionists had the resources for reform, they consistently lacked sufficient political support. McCune Smith explained that absence of decisive intention was why action was not taken. He wondered in print whether supporters of abolition had enough wisdom to see the utility in marrying politics to abolitionism to ensure the ideas of freedom and equality for black African Americans.

For McCune Smith, the greatest stumbling block black Americans faced was the ever-pervasive feeling that white man's failure to bring about social reform implied that political reform was altogether impossible. Black leadership was most concerned that if their white allies could not politically combat the Slave Power, then no one would be able to abolish the oppressive system. McCune Smith rebuked his readers for this line of thought, "Was the white man god, for whom all things were possible?" He noted that black Americans were indeed taught to believe this ridiculous idea, which preserved the idea of white supremacy even concerning emancipation. He suggested that despite the lack of logic in such a notion, it was one held firmly by even the most intelligent black Americans. However, McCune Smith refused to accept erroneous notions that promoted black inferiority and endorsed white leadership as superior. The evidence of successful black resistance was all around.[8]

McCune Smith's strongest argument regarding black humanity came at the end of an article he published about an overseer who was tried for the murder of a slave.[9] In this particular case, the plea stated the enslaved had resisted punishment and, after making an attempt to defend himself, had been murdered by the overseer. Judge Yonger ruled that a slave whose life was imperiled by punishment had the right to defend his person from further harm. The judge convicted the overseer and sentenced him to seven years' imprisonment for his actions. McCune Smith was thrilled with this contrast to the unjust legal proceedings he had seen taking place elsewhere. He called out to his fellows, exclaiming that if African Americans could have this kind of effect in the court of law and in the government, surely there was little outside their power.[10] Even though the enslaved man was killed by his overseer, self-defense or protective violence was deemed legitimate. If using physical force to combat an attacker was within reason for the enslaved and out of bounds for the overseer, then McCune Smith recognized how protective violence could be employed by free black Americans. He was not alone in his sentiments.

Preparing for Violence and Resorting to Revolutions

As a free black American born of free black American parents in Salem, New Jersey, John S. Rock experienced a life of unprecedented privilege. By age twenty-seven, Rock was a teacher, a physician, a dentist, and an abolitionist. He later studied law, passed the bar, and became a lawyer. He championed African American rights and promoted pride within the black community. Rock represented all of the possibilities that parents, whether black or white, would want for their children. As an accomplished man whom some would call "cultured," Rock still saw political violence as the determining factor in the abolition of slavery and in the pursuit of equal rights.

In 1858, almost two years before the start of the Civil War, Rock delivered a powerful speech on the destiny he believed he shared with his free and enslaved black brethren. He warned that America as a country would either learn from its painful history or be doomed to pay the price. He predicted, "Sooner than later, the clashing of arms will be heard in this country, and the black man's services will be needed." Rock contended that a hundred and fifty thousand freemen were capable of bearing arms and were not in the slightest cowards or fools. In addition, he boasted of the "three quarters of a million" enslaved who were, "wild with the enthusiasm caused by the dawn of the glorious opportunity of being able to strike a genuine blow for freedom." Rock firmly believed that together, black Americans possessed a powerful force "which white men will be 'bound to respect.'" Thus, when Rock posed the question "Will the blacks fight?," he responded emphatically, "Of course they will."[11]

As successful as Rock was, he maintained that he would never turn his back on his race, assuring his readers that his own fortunes would rise or fall with those of the cause.[12] He understood that his success was linked directly to that of his enslaved brethren and that theirs was linked to his in return. Despite having never experienced slavery, Rock perceived political violence not merely as an option but as the only road to freedom. He expressed the opinion that, like Nat Turner, "to be free, both slaves and free blacks must fight their own battles."[13]

Two years before the Civil War began, black leaders were strategizing how to move their defensive position to an offensive one. While many wanted to fight, few were sure about how to go about it. In 1858, Charles Remond requested that the Massachusetts State Negro Convention in Bedford "publish an address to the slaves of the South on the subject of the right to and duty to insurrection."[14] The argument that "When I fight, I want to whip somebody" prevailed at the convention.[15] While Remond's peers understood his willingness to ignite a fight, the use of slave rebellions as a technique was still largely rejected as impractical; however, this did not deter leaders from thinking how violence might prove successful.

Remond, like Rock, continued to champion political violence. He predicted that American slavery would go down in blood. He added that not only was he prepared to see it, but that he also longed for the time to come. "I believe it will be a retribution that the American people deserve," declared Remond, "and it will be a lesson by which those who come after them will not fail to profit."[16] Others who, like Remond, felt exasperation began to parody Judge Taney's language ("No rights which the white man was bound to respect") by repeating that the Dred Scott decision was "a foul and infamous lie which neither black men nor white men are bound to respect."[17] In June 1858, a resolution by Lloyd H. Brooks, delivered at the Third Christian Church in New Bedford, Massachusetts, proclaimed: "*Resolved*, That as no attempt for human freedom was ever successful unless perfect union existed in the ranks of the oppressed, we consider it a paramount duty for all *lovers of liberty* to join in waging a war of annihilation against every vestige of oppression under which we are now suffering."[18] All throughout 1858 and 1859, black abolitionists continued to meet, to strategize, and discover ways in which their words and deeds might effect change. However, with each month that passed, a sense of urgency was convincing them to move forward with haste. The tension of the late 1850s was palpable. Everyone involved in the debate about slavery felt that his or her beliefs were being challenged to the point of death.

On December 3, 1859, the day after John Brown's execution, people from the Cincinnati German Freeman Society and the Arbiter Association held a rally in honor of Brown. The crowd was made up of men and women and rather diverse: one-third of the crowd was African American and two-thirds of the crowd were German. Lectures were given in three different languages: English, German, and French. Local newspapers called the gathering a "motley crowd of both sexes, diversified by every hue common to the human species."[19] A white minister of the First Congregational Church, Moncure Conway, spoke at the rally and claimed that American's real revolution was against slavery. "We must die or succeed," he claimed. As Conway was a moral suasionist and former Virginian, violent ultimatums represented quite the ideological leap for him. He recognized that Brown's actions changed the trajectory of the movement. Violent resistance had to be employed, if not, at the very least, considered. On that day, Peter H. Clark was the only African American of the five speakers who spoke. For him, this rally marked the second time in his life when he "truly felt free." He then echoed Conway's sentiments regarding America's unfinished revolution: black freedom. He acknowledged that politically "we are in the midst of a revolution." He firmly believed, as many did that day, that opponents of abolition waged war to secure slavery. Thus, Clark encouraged his comrades to use "all the weapons of freeman" to earn their liberty. He was not speaking in terms of metaphor. Clark believed in moral suasion and the political process, but when all tools had been exhausted, he also firmly believed in violence to achieve emancipation. He warned that people who fought to uphold slavery should be sent to "hospitable graves."[20] Over the course of several months, black leaders and their white allies began to speak out about an impending revolution that would finally address what the American Revolution never accomplished.

On March 5, 1860, Rock gave another speech at Meionaon Hall in Boston to commemorate Crispus Attucks, an African American and the first person to die in the Revolutionary War. The black abolitionist and historian William

C. Nell had instituted such celebrations a few years earlier to acknowledge the start of the American Revolution and pay tribute to black contributions to the country's history. In addition to Rock and Remond, several prominent white abolitionists were in attendance: William Lloyd Garrison, Wendell Phillips, and Theodore Parker. Rock used the occasion to expound upon the ideals represented not only by Attucks but also by the white ally and radical abolitionist, John Brown. Just several months earlier, Brown's raid had changed the climate of antislavery politics. Rock declared, "I believe in insurrections (applause)—and especially those of the pen and of the sword. Wm. Lloyd Garrison is, I think, a perfect embodiment of the moral insurrection of thought." Rock never wanted to discredit the efforts of white abolitionists and Garrisonians, but it was evident which method he saw as more effective. He claimed, "John Brown was, and is, the representative of the potent power, the sword." For him, there was no doubt which method ensured the freedom of black people. Rock declared, "It is a severe method; but to severe ills it is necessary to apply severe remedies." He saw Brown and his men as the first causalities of the oncoming second revolution, just as Crispus Attucks was the first casualty of the American Revolution.[21]

Rock continued to juxtapose Attucks and Brown and admitted that he differed from many abolitionists in terms of the best way to elevate the race. "While I believe that anti-slavery speeches, whether political or otherwise, will do much to correct a cruel and wicked public sentiment," Rock proclaimed, "I am confident that such means alone can never elevate us." He contended the only way black Americans could achieve equality and enfranchisement was through more aggressive efforts. The question of whether freedom or slavery would triumph in the country was soon to be settled. While no one knew whether the shift would come gradually because of spreading antislavery sentiment, or whether abolition would be brought about through more forceful measures, his hopes were that it could all be accomplished peacefully. If war proved inevitable, his greatest hope was that black Americans and white abolitionists alike would not shrink from the responsibility of fighting with courage.[22]

Garrison spoke that day as well. The political climate and recent events had placed his personal beliefs in constant flux with black leadership regarding the use of violence as a tool. Garrison invoked God's call for all people to seek peace. But it appeared that if he were to support any violence, it would be on behalf of the enslaved. He claimed, "I admit, that if any men have a right to fight for liberty with deadly weapons, they are to be found on the

Southern plantations; for no wrongs are like theirs." In the spirit of Attucks, Garrison added that if George Washington and his compatriots had been "justified in taking up arms," then black Americans too, possessed a logical and legitimate right to resort to the same form of armed resistance. This was the same language and reasoning David Walker had employed in his *Appeal*, which Garrison had denounced three decades earlier. Garrison, the same person who had deplored Nat Turner's slave insurrection, wrote a letter to James Redpath several months after his speech in Boston in which he advised, "Brand the man a hypocrite and bastard, who in one breath, exalts in the deeds of Washington and Warren, and in the next, denounces Nat Turner as a monster for refusing to no longer wear the yoke and be driven under the lash and for talking."[23] If violence was going to take place, Garrison rationalized he could be more sympathetic to the enslaved than to free black Northerners calling for violence. Interestingly, his rationale did not account for fugitive slaves, many of whom made up a significant portion of black leadership. Among black abolitionists, white people could not separate free, fugitive, and enslaved black Americans in the same way that one could not parcel out emancipation and equality. Rock was right: free black Americans and the enslaved were inextricably linked. Whether the first blow would be struck by the enslaved or by free black leadership, no one knew, but all stood to face parallel consequences and possessed a legitimate claim for political violence.

The Underwhelming Election of Lincoln

In 1858, during a speech in Chicago, Abraham Lincoln declared, "I have always hated slavery, I think as much as any abolitionist."[24] Undoubtedly, many black abolitionists scoffed at his declaration. Though Lincoln believed the underlying principle of the party was antislavery, in his view, antislavery did not mean equality for black Americans. For black abolitionists, the potential election of Lincoln offered little hope. While many black Americans saw the Republican Party as their best chance for change, few put any stock in the party's ability to alter their situation. Even Frederick Douglass, who supported the Republican Party, was frustrated by the racism of its politicians. For instance, in 1859, William Dennison, the Republican candidate running for governor of the state of Ohio, argued that the Republican Party, "labors for the prosperity and liberty of the white man." As was seen in the conflict over Kansas, free-labor ideology promoted racism as its first principle. Leaders in the Republican political party consistently attempted to assure voters of the idea that "Republican Party is the white man's party." Indeed, much of their campaigns were spent combating the racist propaganda Democrats were spreading about unfounded fears of miscegenation and black rule.[25]

Fear of black Americans' presence and progress was a constant theme among Democrats. In 1859, a Democratic newspaper warned its readers that the success of the Republican Party would encourage black people who immigrated to Canada to return to the state of Ohio. Democrats claimed that Republicans were "pro-Negro." The Democratic Party constantly put the belief before the American people that a vote for Lincoln was a vote in favor of "Negro equality." During the presidential campaign, some New York Democrats went so far as to spread the outlandish rumor that Hannibal Hamlin, the Republican vice-presidential candidate, was a mulatto. All across the country, Democrats used bigotry to stir the emotions of voters. In Wisconsin, Democrats labeled the Republicans the Nigger Party. In addition, the fear of miscegenation had been prevalent since the anti-abolitionist riots of the 1830s. In Indiana, a group of women sympathetic to the Democratic cause marched in a parade with banners that read: "Fathers, save us from nigger husbands."[26]

Conversely, the black press and black leadership recognized all of the political posturing. In 1860, the *Weekly Anglo-African* claimed that to Republicans antislavery meant nothing more than "opposition to the black man."[27] In Framingham, Massachusetts, H. Ford Douglas, a Virginia-born fugitive slave who lived in Illinois, was invited to give a lecture concerning Lincoln's candidacy. He told a predominantly white abolitionist audience that no political party was worthy of their votes "unless that party is willing to extend to the black man all the rights of a citizen."[28] Ford Douglas explained that he knew all about Lincoln and his brand of antislavery. He claimed that Republicans were willing to steal the thunder of abolitionists but unwilling to impose the policies that promoted abolitionism.

Ford Douglas rebuked the party for wanting to take a moderate stance regarding abolition. The party saw abolitionist leaders as radicals who wanted all their goals met immediately. "They say that they cannot go as fast as you antislavery men go in this matter," claimed Ford Douglas, and added, "They want to take time; that they want to do the work gradually. They say, 'We must not be in too great a hurry to overthrow slavery; at least, we must take half a loaf, we cannot get the whole.'" [29] Ford Douglas believed, as did others, that the best way to overthrow slavery in this country was to occupy the highest possible antislavery ground. This meant emancipation and equality now and with all the tools necessary to accomplish it. If this was not going to be the antislavery platform of Lincoln, Ford Douglas wanted nothing of it. He understood that in politics there was often little difference between those who were antislavery and those who were antiblack.

The Mobbing at Tremont Temple

On December 3, 1860, roughly one month after Lincoln's election, abolitionists scheduled an event at Tremont Temple in Boston to commemorate the anniversary of John Brown's raid on Harpers Ferry. Black abolitionists were doing all they could to keep the issue of force at the forefront. Those who attended the meeting did so primarily because they shared Brown's ideology of using political violence to combat slavery. A mix of prominent black and white abolitionists were in attendance. Among them were Frederick Douglass, James Redpath, Franklin Benjamin Sanborn, J. Sella Martin, and others associated with Brown. In the audience were scores of antislavery representatives, along with police officials to maintain an orderly environment.

Hundreds of Bostonians, however, were convinced that abolitionists were responsible for adding fuel to secessionist tensions. These Bostonians were appalled and infuriated by abolitionists who praised Brown when the South was planning succession from the Union. Most white Northerners wanted nothing more than to silence abolitionist agitators who sought to arouse discord. The economies of entire towns surrounding the Boston area and in larger New England were centered on the manufacture of textiles from Southern cotton. Resentment against the abolitionists was not just political or regional; it was economic. Angry anti-abolitionist mobs were beginning to surround the temple to end what they viewed as Northern sedition. The infamous mob violence that took place at Tremont Temple was one of the strongest appeals by black and white abolitionists for both political and protective violence.

The event began when a white abolitionist and writer was jeered off the stage by hecklers intent on silencing the event altogether. It was clear that hecklers prearranged their move to prevent any abolitionists from voicing their opinions. A witness declared that the protestors "resembled the famous mob of 1835" and appeared to be "the sons of gentlemen." These were men heavily invested in the interests of slavery. When a young black clergyman attempted to follow his peer by making a speech, he was taunted with racial epithets, profanity, and shouting. It was not long before the entire room erupted into chaos between those who wished to be heard and those who sought to silence them. Chairs were thrown at the stage, the police were called, and three cheers were shouted when the names of Slave Power leaders were called, such as Governor Wise and Daniel Webster. When Chairman Richard S. Fay, an ex-candidate for Congress, marched to the platform to give a speech on the treasonous acts of Brown, black leaders were outraged. Douglass then stood before the audience in response. He "showered ridicule so plentifully and so effectively among [upon] his opponents" that joint forces began to rise in anger to drown out Douglass's voice.[30] When the angry mob realized they could not silence Douglass, a party rushed the platform to clear it of black leadership. The police managed to interfere against the majority, but within minutes a physical fight had ensued.

Figure 10. "Expulsion of Negroes and Abolitionists from Tremont Temple."
Harper's Weekly, December 3, 1860. Courtesy of Boston Athenaeum.

The *Douglass' Monthly* declared, "On one side cheers for Gov. Wise and the Fugitive Slave Bill were launched—on the other, cheers for freedom and liberty of speech." The commotion could not be quelled. The newspaper described in detail the ensuing brawl: "Men were thrown boldly from the platform down among the audience. . . . The women were greatly frightened, and helped the turbulence by loud cries." Douglass began to fight like "a trained pugilist." When a score of men opposed him, he cleared his way through the crowd and was determined to hold his place. His friends did not come to his aid, and the police managed to drag him away from the podium and throw him down the staircase that led to the floor of the hall. His friend and colleague Sanborn was dragged out by his neck.[31]

Fortunately, no one was severely injured during the skirmish. Nonetheless, the mob at Tremont Temple demonstrated the truth that both anti-abolitionists and abolitionists were out of patience. While the chief of police made a prompt decision to clear the hall, it was announced that another meeting would take place and that the friends of Brown would reassemble in J. Sella Martin's Joy Street Church that evening. As the crowd dispersed, the angry mob continued to harass black Americans and throw rocks through the windows of black homes and businesses. The newspaper declared that pistols had been shot here and there, but it did not appear that anybody was injured as a result.

By late that evening, calm had fallen upon the city. The speakers John Brown Jr., Wendell Phillips, Sanborn, Douglass, Ford Douglas, and others came together again at Martin's church to resume the meeting with the purpose of addressing the question, how can American slavery be abolished? When John Brown Jr. took the stage, he spoke with great conviction. He discussed methods of abolishing slavery and contended that an effective tool was to make the slave owner paranoid concerning the enslaved, as though death and defiance were all around him. Slaveholders could not ensure the longevity of a system that was plagued by rebellion, or even rumors of rebellion. As for free people of color, Brown Jr. instructed them to be thoroughly organized and armed, at which his audience applauded. He then warned that the policy on slave catchers should be to take them "alive, if possible, but secure them, any way—and give them seventy-eight lashes." After being lashed, Brown Jr. suggested, they should be washed down with salt and water. He concluded by telling the assembled crowd that their "watchword should not be, 'Give me liberty or give me death,' but 'Give me liberty, or I will give *you* death.'"[32]

When the white abolitionist and orator Wendell Phillips spoke, he seconded many of the notions Brown Jr. had put forth. He summarized, "John Brown, Jr., has advised colored men to arm themselves with revolvers," and added, "This meeting was a revolver." Phillips claimed that regarding the abolition of slavery, he favored all methods, and particularly freedom of speech, in view of the mob attack at Tremont Temple. After the mobbing, Phillips had to be escorted to his home and even placed men outside to stand guard.[33]

Douglass was not the last to speak, but when he spoke it is likely he commanded the most attention. He clarified that each speaker was expected to present what he regarded as the best way of furthering the abolitionist movement. Douglass declared, "From my heart of hearts I endorse the sentiment expressed by Mr. Phillips." Douglass approved of every method of proceeding against slavery, be it politics, religion, peace, disunion, or war. While he acknowledged that nonviolence and moral suasion had been the method of the last twenty-five years, for Douglass these methods represented a quarter-century of failure. The hour called for radical change in the form of political violence. "I mean the John Brown way," explained Douglass. He reminded his audience that the second purpose of the meeting was to commemorate Brown's contributions to abolition. He suggested employing violence as a method to oppose slavery was the primary reason his peers had faced a mob that day. This method effectively placed all white supremacy at risk. Douglass used the remainder of his speech to advocate for John Brown's way of accomplishing our object.[34]

Douglass also commended John Brown Jr. for having offered sentiments that taught the audience to reach the slaveholder's conscience through his fear of personal danger. He suggested that it was necessary to make the slaveholder live in fear, never knowing when his slaves might dole out violence or death. Douglass explained that the slave owner should feel about his slaves the same way a man feels about a fractious and spirited horse: that he wants to be rid of the troublemaker. The slave owner, Douglass contended, should be made to feel that slavery was exceedingly uncomfortable.[35] Although Douglass did not want his suggestions to be construed as discouragement regarding other efforts that were political or moral, he too had come to believe that violent force was the surest of methods, particularly given what he had experienced by the mob.

Let the Union Perish

Black abolitionists, along with white allies, understood the utility of playing upon the insecurity of the slaveholding South and an economically invested North. Amid rumors of Southern secession, the *Douglass' Monthly* had argued the Union could not and should not be held together at the expense of the enslaved. In retrospect, the Slave Power had been given many victories— mainly, the Fugitive Slave Law and Dred Scott—all to the detriment of black Americans and the Northern political autonomy. If slavery and black disenfranchisement were going to continue, all because the South cried secession, black leadership's response was "Let the Union perish."[36] When others struck first, black abolitionists no longer had to justify retaliation. Furthermore, if black leaders could provoke Southerners and Northerners alike to take up arms and confront conflict head on, they stood a better chance of success.

Within three months of Lincoln's election, seven states seceded from the Union. The first was South Carolina, on December 20, 1860, followed by Georgia, Florida, Alabama, Mississippi, Texas, and Louisiana. Together they formed the Confederate States of America and were later joined by Virginia, Arkansas, North Carolina, and Tennessee. With Southern secession underway and the outbreak of the Civil War, black abolitionists were more prepared for violence than they had ever been in the history of abolitionism.[37] While Southerners saw Lincoln's election as the final political breaking point, black leaders marked it as the beginning of a black war of emancipation. Each succeeding state built upon the momentum of a black carbonari waiting to seize their liberty.

Just two months before Lincoln's inauguration, Douglass wrote that the abolitionists had had enough of talk. He explained, "If speech alone could have abolished slavery, the work would have been done long ago. What we want is anti-slavery government, in harmony with our anti-slavery speech, one which will give effect to our words, and translate them into acts." He surmised, "For this, the ballot is needed, and if this will not be heard or heeded, then the bullet. We have had enough, and are sick of it.[38] Douglass's patience was at an end. Black leadership did not just warn others of war, they welcomed it.

Just two weeks prior to Lincoln's inauguration, Jefferson Davis had been inaugurated as the president of the Confederate States of America. When Lincoln gave his inaugural speech, he had no plans of abolishing slavery where it existed. Indeed, he clarified, "I have no purpose, directly or indirectly, to interfere with the institution of slavery in the States where it exists. I believe I have no lawful right to do so, and I have no inclination to do so."[39] In fact, Lincoln continued in his address to uphold the Fugitive Slave Law. As president, he publicly confessed that his priority was to preserve the Union—if necessary, at the expense of abolition. Lincoln, along with most of the country could not imagine a biracial society.

The prevailing political climate was more than Garrison could bear. In response to President Lincoln's First Inaugural Address, Garrison offered statements that resembled the threats of black abolitionists. Lincoln contended that regarding Southern opposition, he believed bloodshed and violence were not necessary unless they were "forced upon the federal authority."[40] In fierce objection, Garrison charged: "Either blood must flow like water, or Mr. Lincoln and the North must back down, and confess that the American Union is dissolved beyond the power of restoration." Even Garrison saw violence as inevitable if Lincoln sought to maintain the Union without abolishing slavery simultaneously.[41]

Emigration to Haiti as Resistance

Toward the start of the Civil War, certain ideologies within the abolitionist movement were also coming full circle. For those black Americans who believed violence was not the only option, there remained an alternative: emigration. Interestingly, when George Lawrence issued the call for a "Carbonari" during the Harris family arrest in Chicago, many considered fleeing instead of fighting. Within a week of the Harris family capture, over three hundred black residents had abandoned the city for Canada.[42] While the political climate pushed some people toward force, violence against African Americans simultaneously pulled many toward emigration. As the South was making plans for forming their own country, black abolitionists felt some of the strongest pulls to leave the country in decades. For black Chicagoans, fleeing made more sense than fighting.

In some cases, force is not always violent; with emigration, force was flight. The withdrawal of black labor and black bodies was an attack on the slaveholding class.[43] In effect, to "steal away" was a direct personal and political tool among the enslaved that cannot be overlooked. Flight robbed the planter of his economic assets and threatened the very foundation of the slavery. For free black Americans, flight gave them the opportunity to assert their own agency regarding their labor and their refusal to live in the subordinated status of Northern white supremacist laws and norms. Thus, the eve of the Civil War created a tension of push-pull factors for black Americans still advocating for reform. The push was to stay, to fight, and to agitate. Yet the thought of a life free from slavery and the prospects of enslavement propelled many black Americans toward emigration.

Since the 1820s, the impulse to leave America altogether had never completely disappeared. And now Haiti, a country that was still seeking diplomatic recognition from the United States, revamped its programs to bring black Americans to their country. In previous decades, black abolitionists looked to Canada, parts of Mexico, and Haiti as lands in which they could obtain freedom and enfranchisement. For some, Haiti never left black consciousness. The Haitian Revolution represented something inspirational in the pursuit of emancipation and equality. If black abolitionists could not *be* Haitians (in terms of accomplishing success through revolution), then the next best option was to join them. And unlike the failed attempts of the American Colonization Society, emigration was a choice of their own.

Black leaders such as Martin Delany, Henry Highland Garnet, H. Ford Douglas, James Theodore Holly, E. P. Walker, J. M. Whitfield, and William C. Monroe were at the forefront of black American emigration, particularly to the island of Haiti. Such movements dated as far back as the administrations of the Haitian presidents Jean-Jacques Dessalines, Alexandres Pétion, and Jean-Pierre Boyer, all of whom encouraged black Americans to settle in Haiti in the early 1800s. By the late 1850s, the time was ripe for a resurgence of the notion. Then-president of Haiti, Fabre-Nicholas Geffrard, who adamantly supported the abolitionist movement and had even held a funeral for John Brown and donated $2,000 to his widow, continued the policy of recruiting black Americans to the island.[44] The Haitian government developed the Haitian Bureau of Emigration, investing over $20,000 and creating employment for black American leadership that had more stability than they enjoyed stateside. Central to emigrationist ideology was the potential for economic impact.[45] It is routinely forgotten that during the nineteenth century Haiti was a site of agricultural innovation and economic prosperity and boasted one of highest standards of living for black people in the western hemisphere.[46]

No newspaper endorsed emigration more than the *Weekly Anglo-African*, owned by brothers Thomas and Robert Hamilton. In many ways, the paper became the public relations outlet for the Haitian movement as the Civil War approached. Though it was only in existence from July 1859 until March 1861, during its brief tenure the newspaper developed a reputation for its militancy and made sure that readers were aware of the advantages and disadvantages of emigration. James Redpath purchased the newspaper from its original owners in 1859, changing its name to the *Pine and Palm* and using it specifically to advocate for the Haytian emigration movement. When Redpath retired from his position as emigration agent of the Haytian Movement on May 11, 1861, he turned the paper back over to Robert Hamilton. The paper then took up its previous name of the *Anglo-African*. Throughout these changes in the paper's name and ownership, the theme of emigration continued to be broadcast in its pages.[47]

As proof that the topic of emigration was becoming unavoidable among black leaders, those who had previously not favored emigration were beginning to see its utility given Southern succession. Douglass and McCune Smith had previously rejected and ignored the efforts of Martin Delany, the leading emigrationist and Black Nationalist. By 1859, Delany, who initially focused on emigration to Canada and the Caribbean, was now making inroads into West Africa. By the end of 1860, when Delany returned the United States, Douglass's new empathy toward the emigration movement did not go unnoticed.

Although Douglass had never fully embraced emigration, prior to the war he came to see it as a practical option when politics proved useless in attaining black emancipation and equality. During 1861, he began to support emigration and to show that support. He even allowed full-page ads to run in his newspaper, the *Douglass' Monthly*, to recruit black Americans to Haiti. In addition, Douglass planned a trip to Haiti, with all expenses paid by the Haitian government. As he prepared for his trip, he was informed that South Carolina had fired on Fort Sumter. He canceled his trip immediately.[48] Though Douglass chose to wait rather than leave for the island just yet, in May 1861, he wrote in his newspaper: "We propose to act in view of the settled fact that many of them [black Americans] are already resolved to look for homes beyond the boundaries of the United States, and that most of their minds are turned toward Haiti."[49]

During a lecture in Ohio, the abolitionist William J. Watkins explained his position on emigration and the Haytian emigration movement. Watkins saw no hope for gaining equal footing with white Americans. He claimed that everything concerning black Americans was considered unconstitutional. "The social and political disabilities under which we labor crush us to the earth," argued Watkins, adding, "Here in Ohio, our children are not allowed to take their seats in the same school with the whites, but are driven to some nook or corner, in an isolated position, as though they were the special pets of the small pox. Even the churches refuse the recognition of our equal manhood." Watkins then proceeded to discuss the need to change conditions for African Americans. For Watkins to view America as a place worthy of his continued habitation, he had to be able to answer specific questions in the affirmative: "Will the time ever arrive when the colored man will have *equal rights* with the white man? Will he ever have equal access to the Presidential chair, or occupy seats in the Cabinet, or in the Senate, or on the bench of the Supreme Court?" In sum, Watkins was asking, "Will the white man so far forget the black man's complexion that he will consent to be governed by him, or to receive the law from him?" If black men could not hope for recognition in ways that effectively granted equality, Watkins indicated, he saw no reason to stay in America. He urged each of his fellows to place themselves in a country where no barriers would oppose the development of their "mental and moral being, but where his every faculty can proudly sweep the whole circle of human activity."[50]

However, Watkins did not support emigration en masse anywhere, a plan that he labeled both impossible and impractical.[51] He believed that Haiti and Canada, specifically, had some of the strongest appeal. In Haiti, a home was offered where black Americans could demonstrate their capacity for self-government. Watkins explained that emigrants from Toledo could have their passage to the island paid for by the Haitian government. In addition, each head of family would receive sixteen acres of land, and eight acres would be provided for individuals as a payment and investment in the country. The Haitian government had also promised to provide emigrants with subsistence for up to eight days after their arrival. An Ohio newspaper assured its readers that "much interest will be awakened by this lecture."[52] The land incentives in Haiti were not the only attraction. Black Americans saw emigration to Haiti as an opportunity to cultivate Black Nationalism. Haiti offered a national identity that was encouraging and elevating to black Americans after the lamentable Dred Scott decision.

Scholars claim that the additions of Douglass, Wells Brown, and William J. Watkins, who were sympathetic to the emigration movement, marked an end of pro-Americanist sentiment. Even the abolitionist George T. Downing, who was one of the biggest opponents of emigration, shifted his opinions. By the middle of 1861, prominent black leaders who publicly promoted stay-at-home-at-any-cost beliefs were in the minority. Conditions were such that it was difficult not to look favorably upon the plan. While few went as far as to champion emigration as the only true road to progress, it was certainly one road. As one black newspaper rationalized, "Better to make a good run, than a bad stand."[53]

The push-pull factors that affected black abolitionists have several important implications. The push for black abolitionists to advocate the use of political violence and force revealed their willingness to fight for change while simultaneously offering the opportunity for American democracy to correct itself before reaping grievous consequences. The pull of emigration was a way to escape oppression and disenfranchisement. In many ways, Canada, Europe, and Haiti became the equivalent of maroon communities, a haven for runaway slaves and free black Americans seeking refuge.[54] Force and emigration were not the only answers, but in many ways, they appeared to be the best answers.

Ironically, by the start of the Civil War, abolitionists returned to the very ideas they expressed in their early stages. Not moral suasion, but revolutionary politics were again on the table. Along the lines of Walker's *Appeal*, independence (both physical and geographical) was a black agenda. Haiti, too, resurfaced as the echoing call for black self-determination. Pushed into war or pulled into Haiti, black Americans could see themselves at the center of a country that could no longer keep them on the periphery.

The Slave's Farewell

In September 1861, the Civil War was well into being fought when a young black woman by the name of Miss Paulyon stood before the podium to give a lecture at the Zion Baptist Church on Sullivan Street in New York. Although the group had met to pray for the federal government in hope that the enslaved might be liberated, Paulyon had decided to take the discussion and her life in a different direction. As a native of Alabama, Paulyon began her lecture by telling the audience of her early years spent as a slave. Her testimony was so gripping it moved the audience to tears, particularly the women. She spoke at length on the condition of the country, the advantages and disadvantages or black Americans, and what it meant to be a part of what she labeled a "caste." She explained how in her experience, white Americans had taught their children to subordinate black Americans, at which the audience erupted in applause. She was just sixteen years old when she fled from slavery to face hunger, thirst, and cold on her journey north. Now having spent seven years in freedom, Paulyon learned "needle-work, geography, arithmetic, grammar, painting, together with one or two other of the fine arts, all through her own exertions," but she was still left unfulfilled.[55]

In her remarks, she made clear that neither fugitives nor free black Americans were ever truly free. She could no longer see herself staying in America. In two days Paulyon had plans to sail to Haiti for better opportunities. She requested donations to help her purchase several items before she began her journey. Before she left the podium, Paulyon sang a piece of poetry she had written, entitled the "Slave's Farewell," at which point it was difficult to locate a dry eye in the room. Although the historical record and details of Paulyon's life end here, of her hour-and-a-half speech, the newspaper declared, "For our part we never heard anything to equal it."[56] For Paulyon, Haiti had more of an appeal than her peers would ever know. She was departing for Haiti for herself and likely by herself. There is no mention of any accompanying companions. Seeking a better life for one's self was not limited to men's attempt to provide for their families; women too sought something better for themselves. As the allure and potential benefits of Haiti continued to snowball, it is possible that exceptional individuals like Paulyon were essentially no exception when it came to leaving the country of their birth for a better future. Forced migrations brought on by slavery and antiblackness placed all black Americans in a constant search of well-being and belonging that arguably continues today.

Overall, leaving was a short-term solution. Interestingly, Martin Delany was more effective in getting black men to fight than he was in getting them to leave. Delany used his talents to recruit thousands of black men to fight as soldiers to fight for the Union Army. Not only did Delany recruit soldiers, but he became the first black commissioned officer to serve in the military as a major in the 52nd US Colored Troops regiment. Even, Shadd Cary returned to the United States during the war and used her platform to recruit soldiers into fighting for the Union. The Civil War created an opportunity in which the enslaved did not necessarily have to choose. Black men could flee the South and fight at the same time.

Freedoms Won: Leaving the Slave to Free Himself

Over the course of the abolitionist movement, no issues commanded more attention from black leadership than immediate emancipation and equality, political enfranchisement, emigration, and violence. And no issues pushed white leadership to the edges of their beliefs more than equality and violence. Most black Americans, free and enslaved, believed that just as violence could not be separated from their bondage, freedom could not be separated from force. Black leadership was convinced that war would lead to emancipation. Historically, they had every right to believe this; the largest numbers of freed Africans Americans earned their emancipation thorough warfare in the American Revolution and the War of 1812.[57] The Civil War would be no different. Black abolitionists did not cause the war, but they predicted it and prepared for it. Whether Lincoln chose it or not, the Civil War culminated in a black war of emancipation.

Douglass contended that while white abolitionists formalized a movement to free the enslaved, it ended when the enslaved were left to free themselves. The abolitionist movement of the 1830s and 1840s championed given freedom, but slavery collapsed with freedoms won by the black Americans who fought against their oppressors and fled the fields en masse during the outbreak of war. For years, scholars have debated about the leading causes of the Civil War. Contemporary scholars such as W. E. B. Du Bois argued that black Americans sensed what was about to happen. He claimed, "All began carefully to watch the unfolding of the situation." Even before the shot at Fort Sumter was fired, movement had begun across the border. Free and enslaved black Americans were fleeing to the North in unprecedented numbers. Du Bois estimated that roughly two thousand black Americans had left the state of North Carolina alone due to rumors of war.[58] When the war began, it was the enslaved, not Southerners, who mobilized first.

By returning to Martin Luther King Jr.'s belief that "a riot is the language of the unheard," black abolitionists have changed our understanding of violence to see that a revolution is the language of the empowered.[59] Riots guarantee an audience, but revolutions require change. No change remains more radical in American history than the freeing of four million enslaved black men, women, and children. Black abolitionists saw freedom as revolutionary, complex, and multifaceted because it *is* revolutionary, complex, and multifaceted. Black abolitionists understood far more clearly than their white counterparts that liberation was not freedom; freedom was a dynamic that encompassed citizenship (protection) and rights (privileges). Furthermore, black leaders helped to shape the meaning of freedom by what they expected from their government. This empowerment and expectation was cemented in the passing of the Thirteenth, Fourteenth, and Fifteenth Amendments.

In the long view of abolitionist history, scholars continue to grapple with how we should define the success of the movement. This is where politics matters. Historically, white Americans and black Americans have viewed success differently, just as they viewed the war differently. In 1974, when Jane and William Pease wrote *They Who Would Be Free: Blacks' Search for Freedom*, they summarized black abolitionism as a failure, particularly regarding political violence. They argued that rebellion and insurrection were threatened but never came to pass. The population of black Americans never had sufficient numbers or resources to defeat their oppressors. For the Peases, the language of black abolitionists conveyed only the frustrations of powerlessness and no viable solutions.[60] They contended that what white abolitionists saw as a single unified goal, black people saw as complicated and nuanced. Ultimately, the Peases contended that black abolitionists had quarrelsome leaders and lacked organizational efficiency. The lack of political power and resources ensured that to some extent black abolitionists had to consistently rely on white allies. The Peases even went so far as to say that many black leaders had no experience with slavery or with the enslaved for which they advocated.[61] In one word, the Peases concluded that black America was powerless. For them, "the power to effect change was the white man's to give, not the black man's to take."[62]

With new research and scholarship, we know that the perspective of the Peases is not only dated but also inaccurate and incomplete. Though new scholarship honors the many successes of the movement, it is only beginning to see black resistance as the center. Too much credit and attention has been given to white allies at the expense of black abolitionists and women. Even in popular culture, many still cling to the idea Lincoln alone freed the slaves. In fact, it is exactly this line of thinking that leads readers to view the abolitionist movement as a white man's struggle to end slavery. Furthermore, the topic of violence and its utility is too quickly dismissed, lumped in with fanaticism, or monopolized by Southern antics and terrorism. Black resistance continually challenged white supremacy among its enemies and its allies. Black resistance inflicted its own form of terror.

Repeatedly, John Rock and black leadership made it clear that only black

Americans could elevate themselves. "They cannot elevate us. Whenever the colored man is elevated, it will be by his own exertions," declared Rock. He insisted that friends and allies could help as much as possible, but he was quite emphatic concerning who must do the heavy lifting. For Rock, the prime mover was "the colored man who, by dint of perseverance and industry, educates and elevates himself, prepares the way for others, gives character to the race, and hastens the day of general emancipation."[63] Furthermore, black success cannot be examined or determined by white standards. For black abolitionists, the Civil War was their revolution. It would not have been waged without the pressure of black Americans, and it could not have been won without the presence of black Americans. It was black abolitionists who forced an agenda, established international relations with Canada, Haiti, and Europe, and created a template for protest that was used more than a hundred years later during the Civil Rights and Black Power movements. Even black newspapers, literature, and narratives created a canon that authentically communicated their own principles. This was the work of an empowered people—not of freedoms given, but of freedoms hard won. Centering black abolitionists compels us reexamine what we perceive as power, violence, and success.

When the war was over, Douglass gave a speech in which he listed factors in the war's origination. He claimed, "It was begun, I say, in the interest of slavery on both sides." In a list of contrasts, he explained, "The South was fighting to take slavery out of the Union, and the North was fighting to keep it in the Union; the South fighting to get it beyond the limits of the United States Constitution, and the North fighting to retain it within those limits; the South fighting for new guarantees, and the North fighting for the old guarantees." Then Douglass skipped the corollaries and stated where both factions were in agreement: both parties despised black Americans. Both parties insulted their capabilities.[64]

It was not that abolitionists failed, but that society continually failed to recognize the enduring power of the slaverocracy and antiblack sentiments. This lesson remains instructive today. Opposing the slaveholding South and white supremacy nationally, was not just difficult, it was deadly. Understanding black abolitionists' incapacity to act is just as important as knowing what made them successful. The goal was never just emancipation but equality. Black people wanted liberty from both slavery and racism. But rather than live up to American principles, white Americans squandered any moment that would have led to an alternative labor system through moral suasion.

The real bondage was not the chains of the enslaved, but the political, economic, social, and psychological stronghold of white supremacy.

During the 1870s, Douglass also reflected on the course of moral suasion and the effectiveness of its tactics. Douglass recognized that the years of moral suasion had failed to reach the masses by appealing only to the elite of society. He claimed that the "voice of reason" would not influence the masses but that what was required was "the force of events." He added, "The American public . . . discovered and accepted more truth in our four years of Civil War than they learned in forty years of peace." He believed that without the threat and aid of violence, American slavery could have easily persisted for another hundred years.[65]

Today many white Americans romanticize the Civil War era and even the Civil Rights movement, for its leaders' radical ideas regarding nonviolence. However, until America reckons with the disturbing fact that freedom for black Americans has been largely achieved through violence, these invaluable lessons will remain largely untaught and wholly unlearned. Because of white supremacy, black Americans always knew freedom would require force. At the cost of hundreds of thousands of lives, slavery was abolished. The shots fired on Fort Sumter on April 11, 1861, were not only the first shots of the Civil War, they were also shots that pierced the hopes of any American leader who still hoped for nonviolent reform.

EPILOGUE

I never was a true believer in nonviolence.

—Cynthia Washington

Recalling her experience during the Civil Rights movement, the former field secretary of the Student Nonviolent Coordinating Committee Cynthia Washington claimed, "I never was a true believer in nonviolence, but was willing to go along [with it] for the sake of the strategy and goals." She explained that the deaths of the three civil rights workers—James Chaney, Andrew Goodman, and Michael Schwerner—was a turning point for her, especially when she heard that Chaney had been brutally beaten before he was shot to death. Washington acknowledged, "The thought of being beaten to death without being able to fight back put the fear of God in me." She also explained that she was her mother's only child and that it would be an "unforgivable sin" for her to be endangered by white supremacists and go down without a fight. From then on Washington carried a handgun in her handbag. And though she never fired it, she made it clear that she was willing to do so. Even in her advanced age, she expressed the willingness to protect her son, his wife, and her grandson if necessary.[1]

Cynthia Washington's story illustrates that, when faced with violence, more black Americans than commonly believed sought to protect themselves and their community without apology. Washington's words also reveal that women, too, were invested in armed defense and that this stance worked in tandem with their femininity, not against it. Indeed, it was the journalist Ida B. Wells who claimed at the end of the nineteenth century, "A Winchester rifle should have a place of honour in every black home, and it should be used for that protection which the law refuses to give."[2] Decades after the abolition of slavery, the sentiments of Washington and Wells toward self-defense were similar to the claims made by black abolitionists because it was clear that the "spirit of slavery" had lived on.

In 1837, the minister Joshua Easton was right when he claimed the remedy for slavery entailed the death of both the institution and the spirit of slavery. He claimed it was this lingering "spirit" that made color a mark of degradation.[3] Black leaders sought to prove and assert their own humanity while simultaneously proving and asserting the notion that whiteness was not supreme. One of the deadliest tools against white supremacy was unapologetic black self-defense. No greater action demanded the rights and respect of black humanity than physical resistance.

For many black Americans, then, self-defense was godly, and guns were held in honor. Even in 1851, Martin Delany hoped "the grave may refuse my body a resting place, and the righteous Heaven my spirit a home" if he did not make slave catchers who tried to enter his home "a lifeless corpse at my feet."[4] Social liberty and political progress had to be defended. If black resistance was central to emancipation, then self-defense was central to equality. Freedom was fragile and had to be secured at all times.

From the beginning of the antislavery movement, black abolitionists understood their vulnerabilities and strengths. They also understood violence fluently. Violence, for them, was not about vengeance. While general violence as a means of producing liberation was a method of last resort, political violence as a means of protection against individuals and their communities was always a first response. Political violence was about asserting one's humanity, about being seen as a mother, father, son, and daughter before the eyes of God and under the protection of the law.

During the antebellum period, nonviolence could not be separated from the belief in black subordination. In other words, for many black abolitionists, moral suasion was predicated on people's acceptance of black inferiority. Activism or protest against slavery were only acceptable to white abolitionists such as William Lloyd Garrison so long as it did not interfere or threaten their authority. Black abolitionists understood this dynamic well and used the power of violence to challenge it. A San Francisco correspondent for *Frederick Douglass' Weekly* claimed, "The friends of the colored people took part in antislavery work as a matter of duty . . . but they were no more likely to believe that Negroes were naturally equal to whites than they were to believe that chalk was cheese."[5]

From the formalization of abolitionist movement in the 1830s to the militancy of the 1850s, black leaders attempted to push issues of freedom and equality to the forefront of American politics. The shift from moral suasion among black abolitionists to direct, combative, and violent strategies forced

Americans to examine their allegiance to the ideal that "all men are created equal." This principle of the Founding Fathers remains in constant contestation to this day.

For many, it is difficult to believe that one hundred and fifty years after slavery's end, Americans can invoke a similar sense of frustration as black abolitionists did in fighting for equality. But it was James Baldwin who famously wrote to his nephew in 1962, "You know and I know that the country is celebrating one hundred years of freedom one hundred years too early."[6] The lessons of the lingering spirit of slavery have not been learned. We have continually underestimated both black resistance to oppression and white resistance to emancipation and enfranchisement. During slavery, these contests culminated in the Fugitive Slave Law, the Kansas-Nebraska Act, the Dred Scott decision, and even the Emancipation Proclamation. Beyond the Civil War, black codes, *Plessy v. Ferguson*, *Brown v. Board of Education*, and incalculable legal and political agendas ignited battles for African Americans to obtain equal rights. The trajectory of change in black America has almost always depended upon the local, state, and federal government's willingness to accept (or be forced to accept) black humanity.

Ideologically, it is easy to see how slavery is problematic morally, politically, socially, and economically. Contemporary audiences can readily concede that slavery was wrong. They can even concede that violence would have been necessary to overthrow the institution. But it remains difficult for white Americans to separate it from the institutional advantages of antiblackness. In overthrowing the spirit of slavery, it is not violence that is required, but sacrifice. Advantage and equality cannot share the same space. Likewise, one cannot end inequality without sacrifice. The larger lessons of abolitionism have to include the commitment to emancipation and enfranchisement. Frederick Douglass contended, "Until it is safe to leave the lamb in the hold of the lion, the laborer in the power of the capitalist, the poor in the hands of the rich, it will not be safe to leave a newly emancipated people completely in the power of their former masters, especially when such masters have ceased to be such not from enlightened moral convictions but irresistible force."[7] It is impossible to bring about change and transformation without the forfeiture of power.

Throughout the nineteenth century, the enslaved and free black Americans raised their fists and their finances to make themselves seen and heard. They employed both the pen and the pistol to accelerate the road to abolition. They used fear and intimidation in their speeches. They stole themselves away or aided and abetted the stealing of others. They defended themselves and each other. They utilized all necessary means and discarded what failed. They fled and fought and continue to fight. In short, black Americans have always had to force their own freedoms, and forcing freedom is what they will continue to do until white resistance to black humanity has at long last come to an end.

NOTES

Introduction

1. *Frederick Douglass' Paper*, August 8, 1856; as quoted in John Stauffer, ed., *The Works of James McCune Smith: Black Intellectual and Abolitionist* (Oxford: Oxford University Press, 2006), 154.

2. "Masa gib me holiday" is a line from the minstrel song "Dearest May," written by Francis Lynch with music by L. V. H Crosby. See *Frederick Douglass' Paper*, August 8, 1856; Stauffer, *Works of James McCune Smith*, 152–154; 180–181.

3. *Frederick Douglass' Paper*, August 8, 1856; Stauffer, *Works of James McCune Smith*, 154.

4. Manisha Sinha, *The Slave's Cause: A History of Abolition* (New Haven, CT: Yale University Press, 2016), 1–2.

5. For the benefit of the readers, I use the terms "black Americans," "African Americans," and "black people" interchangeably, because they are synonymous in my understanding. I have also elected to use the term "black abolitionists" as synonymous with "black leadership." I have yet to find a black leader who was not an abolitionist or who held a proslavery or apathetic stance. There were, however, black Americans who did not participate in the abolitionist movement. I find the biographical history of black leaders to be an invaluable tool in understanding their political stance. Knowing whether a black American was born free or enslaved, or lived largely as a fugitive slave, can provide important context for understanding his or her particular ideology. In some instances, I refer to fugitive slaves as black abolitionists, not necessarily by their commitment to the organization or leadership, but because they actively participated in attaining their own freedom and thereby contributed to the degradation of the system of slavery. To avoid generalizations and ambiguity, I have attempted to make all subjects' affiliations and ideological beliefs apparent.

6. See John Stauffer, *The Black Hearts of Men: Radical Abolitionists and the Transformation of Race* (Cambridge, MA: Harvard University Press, 2004). Stauffer's work was essential to contemporary understanding of black leadership, white allies, and their relationship to political violence. However, Stauffer concluded that while the interracial friendship of radical abolitionists was exemplary, their mutual commitment to violence was not, even if it was inspired by God.

7. As the historian Steven Hahn argues, the enslaved were well aware of the political climates in which they lived; see *A Nation under Our Feet: Black Political Struggles in the Rural South from Slavery to the Great Migration* (Cambridge, MA: Belknap Press of Harvard University Press, 2003), 52–61.

8. "Give me liberty or give me death" was published in more than thirty-five editions of William Wirt's 1817 biography of Patrick Henry. In addition, excerpts of Henry's speech were included in popular texts and schoolbooks such as William Holmes McGuffey's *Eclectic Readers*,

which ultimately sold between 50 and 120 million copies after their debut in 1836. See François Furstenberg, "Beyond Freedom and Slavery: Autonomy, Virtue, and Resistance in Early American Political Discourse," *Journal of American History* 89, no. 4 (March 2003): 1302.

9. Gayle T. Tate, "Free Black Resistance in the Antebellum Era, 1830–1860," *Journal of Black Studies* 28, no. 6 (July 1998): 778.

10. Franklin W. Knight, "The Haitian Revolution," *American Historical Review* (February 2000):103–115; see also Knight's references to R. R. Palmer, *The Age of the Democratic Revolution*, 2 vols. (Princeton, NJ: Princeton University, 1959); Lester Langley, *The Americas in the Age of Revolution, 1750–1850* (New Haven, CT: Yale University Press, 1996); James H. Billington, *Fire in the Minds of Men: Origins of Revolutionary Faith* (New York: Basic Books, 1980); Alyssa Goldstein Sepinwall, "Regenerating France, Regenerating the World: The Abbé Grégoire and the French Revolution, 1750–1831," PhD diss., Stanford University, 1998.

11. James Theodore Holly, "Vindication," in Howard H. Bell, ed., *Black Separatism and the Caribbean 1860* (Ann Arbor: University of Michigan Press, 1970), 24–25; Matthew Clavin, "A Second Haitian Revolution: John Brown, Toussaint Louverture, and the Making of the American Civil War," *Civil War History* 54, no. 2 (2008): 134.

12. See Edmund Morgan, *American Slavery, American Freedom: The Ordeal of Colonial Virginia* (New York: W. W. Norton, 1975); David Brion Davis, *The Problem of Slavery in the Age of Revolutions 1770–1823* (Oxford: Oxford University Press, 1999); Eric Foner, *The Story of American Freedom* (New York: W.W. Norton, 1999).

13. *North Star*, September 5, 1850, BAP 5:570–573.

14. Leonard Richards, in *"Gentlemen of Property and Standing": Anti-abolition Mobs in Jacksonian America* (New York: Oxford University Press, 1971), examines antislavery mobs and argues that the riots of the 1830s represented the most violent decade than any other previous to the Civil War. He claimed the underlying factor for these riots stemmed from racism and the idea that abolitionists sought miscegenation (in which cases black men were targeted and lynched). The violence of the 1830s represented a desire to preserve the status quo for antiabolitionists. The violence of the 1850s that I am investigating refers largely to attempts to overthrow the status quo.

15. While Maine began its antislavery society in 1834, the state was largely ambivalent toward abolitionism. Economically, Maine relied heavily on shipping up and down the East Coast and to the Caribbean. Along with Maine's cotton mills from Southern slave plantations, many people declined to get involved in any venture that would politically harm their business. Abolitionists often faced hostility on these grounds. Richards, *"Gentlemen of Property and Standing,"* 63–64.

16. *Anglo-African Magazine*, December 1859, 386.

17. Sinha, *Slave's Cause*, 584.

18. Ronald Takaki, *Violence in the Black Imagination: Essays and Documents* (New York: Oxford Press, 1993), 9–10.

19. Manisha Sinha, "'Coming of Age': The Historiography of Black Abolitionism," in Timothy Patrick McCarthy and John Stauffer, eds., *Prophets of Protest: Reconsidering the History of American Abolitionism* (New York: New Press, 2006), 29.

20. See Ernest G. Bormann, ed., *Forerunners of Black Power: The Rhetoric of Abolition* (Englewood Cliffs, NJ: Prentice Hall, 1971); Scot French, *The Rebellious Slave: Nat Turner in American Memory* (Boston: Houghton Mifflin, 2004), 107; and Nathan Wright, *Black Power and Urban Unrest: Creative Possibilities* (New York: Hawthorn Publishing, 1967), 13.

21. Martin Luther King Jr., "The Other America," speech given at Grosse Pointe High School, March 14, 1968. In addition, Carl von Clausewitz's classic, *On War*, explains concepts of war being political in nature. See Clausewitz, *On War*, abridged version translated by Michael Howard and Peter Paret, edited by Beatrice Heuser (Oxford: Oxford University Press, 2007).

22. Massachusetts Anti-Slavery Society, *Fifth Annual Report . . . 1837* (Boston: The Society, 1837), xxxix. See also Merton L. Dillon, *The Abolitionists: The Growth of a Dissenting Minority* (DeKalb: Northern Illinois University Press, 1974), 106–107.

23. *Frederick Douglass' Paper*, August 8, 1856; Stauffer, *Works of James McCune Smith*, 154.

Chapter 1

1. James Sidbury, *Ploughshares into Swords: Race, Rebellion and Identity in Gabriel's Virginia, 1730–1810* (New York: Cambridge University Press, 1998), 39–48.

2. For more on this see Junius Rodriguez, "Rebellion on the River Road: The Ideology and Influence of Louisiana's German Coast Slave Insurrection of 1811" in John McKivigan and Stanley Harrold, eds., *Antislavery Violence: Sectional, Racial, and Cultural Conflict in Antebellum America* (Knoxville: University of Tennessee Press, 1999), 65–88.

3. It is important to note that Gabriel's and Vesey's plots were rebellion scares and not revolts that occurred. However, the plots illustrate how the master classes took the possibility, and thus likely the frequency, of violence very seriously. Much of the earlier literature on revolts saw this early nineteenth-century period as fraught with conspiracies and rebellion. See Herbert Aptheker, *American Negro Slave Revolts* (New York: Cameron Associates, 1943; 1955); see also Vincent Harding, *There Is a River: The Black Struggle for Freedom in America* (Orlando: Harcourt, Brace, 1981); on black resistance as a central role in the support of colonization, see Lacy K. Ford, *Deliver Us from Evil: The Slavery Question in the Old South* (Oxford: Oxford University Press, 2011).

4. McKivigan and Harrold, *Antislavery Violence*, 6. See also Douglas Egerton, *Gabriel's Rebellion: The Virginia Slave Conspiracies of 1800 and 1802* (Chapel Hill: University of North Carolina Press, 1993), x–xi; Eugene Genovese, *From Rebellion to Revolution: Afro-American Slave Revolts in the Making of the Modern World* (New York: Vintage Books, 1981), 45; Merton L. Dillon, *Slavery Attacked* (Baton Rouge: Louisiana State University Press, 1990), 59.

5. In 1969, Benjamin Quarles argued in his book *Black Abolitionists* (New York: Oxford University Press, 1969) that black abolitionism was developed out of a response to the American colonization movement (see pp. 3–22). While Quarles believed that African Americans were the pioneers of the movement, he dated their formal involvement around 1817. Today, work being done by scholars such as Manisha Sinha dates the black abolitionist movement back to the Revolutionary period. I would add that using the ACS as an ideological starting point for black abolitionism serves to perpetuate ideas that black Americans are always forming their ideas in response to white Americans and never out of their own agency.

6. Scholars now see the ACS as a reactionary response to emancipation and free black communities in the United States; it was not necessarily antislavery as much as it was anti–free black Americans. See William Lloyd Garrison, *Thoughts on African Colonization: Or an Impartial Exhibition of the Doctrines, Principles and Purposes of the American Colonization Society; Together with the Resolutions, Addresses and Remonstrances of the Free People of Color* (Boston: Garrison & Knapp, 1832); and Eric Burin, *Slavery and the Peculiar Solution: A History of the American Colonization Society* (Gainesville: University of Florida, 2008).

7. See Clavin, "Second Haitian Revolution," 119; the canon is that the ideological roots of violent black abolitionism began with Walker and later Garnet, but that they were building on a tradition long in the making.

8. Peter Hinks, ed., *David Walker's Appeal to the Colored Citizens of the World* (University Park, PA: Penn State University Press, 2000), 126n81.

9. In lieu of the ACS's attempt to encourage emigration to Liberia, President Boyer constructed a plan that would aid Haiti's economy and marshal support for formal diplomatic recognition by the United States. Boyer used Pierre Joseph Marie Granville, also known as Jonathan Granville, to help recruit free African Americans living in the US. Boyer provided Granville with fifty thousand pounds of coffee and promised to pay the full fare for passage to Haiti. After Granville's tour in the US, approximately six thousand black Americans left for Haiti. Later that number would rise to almost thirteen thousand people, leaving from places such as Maryland, Delaware, and New York. See *Niles' Weekly Register*, July 1, 1820; Chris Dixon, *African America and Haiti: Emigration and Black Nationalism in the Nineteenth Century* (Westport, CT: Greenwood Press, 2000); Eric Anderson, "Black Émigrés: The Emergence of Nineteenth-Century United States Black Nationalism in Response to Haitian Emigration, 1816–1840," *49th Parallel: An Interdisciplinary Journal of North American Studies* 1 (Winter 1999).

10. Peter Hinks, *To Awaken My Afflicted Brethren: David Walker and the Problem of Antebellum Slave Resistance* (University Park, PA: Pennsylvania State University Press, 1997), 198.

11. Alfred Hunt, *Haiti's Influence on Antebellum America: Slumbering Volcano in the Caribbean* (Baton Rouge: Louisiana State University Press, 1988), 148; Herbert Aptheker, *One Continual Cry: David Walker's Appeal to the Colored Citizens of the World (1829–1830)* (New York: Published for A.I.M.S. by Humanities Press, 1965), 60; for reactions to Walker's *Appeal* in the Southern states, see William Pease and Jane Pease, "Walker's Appeal Comes to Charleston: A Note and Documents," *Journal of Negro History* 59, no. 3 (1974): 287–292.

12. David Walker, *Walker's Appeal* (Boston: September 28, 1829), 29–30; see also *Freedman's Journal*, December 19, 1828.

13. Walker, *Walker's Appeal*.

14. Hinks, *To Awaken My Afflicted Brethren*, 111–112.

15. Ibid.

16. *Boston Daily Advertiser, Evening Journal Transcript*, September 28, 1830, as quoted in Hinks, *To Awaken My Afflicted Brethren*, 151.

17. Samuel J. May, *Some Recollections of Our Antislavery Conflict* (Boston: Fields, Osgood, 1869), 133.

18. According to the *Boston Daily Courier* (August 10, 1830), seven people died in the same week of lung complications. See Hinks, *To Awaken My Afflicted Brethren*, 269–270.

19. William Lloyd Garrison and Isaac Knapp, "*Shall the Liberator Die?*" (1834), Antislavery Collection Letters Boston Public Library; C. Peter Ripley, ed. *The Black Abolitionist Papers*, vol. 3, *The United States, 1830–1846* (Chapel Hill: University of North Carolina Press, 1991), 9.

20. *Liberator*, January 4, 1834, 2.

21. Carleton Mabee, *Black Freedom: The Nonviolent Abolitionists from 1830 Through the Civil War* (New York: Macmillan, 1970), 51.

22. See Edward Bartlett Rugemer, *The Problem of Emancipation: The Caribbean Roots of the American Civil War* (Baton Rouge: Louisiana State Press, 2008); Abigail B. Bakan, *Ideology and Class Conflict in Jamaica: The Politics of Rebellion* (Quebec: McGill-Queen's University Press, 1990); Nigel Bolland, "The Politics of Freedom in the British Caribbean," in Frank McGlynn and

Seymour Drescher, eds., *The Meaning of Freedom: Economics, Politics, and Culture After Slavery* (Pittsburgh: University of Pittsburgh Press, 1992), 118.

23. Aileen Kraditor, *Mean and Ends in American Abolitionism: Garrison and His Critics on Strategy and Tactics, 1834–1850* (New York, Pantheon Books, 1969), 3–5.

24. Meeting, Philadelphia, March 12, 1831, Frederick A. Hinton, chairman, William Whipper and James Cornish, secretaries, *Liberator*, March 12, 1831

25. John Demos, "The Antislavery Movement and the Problem of Violent 'Means,'" *New England Quarterly* 37, no. 4. (December 1964): 505.

26. Demos, "Antislavery Movement," 503; *Liberator*, October 10, 1835, p. 163.

27. *Liberator*, January 20, 1831, and letter to the editor, January 29, 1831.

28. Anonymous, BAP, reel 1, frame 70.

29. *National Enquirer*, January 28, 1837, BAP, reel 1: frame 920.

30. Quotation from *Proceedings of a Crowded Meeting of the Colored People of Boston: Assembled July 15th, 1846* (Dublin, Ireland: Webb and Chapman, 1846), 11; Quarles, *Black Abolitionists*, 19–22; C. Ripley, *Black Abolitionist Papers*, 3:9–10.

31. Anonymous, BAP 1:70.

32. Ibid.

33. Dr. Franklin, *Liberator*, February 12, 1831.

34. Colored Philadelphian [pseud.], *Liberator*, August 20, 1831.

35. Man of Color [pseud.], *Liberator*, January 22, 1831.

36. *Liberator*, September 17, 1831 Demos, "Antislavery Movement," 504.

37. *Liberator*, September 3, 1831.

38. William Lloyd Garrison, "Some Remarks on the Former and Present State of St. Domingo and Hayti," *Liberator*, March 10, 1832; William Wells Brown, *The Black Man, His Antecedents, His Genius, and His Achievements* (New York: Thomas Hamilton, 1863), 105; J. Dennis Harris, *A Summer on the Border of the Caribbean Sea* (New York, 1860), 115; Hunt, *Haiti's Influence*, 92–93.

39. *Liberator*, January 7, 1832, 2; June 30, 1832, 163; Mabee, *Black Freedom*, 52.

40. May, *Some Recollections*, 134.

41. Ripley, *The Black Abolitionist Papers*, (Chapel Hill: University of North Carolina Press, 1991), 4:26–27n18.

42. Edwin G. Burrows and Mike Wallace, "White, Green and Black," in *Gotham: A History of New York City to 1898* (Oxford: Oxford University Press, 1999), 542–562, on the riots (556–559) and their causes.

43. Burrows and Wallace, *Gotham*, 558.

44. Richards, *"Gentlemen of Property and Standing."*

45. *Liberator*, April 26, 1834, 68.

46. Demos, "Antislavery Movement," 506; see also David Grimsted, *American Mobbing, 1828–1861: Toward Civil War* (Oxford: Oxford University Press, 1998).

47. Quotations from Maria Stewart, "Productions" address delivered at the African Masonic Hall in Boston, 1832, printed in *Liberator*, November 17, 1832.

48. Maria Stewart, "Productions"; Richard Newman, Patrick Rael, and Phillip Lapsansky, eds., *Pamphlets of Protest: An Anthology of Early African-American Protest Literature, 1790–1860* (New York: Routledge, 2001), 25.

49. Marilyn Richardson, *Maria W. Stewart: America's First Black Woman Political Writer* (Bloomington: Indiana University Press, 1987), 30.

50. *Liberator*, April 11, 1835, 59, and April 18, 1835, 62; Demos, "Antislavery Movement," 506.

51. *Liberator*, December 1, 1837, 194.

52. From the *Friend of Man*. Quoted in *Liberator*, September 6, 1839, 141; Demos, "Antislavery Movement," 508.

53. This notion stems from the saying once put forth by Mahatma Gandhi that "it is better to be violent, if there is violence in our hearts, than to put on the cloak of nonviolence to cover impotence."

54. Henry Mayer, *All on Fire: William Lloyd Garrison and the Abolition of Slavery* (New York: St. Martin's Griffin Press, 1998), 237–239.

55. Isaac Parrish, *Brief Memoirs of Thomas Shipley and Edwin P. Atlee* (Philadelphia: Merrihew & Gunn, printers, 1838), 8–11.

56. Peter Paul Simons Speech, *Colored American*, June 1, 1839.

57. Tate, "Free Black Resistance," 768.

58. Ibid., 769. See also Philip S. Foner, *The History of Black Americans*, vol. 2, *From the Emergence of the Cotton Kingdom to the Eve of the Compromise of 1850* (Westport, CT: Greenwood Press, 1983), 207.

59. Eric Foner, *Free Soil, Free Labor, Free Men: The Ideology of the Republican Party Before the Civil War* (New York: Oxford University Press, 1970), 261.

60. Tate, "Free Black Resistance," 769.

61. Furstenberg, "Beyond Freedom and Slavery," 1306.

62. Gayle T. Tate, "Prophesy and Transformation: The Contours of Lewis Woodson's Nationalism," *Journal of Black Studies* 29, no. 2 (November 1998): 215–217.

63. Augustine, *Colored American*, July 28, 1838 (Augustine was a pseudonym for Lewis Woodson writing in the *Colored American*); see Tate, "Free Black Resistance," 771–772.

64. David Ruggles, *First Annual Report of the New York Committee of Vigilance for the Year 1837* (New York: Piercy and Reed, 1837). In 1836, Ruggles attempted, unsuccessfully, to rescue slaves from the *Brillante*, a Brazilian ship owned by the mayor of Rio de Janeiro. As a result, Ruggles was jailed on charges of aiding in a slave escape and inciting a riot. See *Weekly Advocate*, January 14, 1837; Jane H. Pease and William Pease, *They Who Would Be Free: Blacks' Search for Freedom, 1830–1861* (New York: Atheneum, 1974), 209–210.

65. Graham Russell Gao Hodges, *David Ruggles: A Radical Black Abolitionist and the Underground Railroad in New York City*. John Hope Franklin Series in African American History and Culture (Chapel Hill: University of North Carolina Press, 2010).

66. Philip A. Bell, *Weekly Advocate*, January 14, 1837, UDM, Black Abolitionist Archive, doc. no. 10536.

67. Peter Paul Simmons, speech, "We Must Remain Active" (New York), *Colored American*, June 1, 1839.

68. See Mabee, *Black Freedom*, 59. For more on Garnet and Douglass, see Robert S. Levine, *The Lives of Frederick Douglass* (Cambridge, MA: Harvard University Press, 2016); James Oakes, *The Radical and the Republican: Frederick Douglass, Abraham Lincoln, and the Triumph of Antislavery Politics* (New York: W. W. Norton, 2008).

69. Quotation from Hamilton Child, *Gazetteer of Grafton County, N. H. 1709–1886* (Syracuse, New York, 1886), 216–235; see also Craig Steven Wilder, lecture, "Noyes Academy: A New Hampshire Struggle for a Black College," presented April 5, 2006, Dartmouth College, Hanover, New Hampshire.

70. US Census, New Hampshire Race and Hispanic Origin, 1790–1990. In 1830, of the 607 who were African American, 3 were enslaved and 604 were free.

71. Quotation from Craig Steven Wilder, lecture, "Noyes Academy: A New Hampshire Struggle for a Black College," presented April 5, 2006, Dartmouth College, Hanover, New Hampshire. Wilder claimed that the context of the Canaan school attack stemmed from a pro-slavery consensus and the rise of Democratic power. He added that Northern voters who had no real immediate ties to slavery, but something to be gained at the local level, possessed a willingness to turn a blind eye to what was happening at the national level in terms of slavery.

72. See Steven H. Shiffrin, "The Rhetoric of Black Violence in the Antebellum Period: Henry Highland Garnet," *Journal of Black Studies* 2, no. 1 (September 1971): 49.

73. *National Reformer*, October 1839, 155–156; see also Mabee, *Black Freedom*, 59.

74. Garnet, "Address to the Slaves of the United States of America," 1843, reprinted in Garnet, *A Memorial Discourse by Rev. Henry Highland Garnet* (Philadelphia: Joseph M. Wilson, 1865), 44–51.

75. Ibid.

76. Henry Highland Garnet to Mrs. Maria W. Chapman, November 27, 1843, in Carter G. Woodson, ed., *The Mind of the Negro as Reflected in Letters Written During the Crisis, 1800–1860* (Washington, DC: 1826), 194; Leon F. Litwack, "The Emancipation of the Negro Abolitionist," in Martin Duberman, ed., *The Antislavery Vanguard: New Essays on the Abolitionists* (Princeton, NJ: Princeton University Press, 1965), 146.

77. *North Star*, August 10, 1849; Foner, *Life and Writings*, 1: 398–399; Leslie Friedman Goldstein, "Violence as an Instrument for Social Change: The Views of Frederick Douglass, 1817–1895," *Journal of Negro History* 61, no. 1 (1976), 68.

78. Shiffrin, "Rhetoric of Black Violence," 53; italics added.

79. *North Star*, September 7, 1849, BAP, reel 6, frame 136.

80. Henry Highland Garnet, *Impartial Citizen*, August 8, 1849, UDM, Black Abolitionist Archive, doc. no. 09908.

81. Tate, "Free Black Resistance," 772.

82. Goldstein, "Violence as an Instrument," 65.

83. Ibid., 66. See Philip S. Foner, *The Life and Writings of Frederick Douglass* (New York: International Publishers, 1950–1975), vol. 1, 114–115, 146–147, 164, 227; *North Star*, September 7, 1849, BAP, reel 6, frame 136; Frederick Douglass, *The Life and Times of Frederick Douglass: His Early Life as a Slave, His Escape from Bondage, and His History Complete* (Hartford, CT: Park Publishing, 1881; repr., New York: Citadel Press, 1995), 275.

84. Douglass, *Life and Times*, 287–288; Foner, *Life and Writings* 1: 57, 181–182.

85. Douglass to Hinton, January 17, 1893, Columbia University Library, Rare Book Division, Special Collections. See also Goldstein, "Violence as an Instrument," 64.

86. Goldstein, "Violence as an Instrument," 64.

87. Ibid., 63.

88. *North Star*, January 14, 1848, Frederick Douglass Papers, Library of Congress.

89. Ibid.

90. Douglass, *Life and Times*, 282.

91. Mayer, *All on Fire*, 430. For Garrison's answer to Ward, see *Liberator*, July 4, 1851.

92. *Liberator*, July 4, 1851.

93. Foner, *Life and Writings*, 1: 359–360; *North Star*, February 9, 1849; see also Robert C. Dick, *Black Protest Issues and Tactics* (Westport, CT: Greenwood Press, 1974), 138.

94. Speech published November 2, 1845, by H. T. Wells, BAP 5:94–98.

95. *Liberator*, July 9, 1847, 109.

96. Howard Holman Bell, *A Survey of the Negro Convention Movement, 1830–1861* (New York: Arno Press and *New York Times*, 1969), 115.

97. The special edition and reprinting of David Walker's *Appeal* and Garnet's speech was published by J. H. Tobitt, in Troy, New York, in 1848, with permission from David Walker's widow, Mrs. Eliza Dewson.

98. Bell, *Survey of the Negro Convention Movement*, 115.

99. *Liberator*, January 26, 1849, 14; Demos, "Antislavery Movement," 520.

100. See Demos, "Antislavery Movement," 519.

101. Henry Steele Commager, *Theodore Parker* (Boston: Little, Brown, 1936), 193; also quoted in Demos, "Antislavery Movement," 519.

102. Peter Simmons, *Colored American*, June 1, 1839, BAP reel 3, frame 0076.

103. William Whipper, *Colored American*, July 1838, BAP, reel 2, frame 0541.

104. On January 2, 1893, Frederick Douglass gave a speech on Haiti at the World's Fair in Jackson, Park, Chicago, IL. In his speech he proclaimed,

> I can speak of her [Haiti], not only words of admiration, but words of gratitude as well. She [Haiti] has grandly served the cause of universal human liberty. We should not forget that the freedom you and I enjoy to-day; that the freedom that eight hundred thousand colored people enjoy in the British West Indies; the freedom that has come to the colored race the world over, is largely due to the brave stand taken by the black sons, of Haiti ninety years ago. When they struck for freedom, they builded better than they knew. Their swords were not drawn and could not be drawn simply for themselves alone. They were linked and interlinked with their race, and striking for their freedom, they struck for the freedom of every black man in the world.

105. Tate, "Free Black Resistance," 766.

Chapter 2

1. The term "Slave Power" was often used as a pejorative for distrust of slave owners. The disdain did not develop out of the treatment of African Americans but of free-labor whites who believed slavery undercut their economic and political livelihood. See Leonard L. Richards, *The Slave Power: The Free North and Southern Domination, 1780–1860* (Baton Rouge: Louisiana State Press, 2000). See also John Elliott Cairnes, *The Slave Power: Its Character, Career, and Probable Designs: Being an Attempt to Explain the Real Issues Involved in the American Contest* (New York: Carleton, 1862; repr., Columbia: University of South Carolina, 2003).

2. Charles L. Remond, North Star, May 10, 1850, UDM, Black Abolitionist Archive Black Abolitionist Archives, doc. no. 10722, p. 1.

3. For more on Border States and interstate conflict, see Stanley Harrold, *Border War: Fighting over Slavery Before the Civil War* (Chapel Hill: University of North Carolina Press, 2010).

4. See Erica Armstrong Dunbar, *Never Caught: The Washington's Relentless Pursuit of their Runaway Slave, Ona Judge* (New York: Aria Books, 37Ink, 2017).

5. Runaway slaves often changed their names. Among the famed black abolitionists who had been fugitives were Frederick Douglass, formerly Frederick Bailey; Harriet Tubman, who was born Araminta Ross; Jermain Wesley Loguen, who was known as Jermain Logue, and

William Wells Brown, who later adopted the name Wells Brown from a Quaker who helped him obtain his freedom. Many took the surname of Freeman to mark their new status.

6. See Erica Ball, *To Live an Antislavery Life: Personal Politics and the Antebellum Black Middle Class* (Athens: University of Georgia Press, 2012).

7. Jayme Sokolow, "The Jerry McHenry Rescue and the Growth of Northern Antislavery Sentiment During the 1850s," *Journal of American Studies* 16, no. 3 (1982): 427–445.

8. *Chicago Journal*, June 13, 1851, and reprinted in the *Liberator*, July 11, 1851.

9. Frederick Douglass, *Life and Times of Frederick Douglass* (Hartford, CT: Park Publishing, 1881), 287.

10. The quotation by William Wells Brown relates to biblical scripture of James 4:7, New International Version: "Therefore, submit yourselves to God. Resist the devil, and he will run away from you." See *National Anti-Slavery Standard*, May 18, 1848, BAP 5:636.

11. Bell, *Survey of the Negro Convention Movement*, 111–113.

12. Robert C. Dick, *Black Protest Issues and Tactics* (Westport, CT: Greenwood Press, 1974), 141.

13. *National Anti-Slavery Standard*, October 10, 1850; the *National Anti-Slavery Standard* was edited by Lydia Marie Child and David Lee Child; Pease and Pease, *They Who Would Be Free*, 218.

14. Howard Bell, ed. and comp., *Minutes of the Proceedings of the National Negro Conventions, 1830–1864* (New York: Arno Press, 1969), 162.

15. J. D. B. DeBow, *Statistical View of the United States: Embracing its territory, population—white, free colored, and slave—moral and social condition, industry, property, and revenue: The detailed statistics of cities, towns and counties: Being a compendium of the seventh census, to which are added the results of every previous census, beginning with 1790* (Washington, DC, 1854), 63–65. For more on the Fugitive Slave Law in Pennsylvania, see David G. Smith, *On the Edge of Freedom: The Fugitive Slave Issue in South Central Pennsylvania, 1820–1870* (New York: Fordham University Press, 2012); Jim Remsen, *Embattled Freedom: Chronicle of a Fugitive-Slave Haven in the Wary North* (Boiling Springs, PA: Sunbury Press, 2017); and Richard Blackett *Making Freedom: The Underground Railroad and the Politics of Slavery* (Chapel Hill: University of North Carolina Press, 2017).

16. For more, see Stanley W. Campbell, *The Slave Catchers: Enforcement of the Fugitive Slave Law, 1850–1860* (Chapel Hill: University of North Carolina Press, 1970); John Hope Franklin and Loren Schweninger, *Runaway Slaves: Rebels on the Plantation, 1790–1860* (New York: Oxford University Press, 1999).

17. William Parker, "The Freedman's Story," *Atlantic Monthly*, February 1866, 161.

18. Ibid.

19. Ibid., 281–282.

20. Ibid., 282.

21. Ibid., 154.

22. Ibid., 165.

23. Ibid.

24. *New York Herald*, August 2, 1852; Benjamin Quarles, "Abolition's Different Drummer," in Duberman, *Antislavery Vanguard*, 124.

25. Parker, "Freedman's Story," 283.

26. *Frederick Douglass' Paper*, September 25, 1851; Ella Forbes, "'By My Own Right Arm': Redemptive Violence and the 1851 Christiana, Pennsylvania Resistance," *Journal of Negro History* 83, no. 3 (Summer 1998): 159–167.

27. Forbes, "'By My Own Right Arm,'" 164.

28. Parker, "Freedman's Story," 288.

29. Douglass, *Life and Times*, 334.

30. Ibid.

31. Ibid.

32. Thomas P. Slaughter, *Bloody Dawn: The Christiana Riot and the Racial Violence in the Antebellum North* (New York: Oxford University Press, 1991), 97–99.

33. Ibid. The 1847 anti-kidnapping act worked to severely limit the local efforts to assist in the recapture of fugitive slaves. Governor Johnston was known to be a Free Soiler, and in 1847 he switched party lines from the Democratic Party to the Whig Party in order to run for the Pennsylvania Senate. After the Christiana Resistance, Johnston lost his reelection bid.

34. Ibid.

35. Slaughter, *Bloody Dawn*, 96–97; *Pennsylvania Freeman*, September 1851, reprinted from the *New York Independent*.

36. Slaughter, *Bloody Dawn*, 96–97.

37. E. K., preface to "The Freedman's Story," *Atlantic Monthly*, February 1866, 153; Slaughter, *Bloody Dawn*, 182.

38. E. K., preface to "The Freedman's Story," *Atlantic Monthly*, February 1866, 153.

39. Frank A. Rollin, *Life and Public Services of Martin R. Delany* [...] (Boston: Lee and Shepard, 1868; repr., New York: Arno Press, 1969), 76; Pease and Pease, *They Who Would Be Free*, 218.

40. Margaret Hope Bacon, *But One Race: The Life of Robert Purvis* (Albany: State University of New York, 2007), 21–23. The wealth from the Purvis family served to finance many of their abolitionist activities, particularly with the Underground Railroad.

41. *Pennsylvania Freeman*, January 9, 1851; Harrold, *Border War*, 150. Despite the enactment of the Fugitive Slave Law, there remained a staunch group of white abolitionists, mostly Quakers, who refused to advocate violence or self-defense because it violated their religious ideology.

42. Quarles, *Black Abolitionists*, 201. See also Rollin, *Life and Public Services*, 76; Pillsbury to Oliver Johnson, October 18, 1850, in the *Anti-Slavery Bugle*, November 3, 1850.

43. Harrold, *Border War*, 150.

44. Parker, "Freedman's Story," 162.

45. Ibid.

46. Ibid., 162–163.

47. J. R. Kerr-Ritchie, "Rehearsal for War: Black Militias in the Atlantic World," in *Rites of August First: Emancipation Day in the Black Atlantic World* (Baton Rouge: Louisiana State University Press, 2007), 172.

48. *Pittsburgh Gazette*, February 16 and 18, 1853.

49. Ibid.

50. Ibid.

51. Parker, "Freedman's Story," 282.

52. Benjamin Stanley, *National Anti-Slavery Standard*, October 10, 1850, UDM, Black Abolitionist Archive, doc. no. 10926(a).

53. Ibid.

54. Angela Murphy, "'It Outlaws Me, and I Outlaw It': Resistance to the Fugitive Slave Law in Syracuse, New York," *Afro-Americans in New York Life and History* 28, no. 1 (January 2004): 2.

55. *Syracuse Standard*, October 3, 1850. For a more in-depth history on black resistance in Syracuse and the Jerry Rescue, see Angela Murphy, *The Jerry Rescue: The Fugitive Slave Law, Northern Rights, and the American Sectional Crisis* (Oxford: Oxford University Press, 2015).

56. *Impartial Citizen*, October 26, 1850, BAP 6:650.

57. Loguen's daughter Amelia married Frederick Douglass's son, Lewis, in Loguen's home in 1869.

58. Jermain Loguen, *The Rev. J. W. Loguen, as a Slave and as a Freeman: A Narrative of Real Life* (Syracuse, NY, 1859), 391–394.

59. Rev. Jermain Wesley Loguen, speech, "I Won't Obey the Fugitive Slave Law," 1850; Loguen, *Rev. J. W. Loguen*, 391–394.

60. Loguen, "I Won't Obey the Fugitive Slave Law"; Loguen, *Rev. J. W. Loguen*, 391–394.

61. Loguen, *Rev. J. W. Loguen*, 391–394.

62. Daniel Webster, *The Writings and Speeches of Daniel Webster* (Boston: Little, Brown, 1903), 419–20; Murphy, "'It Outlaws Me, and I Outlaw It!,'" 1.

63. *New York Tribune*, October 4, 1851.

64. Loguen, *Rev. J. W. Loguen*, 410–411.

65. Loguen, *Rev. J. W. Loguen*, 391–394.

66. "Merrick Reminiscences, 1893," in Franklin H. Chase, ed., *The Jerry Rescue* (Syracuse: Onondaga Historical Association, 1924); Loguen, *Rev. J. W. Loguen*, 411. Murphy explains both in her book and her article that the presence and importance of women. She contends, "Few sources indicate a central role for any women in the rescue or in the agitation against the Fugitive Slave Law." See Carol Hunter, *To Set the Captives Free: Reverend Jermain Wesley Loguen and the Struggle for Freedom in Central New York 1835–1872* (Arlington, VA: Hyrax Publishing, 2013), 116; Ellen Birdseye Wheaton, *Diary, 1846–1857* (Boston: Marymount Press, 1923); Murphy, "'It Outlaws Me, and I Outlaw It!,'" 5n51.

67. *New York Tribune*, October 27, 1851.

68. "Address, Reported by Gerrit Smith to the Jerry Rescue Convention, held in Syracuse October 1," 1857, Lysander Spooner Papers, Slavery Collection, New-York Historical Society.

69. Frederick Douglass to Gerrit Smith, November 6, 1852, Gerrit Smith Papers, Syracuse, NY. "The Jerry Level" was a statement often used to urge people to rise to the level of resistance found in Syracuse during the Jerry Rescue. Resistance meant a refusal to compromise with slave owners in any way. Smith and others used the term quite a bit after the Republican Party attracted many of the former Libertyites in New York away from their stricter form of antislavery. See Murphy, *Jerry Rescue*, 151–154.

70. *Speech of Rev. Samuel J. May, to the Convention of Citizens, of Onondaga County* (Syracuse: Agan and Summers, 1851).

71. Samuel J. May to William Lloyd Garrison, December 6, 1851, Antislavery Letters, Boston Public Library.

72. Murphy, "'It Outlaws Me, and I Outlaw It!,'" 3.

73. *Frederick Douglass' Paper*, August 21, 1851, BAP 6: 813.

74. Ibid.

75. Lewis Hayden to Sydney Howard Gay, undated, Sydney Howard Gay Papers, Columbia University Libraries Special Collection. See also Randolph Paul Runyon, *Delia Webster and the Underground Railroad* (Lexington, University Press of Kentucky, 1996), 114–115. Howard Gay was the editor of the *National Antislavery Standard* (the official publication of the American Antislavery Society).

76. *Liberator*, October 4, 1850.

77. Ibid.

78. Joel Strangis, *Lewis Hayden and the War Against Slavery* (New Haven, CT: Linnet Books, 1999), 61–62.

79. Goldstein, "Violence as an Instrument," 68–69.

80. *Boston Herald*, October 15, 1850; *Liberator*, October 18, 1850; Quarles, *Black Abolitionists*, 202–203.

81. *Congressional Globe*, 31st Congress, 2, Session 596-97, quoted in Melba Porter Hay, ed., *The Papers of Henry Clay* (Lexington: University Press of Kentucky, 1999), 10:863.

82. Charles F. Adams, *Richard Henry Dana* (Boston: Houghton Mifflin, 1891), 2:217; Strangis, *Lewis Hayden*, 77–79.

83. See Manisha Sinha, "The Caning of Charles Sumner: Slavery, Race, and Ideology in the Age of the Civil War," *Journal of the Early Republic* 23, no. 2 (Summer 2003): 233–262.

84. Gordon S. Barker, *Imperfect Revolution: Anthony Burns and the Landscape of Race in Antebellum America* (Kent, OH: Kent State University Press, 2011), 130n37.

85. William F. Channing to Thomas Wentworth Higginson, February 6, 1898, Thomas Wentworth Higginson Papers, Houghton Library, Harvard University.

86. *Frederick Douglass' Paper*, June 2, 1854.

87. *Frederick Douglass' Paper*, February 9, 1855. For more on Watkins' militancy, see *Frederick Douglass' Paper*, March 2, 1855; Zachary J. Lechner, " 'Are We Ready for the Conflict?' Black Abolitionist Response to the Kansas Crisis, 1854–1856," *Kansas History: A Journal of the Central Plains* 31 (Spring 2008): 30.

88. See also Barker, *Imperfect Revolution*.

89. James M. McPherson, *Battle Cry of Freedom: The Civil War Era* (New York: Bantam Books, 1989), 120.

90. *Frederick Douglass' Paper*, September 1, 1854.

91. Ernest G. Bormann, *Forerunners of Black Power: The Rhetoric of Abolition* (Englewood Cliffs, NJ: Prentice-Hall, 1971), 173.

92. The group was described as the following: "The above-mentioned four, were all young and likely. Barnaby was twenty-six years of age, mulatto, medium size, and intelligent—his wife was about twenty-four years of age, quite dark, good-looking, and of pleasant appearance. Frank was twenty-five years of age, mulatto, and very smart; Ann (an alias for Emily) was twenty-two, good-looking, and smart." See William Still, *The Underground Rail Road: A Record of Facts, Authentic Narrative, Letters, & C., Narrating the Hardships, Hair-Breadth Escapes and Death Struggles of the Slaves in their Efforts of Freedom, as Related by Themselves and Others, or Witnessed by the Author; Together with Sketches of Some of the Largest Stockholders, and Most Liberal Aiders and Advisors, of the Road* (Philadelphia: Porter & Coates, 1872; repr., Medford, NJ: Plexus Publishing, 2005), 83–84.

93. Still, *Underground Rail Road*, 84.

94. Ibid.

95. Ibid., 85–87. Frank Wanzer's joy in Canada was short-lived when he arrived, for he was grieved by the fact that his mother and sisters remained in bondage. Without telling anyone of his plan, he single-handedly (without the aid of a vigilance committee or the Underground Railroad) returned to Virginia with three pistols and $22 and was able to retrieve a sister, her husband, and a friend. The abolitionist community was shocked by his bravery and determination.

96. John Anderson, *Toronto Globe*, July 5, 1861, UDM, Black Abolitionist Archive, doc. no. 24151.

97. Ibid.

98. Dick, *Black Protest Issues and Tactics*, 147–157.

99. *North Star*, September 5, 1850, BAP 6:570–573.

100. Goldstein, "Violence as an Instrument," 69; *National Anti-Slavery Standard*, November 28, 1850; *North Star*, January 16, 1851; August 21, 1851; September 24, 1851; Foner, *Life and Writings*, 2: 206–208 (August 1852), 284–289 (June 1854), 435,437–439 (May 1857), 462 (October 1859), 458–460 (November 1859), 487–488 (June 1860), 537 (January 1861); Douglass, *Life and Times*, 105–106, 311–112.

101. Loguen, *Rev. J. W. Loguen*, 391–394.

102. Scripture is taken from Deuteronomy 23:15 of the King James Version. The scripture goes on to say: "He shall dwell with thee, even among you, in that place which he shall choose in one of thy gates, where it liketh him best: thou shalt not oppress him" (verse 16).

103. Charles Remond comments from *Liberator*, February 4, 1853, the twenty-first annual meeting of the Massachusetts Antislavery Society, BAP 8: 119. John C. Calhoun died on March 31, 1850; Henry Clay and Daniel Webster died in 1852 (in June and October, respectively).

104. *Official Proceedings of the Ohio State Convention of Colored Freeman*, Columbus, 1853 (Cleveland: Printed by W. H. Day, Aliened American Office, 1853). 5; Dick, *Black Protest Issues and Tactics*, 144.

Chapter 3

1. Loguen to Douglass, August 5, 1853, in *Frederick Douglass' Paper*, August 12, 1853; Quarles, *Black Abolitionists*, 228.

2. *Anti-Slavery Advocate*, January 1, 1856, BAP 10:8.

3. J. R. Kerr-Ritchie, *Rites of August First: Emancipation Day in the Black Atlantic World* (Baton Rouge: Louisiana State University, 2007), 172.

4. Quote taken from Justice Roger B. Taney, Supreme Court Decision on Dred Scott, 1857.

5. *Provincial Freeman*, April 21, 1855; Lechner, "'Are We Ready?,'" 27.

6. *Frederick Douglass' Paper*, September 1, 1854.

7. *Frederick Douglass' Paper*, June 9, 1854; Lechner, "'Are We Ready?,'" 30.

8. For more, see Nicole Etcheson, *Bleeding Kansas: Contested Liberty in the Civil War Era* (Lawrence: University Press of Kansas, 2004); Kristen Tegtmeier Oertel, *Bleeding Borders: Race, Gender, and Violence in Pre-Civil War Kansas* (Baton Rouge: Louisiana State University Press, 2009).

9. David M. Potter, *The Impending Crisis, 1848-1861*, completed and edited by Don E. Fehrenbacher (New York: Harper & Row, 1976), 203. See also Stephen B. Oates, *To Purge This Land with Blood: A Biography of John Brown* (Amherst: University of Massachusetts Press, 1984), 89.

10. *Provincial Freeman*, April 21, 1855 and January 20, 1855.

11. *Provincial Freeman*, December 6, 1856.

12. *Frederick Douglass' Paper*, April 5, 1856; Leon F. Litwack, "The Emancipation of the Negro Abolitionist," in Duberman, *Antislavery Vanguard*, 150.

13. *Liberator*, February 4, 1853, BAP 8:119.

14. *Frederick Douglass' Paper*, December 15, 1854; see also Lechner, "'Are We Ready?,'" 18.

15. Ibid.

16. *Frederick Douglass' Paper*, March 3, 1854; Lechner, "'Are We Ready?,'" 19.

17. William J. Watkins, *Frederick Douglass' Paper*, August 18, 1854, UDM, Black Abolitionist Archive, doc. no. 15548, 19–23. Watkins' speech was delivered on the anniversary of the emancipation of the British West Indies. His intent was to honor the occasion while simultaneously stressing the need to abolish slavery in America.

18. Ibid.

19. Stauffer, *Black Hearts of Men*, 16–17.

20. James McCune Smith to Gerrit Smith, March 31, 1855, reprinted in BAP 4: 275; Stauffer, *Works of James McCune Smith*, xxvii.

21. *Frederick Douglass' Paper*, August 8, 1856.

22. See *Proceedings of the Convention of Radical Political Abolitionists, held at Syracuse, N. Y., June 26th, 27th, and 28th, 1855* (New York: Central Abolition Board, 1855); Stauffer, *Black Hearts of Men*, 9, 13, 23, 25, 42; Nikki Taylor, *America's First Black Socialist: The Radical Life of Peter H. Clark* (Lexington, University of Kentucky Press, 2013) 88–89.

23. *Proceedings of the Convention of Radical Political Abolitionists*.

24. Ibid.

25. Martin R. Delany, *The Condition, Elevation, Emigration, and Destiny of the Colored People of the United States* (Philadelphia: Author, 1852), 14–15.

26. Ibid.; Quarles, *Black Abolitionists*, 167.

27. Sinha, "Caning of Charles Sumner," 241–242.

28. David Herbert Donald, *Charles Sumner and the Coming Civil War* (New York: Knopf, 1960), 286.

29. For more on the canning of Sumner, see William James Hull Hoffer, *The Caning of Charles Sumner: Honor, Idealism, and the Origins of the Civil War* (Baltimore, MD: Johns Hopkins University Press, 2010); Sinha, "Caning of Charles Sumner," 233–262.

30. *Liberator*, July 18, 1856; Sinha, "Caning of Charles Sumner," 250.

31. Ripley, *Black Abolitionist Papers* 5:350.

32. *New Orleans Daily Creole*, December 6, 1856, 2.

33. Douglass, *Life and Times*, 304–306.

34. John Brown Jr. to John Brown, care of Henry and Ruth Thompson, May 20, 1855, Dreer Collection, Historical Society of Pennsylvania; Louis A. DeCaro Jr., *John Brown: The Cost of Freedom, Selections from His Life & Letters* (New York: International Publishers, 2007), 44.

35. DeCaro, *John Brown*, 44.

36. Demos, "Antislavery Movement," 524.

37. Ibid.

38. *New York Tribune*, February 8, 1856.

39. August 16, 1858, Gerrit Smith Papers, MSRC, Howard University, Washington, DC, box 92-1, folder 5.

40. Ralph Volney Harlow, *Gerrit Smith: Philanthropist and Reformer* (New York: Henry Holt, 1939), 305; Demos, "Antislavery Movement," 525.

41. Dillon, *Abolitionists*, 228.

42. *Christian Recorder*, October 18, 1854; *Frederick Douglass' Paper*, September 22, 1854.

43. Deborah Pickman Clifford, *Crusader for Freedom: A Life of Lydia Maria Child* (Boston: Beacon Press, 1992), 226–228; Carolyn L. Karcher, ed., *A Lydia Maria Child Reader* (Durham, NC: Duke University Press, 1997), 142.

44. Angelina Grimké Weld to "a friend" in Brookline, MA, reprinted in *Liberator*, July 7, 1854, 106.

45. *Liberator*, February 13, 1857; Dillon, *Abolitionists*, 223–227. See Dorothy Sterling, *Ahead of Her Time: Abbey Kelly and the Politics of Antislavery* (New York: W. W. Norton, 1991).

46. It should be noted that there were also Quakers who were slaveholders as well. See Herbert Aptheker, "The Quakers and Negro Slavery," *Journal of Negro History* 25, no. 3 (July 1940), 331–362.

47. Demos, "Antislavery Movement," 522.

48. *Liberator*, December 24, 1855, January 4 and February 15, 1856.

49. *Liberator*, February 15, 1856, 27; Demos, "Antislavery Movement," 523.

50. *Liberator*, January 4, 1856, 2; Demos, "Antislavery Movement," 523.

51. Mayer, *All on Fire*, 492.

52. *Liberator*, February 4, 1859, 19.

53. "Massachusetts Anti-Slavery Meeting," *Liberator*, April 15, 1859, 59.

54. Demos, "Antislavery Movement," 525–526.

55. Lechner, " 'Are We Ready?,' " 15.

56. Pease and Pease, *They Who Would Be Free*, 242–243.

57. Bell, *Survey of the Negro Convention Movement*, 117.

58. *Liberator*, December 3, 1858, 194.

59. Bell, *Survey of the Negro Convention Movement*, 118.

60. Bell, *Survey of the Negro Convention Movement*, 121. Though conducted in 1953, Bell's work remains one of the most useful examinations of black conventions and meetings during the antebellum period. Today, many of the notes and minutes of these conventions have been digitalized and available for public use. See Colored Conventions: Bringing Nineteen Century Black Organizing to Digital Life, University of Delaware, http://coloredconventions.org/.

61. William J. Watkins, February 24, 1853, *Our Rights as Men. An Address Delivered in Boston, Before the Legislative Committee on the Militia*, presscopy from Harvard University, Widener Library, Anti-Slavery Pamphlets in UDM, Black Abolitionist Archive, doc. no. 13923.

62. Ibid.

63. *New York Daily Times*, August 2, 1855; Samuel R. Ward, *Autobiography of a Fugitive Negro: His Antislavery Labors in the United States, Canada, & England* (London: John Snow, 1855), 99; Kerr-Ritchie, *Rites of August First*, 173.

64. For a more complete listing of the Organization of Black Militias from 1848 to 1863, see Table 6.1 in Kerr-Ritchie, *Rites of August First*, 177.

65. Mitch Kachum, *Festivals of Freedom: Meaning and Memory in African American Emancipation Celebrations, 1808–1915* (Amherst: University of Massachusetts Press, 2003), 76.

66. Ibid. Benjamin Quarles remarks that the local paper in Harrisburg, the *Patriot and Union* disapproved of the company and its name declaring them "rank and file, but mostly rank." The paper reviled Garnet as a "foul-mouthed, depraved, and vicious, and having done more 'to excite the colored people of the north' than anywhere else." Most likely, Garnet was referred to in this way for his famous *Address to the Slaves* speech calling slaves to revolt against their masters. See Benjamin Quarles's *Allies for Freedom: Blacks and John Brown* (New York: Oxford University Press, 1974), 69–70.

67. Kachum, *Festivals of Freedom*, 76.

68. *Frederick Douglass' Paper*, August 10, 1855.

69. Kerr-Ritchie, *Rites of August First*, 185.

70. Dred Scott v. Sanford, 60 U.S. (19 How.) 393 (1857).

71. Charles Lenox Remond, August 3(?), 1857, Rhode Island Historical Society, Newspaper Clipping File, UDM, Black Abolitionist Archive, doc. no. 18864.

72. Robert Morris, August 3 (?), 1857, New Bedford, Massachusetts, Rhode Island Historical Society, Newspaper Clipping File, UDM, Black Abolitionist Archive, doc. no. 18863.

73. Ibid.

74. Ibid.

75. William Wells Brown, August 3 (?), 1857, New Bedford, Massachusetts, Rhode Island Historical Society, Newspaper Clipping File, UDM, Black Abolitionist Archive, doc. no. 18864(b).

76. William J. Watkins, *Anti-Slavery Bugle*, November 28, 1857, UDM, Black Abolitionist Archive, doc. no. 19202.

77. Pease and Pease, *They Who Would Be Free*, 245; Foner, *Life and Writings*, 2:436–437; *Liberator*, August 13, 1858; *Weekly Anglo-African*, July 23, 1859; *Liberator*, August 19, 1859.

78. *Provincial Freeman*, April 8, 1857.

79. *New York Daily Times*, May 18, 1857, p. 5.

80. Bell, *Survey of the Negro Convention Movement*, 162.

81. Frederick Douglass, *Two Speeches by Frederick Douglass: West India Emancipation . . . And the Dred Scott Decision* (C. P. Dewey, Rochester, New York, August 4, 1857), https://www.loc.gov/item/mfd.21039/.

82. Ibid.

83. Charles L. Remond, speech delivered at Mozart Hall, New York, NY, May 13, 1858, *Liberator*, March 12 and May 21, 1858, BAP 11:176.

84. The full letter can be found in Roy B. Basler, ed., *Collected Works of Abraham Lincoln, 1832–1865* (New Brunswick, NJ: Rutgers University, 1990).

85. James McCune Smith, "Lecture on the Haytien Revolutions," February 26, 1841, in Stauffer, *Works of James McCune Smith*, 36.

86. Gerrit Smith Papers, August 27, 1859, MSRC, Howard University, Washington, DC, box 92-1, folder 1.

87. Ibid.

88. *Douglass' Monthly*, January 1860; Foner, *Life and Writings*, 2:51, 487; Demos, "Antislavery Movement," 501–526.

Chapter 4

1. The spelling of Harpers Ferry, or Harper's Ferry, varies among scholars. During the time of Brown, Harper's Ferry was in the Commonwealth of Virginia. It is now a part of the state West Virginia and the apostrophe has been dropped. I have chosen to use to "Harpers Ferry" to reflect the way in which it would be spelled today.

2. Some of the earliest biographies of Brown, such as Oswald Garrison Villard's *John Brown, 1800–1859: A Biography Fifty Years After* (Boston: Houghton Mifflin, 1910; repr., Gloucester, MA: Peter Smith, 1965) make little connection to the black community and the support he received. Villard was more interested in restoring a favorable view of Brown. In 1942, James Malin wrote *John Brown and the Legend of Fifty-Six* (Philadelphia: American Philosophical Society, 1942), but his reading of Brown was both critical and condescending and failed to include any of the relationships Brown had with African Americans. In 1970, Stephen Oates published the first

revisionist account of Brown, *To Purge This Land with Blood: A Biography of John Brown*. While Oates put forth a neutral telling of Brown, his white comrades are still placed at the center of his text. In 1974, Benjamin Quarles debuted *Allies for Freedom*, but the work focuses more on black admiration for Brown and less on their contributions. Today, more contemporary biographies, such as David Reynold's *John Brown, Abolitionist: The Man Who Killed Slavery, Sparked the Civil War, and Seeded Civil Rights* (New York: Vintage, 2005); Evan Carton's *Patriotic Treason: John Brown and the Soul of America* (New York: Free Press, 2006); Tony Horowitz's *Midnight Rising: John Brown and the Raid That Sparked the Civil War* (New York: Henry Hold, 2012); and Ted A. Smith, *Weird John Brown: Divine Violence and the Limits of Ethics* (Stanford, CA: Stanford University Press, 2015) all largely focus on Brown as a man that compels Americans to rethink his push for civil rights, justice, and morality. Overall, Brown is upheld as a leader and not as a follower of black abolitionist ideals.

3. The Secret Six, or the Secret Committee of Six, comprised Thomas Wentworth Higginson, Samuel Gridley Howe, Franklin Benjamin Sanborn, Gerrit Smith, Theodore Parker, and George Luther Stearns. This group of white men collectively believed slavery would be abolished only by violent means and secretly funded Brown's raid on Harpers Ferry. See Jeffery Rossbach, *Ambivalent Conspirators: John Brown, the Secret Six, and a Theory of Slave Violence* (Philadelphia: University of Pennsylvania Press, 1982); Edward Renehan, *The Secret Six: The True Tale of the Men Who Conspired with John Brown* (Columbia: University of South Carolina Press, 1997).

4. The best example of a portrait of the lives of the five African Americans who joined Brown can be found in Benjamin Quarles's book, *Allies for Freedom*, which examines Brown's relationships with African Americans before, during, and after Harpers Ferry. The most recent book from the law professor Steven Lubet, *The "Colored Hero" of Harper's Ferry: John Anthony Copeland and the War Against Slavery* (New York: Cambridge University Press, 2015), is the first in-depth study to solely focus on one of Brown's followers who faced the gallows for his efforts.

5. See Hunt, *Haiti's Influence*, 140–141; See also Clavin, "Second Haitian Revolution," 117–145.

6. Villard, *John Brown, 1800–1859*, 563–564.

7. Ibid., 142.

8. For more on Harriet Martineau, see Susan Belasco, "Harriet Martineau's Black Hero and the American Antislavery Movement," *Nineteenth-Century Literature* 55, no. 2 (September 2000), 157–194.

9. Clavin, "Second Haitian Revolution," 123.

10. James Redpath, ed., *A Guide to Hayti* (New York: Haytian Bureau of Migration, 1861), 9. Clavin, "Second Haitian Revolution," 135.

11. Letter to Brown's wife, Mary, Springfield, MA, November 28, 1850, in Boyd B. Stutler Collection of the John Brown Papers, Ohio Historical Society (Columbus), roll no. 1; Quarles, *Allies for Freedom*, xii.

12. An admirer of black heroes who employed violence, Langston named his son Nathaniel Turner Langston and his foster son Dessalines, after the Haitian ruler. He is also known for being the grandfather to the famed poet Langston Hughes.

13. Reynolds, *John Brown, Abolitionist*, 103.

14. John Brown quoted by Henry David Thoreau in "A Plea for Captain John Brown," in Richard Scheidenhelm, ed., *The Response to John Brown* (Belmont, CA.: Wadsworth, 1972), 58.

15. Douglass, *Life and Times*, 277; Quarles, *Allies for Freedom*, xii.

16. Richard O. Boyer, *The Legend of John Brown* (New York: Knopf, 1973); also in R. A., "John Brown's Raid–Guns Against Slavery," *Progressive Labor Magazine* 12, no. 4 (Fall 1979): 32.

17. Catherine Clinton, *Harriet Tubman: The Road to Freedom* (New York: Little, Brown, 2004), 90–91.

18. Kate Clifford Larson, *Bound for the Promised Land: Harriet Tubman, Portrait of an American Hero* (New York: Ballantine Books, 2004), 157.

19. Jean M. Humez, *Harriet Tubman: The Life and the Life Stories* (Madison: University of Wisconsin Press, 2003), 34.

20. Clinton, *Harriet Tubman*, 132.

21. Ibid., 156.

22. For more on Pleasant, see Lynne Hudson, *The Making of Mammy Pleasant: A Black Entrepreneur in Nineteenth-Century San Francisco* (Urbana: University of Illinois Press, 2003).

23. Mary Ellen Pleasant, interview by Sam P. Davis, "How a Colored Woman Aided John Brown: A Piece of Unwritten History Disclosing the Identity of the Mysterious Backer of the Hero of Harpers Ferry," *People's Press*, January 5, 1904.

24. Ibid.

25. Taken from the *Boston Traveller* in the Boyd Stutler Collection, quoted in Jean Libby, *Black Voices from Harpers Ferry: Osborne Anderson and the John Brown Raid* (Palo Alto, CA: Libby, 1979), 101.

26. It is also important to note that financial support from the black community was not as exceptional as one might think. Donating and supporting abolitionists' activities was a primary practice of black Northerners and of black women in particular. Black readers largely financed newspapers such as Garrison's *Liberator*. It was also common practice for black women to organize bazaars, sewing circles, and fundraisers to finance the help offered to antislavery newspapers, vigilant societies, and runaway slaves. See Margaret Washington, "Rachel Weeping for Her Children: Black Women and the Abolition of Slavery," Gilder Lerhman Institute of American History, accessed August 17, 2015, http://www.gilderlehrman.org/history-by-era/slavery-and-anti-slavery/essays/"rachel-weeping-for-her-children"-black-women-and-abo.

27. Ibid.

28. From the *Boston Traveller* in the Boyd Stutler Collection, quoted in Libby, *Black Voices from Harpers Ferry*, 101.

29. Douglass, *Life and Times*, 277–280.

30. Douglass, *Life and Times*, 279; Goldstein, "Violence as an Instrument," 66–67. Goldstein sees Douglass's "about-face" from the moral suasion campaign as "a sizeable shift, and it developed via a gradual and somewhat complex process."

31. Douglass, *Life and Times*, 280.

32. Frederick Douglass to "My Dear [William C.] Nell," February 5, 1848, in "Editorial Correspondence," *North Star* (February 11, 1848), p. 2; Reynolds. *John Brown, Abolitionist*, 104; Leon Litwack, *North of Slavery: The Negro in the Free States, 1790–1860* (Chicago: University of Chicago Press, 1961), 244–246; Quarles, *Allies for Freedom*, 67 and 209nn10, 11. For more on John Brown's "Black Heart," see Stauffer, *Black Hearts of Men*.

33. Douglass, *Life and Times*, 325.

34. Ibid., 324.

35. Reynolds, *John Brown, Abolitionist*, 262.

36. Quarles, *Allies for Freedom*, 6.

37. Pease and Pease, *They Who Would Be Free*, 247; Ward, *Autobiography of a Fugitive Negro*,

246–247. See also *Weekly Anglo-African*, November 12, 1859; Fred Landon, "Canadian Negroes and the John Brown Raid," *Journal of Negro History* 6, no. 2 (April 1921), 174–175; W. E. B. Du Bois, *John Brown* (Philadelphia: G. W. Jacobs, 1909), 259–266; Rollin, *Life and Public Services*, 87–89; Fred Landon, "From Chatham to Harpers Ferry," *Canadian Magazine* 53 (October 1919), 447–448.

38. Oates, *To Purge This Land*, 283.

39. Osborne Anderson, *A Voice from Harpers Ferry*, in Libby, *Black Voices from Harpers Ferry*, 35. While many could rejoice over the raid, few could actually be made ready to leave. The logistical questions of moving the elderly and children needed to be addressed. The question of how the conspirators intended to achieve a mass exodus of enslaved black people undetected or unopposed all the way to Canada remained unanswered. Furthermore, the enslaved population in the area of western Virginia was not comparable to the population of slaves that were located in the lower or Deep South.

40. Anderson, *Voice from Harpers Ferry*, in Libby, *Black Voices from Harpers Ferry*, 59–60. *A Voice from Harpers Ferry* was originally published in Boston for the author in 1861 as *A Voice from Harpers Ferry: A Narrative of Events at Harpers Ferry: Incidents Prior and Subsequent to Its Capture by Captain John Brown and His Men*.

41. Ibid.

42. Ibid., 40.

43. Douglass, *Life and Times*, 387–391.

44. Ibid.

45. See Sinha, *Slave's Cause*, 553. John Brown's son Owen was able to escape along with Osborne P. Anderson. Both men published detailed accounts of their experiences. See Richard J. Hinton, *John Brown and His Men: With Some Account of the Roads They Traveled to Reach Harpers Ferry* (New York: Funk & Wagnalls, 1894); Anderson, *A Voice from Harpers Ferry*.

46. Copeland to his brother Henry, Charlestown, VA, December 10, 1859, John A. Copeland Papers, MSRC, Howard University, Washington DC, box 13, folder 49.

47. "Speech of Rev. J. S. Martin," *Liberator*, December 9, 1859, BAP, reel 12: 21450.

48. Daniel C. Littlefield, "Blacks, John Brown, and a Theory of Manhood," in Paul Finkelman, ed., *His Soul Goes Marching On: Responses to John Brown and the Harper's Ferry Raid* (Charlottesville: University Press of Virginia, 1995), 75.

49. *Liberator*, December 9, 1959; Pease and Pease, *They Who Would Be Free*, 245; Ward, *Autobiography of a Fugitive Negro*, 249.

50. *Liberator*, December 9, 1959.

51. "Celebration at North Elba," *Douglass Monthly*, September 1860.

52. Ibid.

53. *Valley Spirit*, October 26, 1859.

54. Abraham Lincoln, address at Cooper Institute, New York, February 27, 1860, in Roy P. Basler, ed., *Abraham Lincoln: His Speeches and Writings, 1859–1865* (New York: World Publishing, 1946), 125.

55. French, *Rebellious Slave*, 107.

56. Daniel C. Littlefield, "Blacks, John Brown, and a Theory of Manhood," in Finkelman, *His Soul Goes Marching On*, 82.

57. Newspaper clipping, unknown, Frederick Douglass Collection, MSRC, box 28-6, folder 216.

58. For more details, see Du Bois, *John Brown*, 211–212; and Quarles, *Allies for Freedom*, 107–108.

59. Quarles, *Allies for Freedom*, xiv.

60. Murat Halstead, "The Execution of John Brown," *Ohio State Archaeological and Historical Quarterly* (July 1921): 291; *Boston Daily Advertiser*, December 3, 1859; Lee to Henry Carter Lee, December 6, 1859, in Robert Carter Lee Papers, Virginia Historical Society, Richmond, VA; Quarles, *Allies for Freedom*, 108.

61. Du Bois, *John Brown*, 211–212. Du Bois explained that in the three counties that bordered Harpers Ferry (Loudoun and Jefferson in Virginia and Washington in Maryland), the number of slaves had decreased by 10 percent, from 17,647 slaves in 1850 to 15,996 in 1860.

62. Quarles, *Allies for Freedom*, 106–107.

63. *Cleveland Plain Dealer*, November 18, 1859.

64. "Correspondence of Lydia Maria Child and Governor Wise and Mrs. Mason of Virginia," in *Anti-Slavery Tracts* (Boston, 1860); Hunt, *Haiti's Influence*, 141.

65. *Washington Post*, August 28, 1899; Frederick Douglass Collection, MSRC, box 28-6, folder 216; Thomas Featherstonhaugh, "The Final Burial of the Followers of John Brown," *New England Magazine* (1901), in John Brown Pamphlets, vol. 3, Boyd B. Stutler Collection, West Virginia State Archives, Charleston, WV.

66. Douglass, *Life and Times*, 311.

67. Ibid., 312–313.

68. Speech by H. Ford delivered at the Town Hall in Salem Ohio; *Anti-Slavery Bugle*, October 6, 1860; Ripley, *Black Abolitionist Papers*, 4:88–95.

69. *Liberator*, December 16, 1859.

70. Frederick Douglass to James Redpath, June 29, 1860, *Liberator*, July 27, 1860; Pease and Pease, *They Who Would Be Free*, 245; Ward, *Autobiography of a Fugitive Negro*, 248; Foner, *Life and Writings*, 2:535.

71. Pease and Pease, *They Who Would Be Free*, 245; Ward, *Autobiography of a Fugitive Negro*, 249; *Anglo-African Magazine* 1 (December 1859), 386.

72. Frederick Douglass, *John Brown: An Address at the 14th Anniversary of Storer College*, May 30, 1881 (Dover, NH: Morning Star Job Printing House, 1881).

73. Douglass, *Life and Times*, 456–457.

74. Ibid., 456.

75. Frederick Douglass, "John Brown: An Address at the 14th Anniversary of Storer College," May 30, 1881 (Dover, NH: Morning Star Job Printing House, 1881).

76. For more commentary on Freedman's Memorial, see Kirk Savage, *Standing Soldiers, Kneeling Slaves: Race, War, and Monument in Nineteenth-Century America* (Princeton, NJ: Princeton University Press, 1997).

77. Philip S. Foner, ed., *Frederick Douglass: Selected Speeches and Writings* (Chicago: Lawrence Hill, 1999), 616–624.

78. Benjamin Quarles quote taken from https://www.nps.gov/articles/niagara-movement -cornerstone-of-the-modern-civil-rights-movement.htm.

79. Anderson, *Voice From Harpers Ferry, 1861*.

80. See David Roediger's introduction to David Roediger, ed., *John Brown, by W. E. B. Du Bois* (New York: Modern Library, 2001), xx–xxi. In 1962, W. E. B. Du Bois republished his biography, *John Brown*, to celebrate the centennial of the Emancipation Proclamation.

81. Lubet, *"Colored Hero,"* 9.

Chapter 5

1. *Weekly Anglo-African*, April 13, 1861.

2. Ibid.

3. Ibid.

4. Demos, "Antislavery Movement," 502–503.

5. *Frederick Douglass' Paper*, April 16, 1858.

6. The proposed constitution stirred controversy throughout the Democratic Party, and debate ensued for several months. Ultimately, the proposed constitution was defeated by the people of Kansas, but the debate over it tore apart the Democratic Party, and some would argue that the conflict helped to pave the way for Abraham Lincoln's election in 1860. Kansas was not admitted to the Union as a free state until 1861. See Kenneth M. Stampp, *America in 1857: A Nation on the Brink* (Oxford: Oxford University Press, 1992), 167–180.

7. *Frederick Douglass' Paper*, April 16, 1858.

8. Ibid.

9. *Tribune*, April 16, 1858.

10. Ibid.

11. John S. Rock, "I Will Sink or Swim with My Race," *Liberator*, March 12, 1858.

12. Ibid.

13. *Liberator*, March 16, 1860.

14. *Liberator*, August 13, 1858, 132. Later, Charles Remond organized black troops during the Civil War. His sister Sarah Parker Remond was also very active in the movement.

15. Quotation from ibid.; Dick, *Black Protest Issues and Tactics*, 147–148.

16. *National Anti-Slavery Standard*, June 4, 1859, 2; Dick, *Black Protest Issues and Tactics*, 150.

17. Ripley, *Black Abolitionist Papers*, 5:391.

18. *Liberator*, July 9, 1858, BAP, reel 11, frame 0173-76.

19. Quotation from Taylor, *America's First Black Socialist*, 99–100; *Cincinnati Daily Commercial*, December 5, 1859; *Cincinnati Enquirer*, December 6, 1859; *Cincinnati Daily Times*, December 5, 1859. This gathering is perhaps one of only a few times when German immigrants and black Americans came together in their activism. Taylor notes that most German radicals were morally opposed to slavery; slave owners reminded them of the aristocratic class in Germany. They hailed Brown because his courage to strike against slavery reminded them of the Revolution of 1848. Politically, most German immigrants aligned themselves with Free Soilers or the Republican Party. See also Bruce Levine, *The Spirit of 1848: German Immigrants, Labor Conflict, and the Coming of the Civil War* (Urbana: University of Illinois Press, 1992).

20. Taylor, *America's First Black Socialist*, 100.

21. Quotations from *Liberator*, March 16, 1860; James Oliver Horton and Lois E. Horton, *Black Bostonians: Family Life and Community Struggle in the Antebellum North* (New York: Holmes & Meier, 1979), 119–120.

22. *Liberator*, March 16, 1860.

23. William Lloyd Garrison to James Redpath, Boston, December 1, 1860, William Lloyd Garrison Collection, Boston Public Library, Ms. A. 1. V. 5, 115.

24. Quotation from Foner, *Free Soil, Free Labor, Free Men*, 215; Roy P. Basler, ed., *The Collected Works of Abraham Lincoln Works* (New Brunswick, NJ: Rutgers University Press, 1953–) 2:492, 3:482.

25. *Ohio State Journal*, August 5 and 12, 1859; Dillon, *Abolitionists*, 240; V. Jacque Voegeli, *Free but Not Equal: The Midwest and the Negro During the Civil War* (Chicago: University of Chicago Press, 1967) documents the political turmoil produced by the issue of race.

26. Foner, *Free Soil, Free Labor, Free Men*, 263–264; Francis P. Blair to Abraham Lincoln, May 26, 1860, Robert Todd Lincoln Papers, Library of Congress; Aaron M. Boom, "The Development of Sectional Attitudes in Wisconsin, 1848–1861," (PhD diss., University of Chicago, 1948), 134; J. A. Lemcke, *Reminiscences of an Indianian* (Indianapolis: Hollenbeck Press, 1905), 196; *New York Tribune*, September 18, 1858.

27. Douglas R. Egerton, *Year of Meteors: Stephen Douglas, Abraham Lincoln, and the Election That Brought on the Civil War* (New York: Bloomsbury Publishing, 2010), 102–103.

28. *Liberator*, July 13, 1860.

29. Ibid.

30. *Liberator*, December 14, 1861.

31. *Douglass' Monthly*, January 1861.

32. Ibid.

33. Ibid.

34. "Free Speech Outrage. An Anti-Slavery Meeting Broken Up by a Mob in Boston," *Douglass' Monthly*, January 1861.

35. Ibid.

36. Ibid.

37. Ibid.

38. Ibid.

39. Abraham Lincoln, "First Inaugural Address," March 4, 1861.

40. Ibid.

41. "Mr. Lincoln's Inaugural Address," *Liberator*, March 8, 1861.

42. *Chicago Times*, April 4 and 6, 1861; Ripley, *Black Abolitionist Papers*, 5:112; Paul M. Angle, *"Here I Have Lived": A History of Lincoln's Springfield, 1821–1865* (Springfield, IL: Abraham Lincoln Association, 1935; repr., New Brunswick, NJ: Rutgers University Press, 1950, 226), see https://babel.hathitrust.org/cgi/pt?id=wu.89100043033;view=1up;seq=6.

43. Chris Dixon, "An Ambivalent Black Nationalism: Haiti, Africa, an Antebellum African-American Emigrationism," *Australasian Journal of American Studies* 10, no. 2 (December 1991): 14; Dixon, *African America and Haiti.*

44. Laurent Dubois, *Haiti: The Aftershocks of History* (New York: Henry Holt, 2012), 135; Sinha, *Slave's Cause*, 563.

45. *Weekly Anglo-African*, April 20, 1860; Dixon, "Ambivalent Black Nationalism," 14.

46. Laurent Dubois and Deborah Jenson, "Haiti Can Be Rich Again," *New York Times*, January 8, 2012. The island did not limit its support to black Americans alone. In fact, during the Civil War, Haiti was one of the few Caribbean islands that welcomed the US Navy and helped to maintain the Union blockade in the Florida Straits—a strategically important point during the war (Dubois, *Haiti: Aftershocks of History*, 153). It was also during this time that the United States gave diplomatic recognition to Haiti for its efforts. Haiti also filled the gap left by the American South by exporting cotton to the United States until the war was over. Given this favorable atmosphere, by 1861 the black abolitionist James Theodore Holly, who later became the first black Episcopal missionary bishop of Haiti, had succeeded in settling a group of black Americans east of Croix-des-Boiquets. See James Theodore Holly, *A Vindication of the Capacity of the Negro Race for Self-Government and Civilized Progress as Demonstrated by Historical*

Events of the Haytian Revolution; and Subsequent Acts of that People since their National Independence (New Haven, CT: printed by W. H. Stanley and published for the Afric-American Printing, 1857). See also Maurice Jackson and Jacqueline Bacon, eds., *African Americans and the Haitian Revolution: Selected Essays and Historical Documents* (New York: Routledge, 2010).

47. I. Garland Penn, *The Afro-American Press and Its Editors* (Springfield, Mass: Willey, 1891), 86–88; Ripley, *Black Abolitionist Papers*, 5:28–29.

48. Quarles, *Black Abolitionists*, 222.

49. *Douglass' Monthly*, May 1861, 449–450; Bell, *Survey of the Negro Convention Movement*, 221; David Geggus, ed., preface to *Impact of the Haitian Revolution in the Atlantic World* (Columbia: University of South Carolina, 2001), xvi.

50. William J. Watkins, *Pine and Palm*, November 23, 1861, UDMUDM, Black Abolitionist Archives, doc. no. 24731.

51. Ibid.

52. Ibid. This article was reprinted in the *Pine and Palm*, but researchers believe it to have been printed originally in a western newspaper, most likely the *Toledo Daily*.

53. *National Anti-Slavery Standard*, August 14, 1858.

54. For more on the North as a maroon community, see Steven Hahn, *The Political Worlds of Slavery and Freedom* (Cambridge, MA: Harvard University Press, 2009).

55. Miss Paulyon's first name is unknown. *Weekly Anglo-African*, September 7, 1861, Miss Paulyon, UDM, Black Abolitionist Archive, doc. no. 24399.

56. Ibid.

57. During the War of 1812, over four thousand people were freed by the British from slavery. It was the largest emancipation that took place in the US until the Civil War.

58. W. E. B. Du Bois, *Black Reconstruction in America, 1850–1880* (New York: Harcourt, Brace, 1935), 59.

59. Martin Luther King Jr., "The Other America," speech given at Grosse Pointe High School, March 14, 1968. In addition, Carl von Clausewitz's classic, *On War*, explains concepts of war being political in nature. See Carl von Clausewitz, *On War*, abridged ed. translated by Michael Howard and Peter Paret, edited by Beatrice Heuser (Oxford: Oxford University Press, 2007).

60. Pease and Pease, *They Who Would Be Free*, 250.

61. For many of the major leaders in the movement, this statement is completely false. Black leadership was intimately connected to the institution of slavery. Frederick Douglass was a slave for more than twenty years. Harriet Tubman was a slave for twenty-eight years. Martin Delany's father was enslaved, and when Delany was a child, attempts were made to enslave him and his sibling. Henry Highland Garnet was born a slave in Maryland and upon escaping faced constant threats from slave catchers. William Wells Brown was enslaved for eighteen years in Kentucky and Missouri before he escaped to freedom. James McCune Smith's mother was a former slave. Jermain Loguen was enslaved for over twenty-one years before he was able to escape to freedom from Tennessee. Samuel R. Ward escaped slavery as young child when he fled with his parents to New Jersey. These life experiences informed their political ideologies.

62. Pease and Pease, *They Who Would Be Free*, 298–299.

63. Rock, "I Will Sink or Swim with My Race," *Liberator*, March 12, 1858.

64. Frederick Douglass, "What the Black Man Wants," speech given at the Annual Meeting of the Massachusetts Anti-Slavery Society in Boston, April 1865.

65. Frederick Douglass Papers, Library of Congress, microfilm, reel 14—"On John Brown"

(1883), reel 15—"Recollections on the Anti-Slavery Conflict (1873), reel 17—"Reminiscences of the Anti-Slavery Conflict" (1872–1873) and "Discussion of Dutch Wars" (n.d.); Goldstein, "Violence as an Instrument," 72.

Epilogue

1. Cynthia Washington, quoted in Charles E. Cobb Jr., *This Nonviolent Stuff'll Get You Killed: How Guns Made the Civil Rights Movement Possible* (Durham, NC: Duke University Press, 2014), vii.

2. Ida. B. Wells, *Southern Horrors: Lynch Law in All Its Phases* (New York: New York Age, 1892), 26. When I began writing this book, only a few scholars were beginning to examine the role of political violence in the black community with special attention to arms or self-defense. See Nicholas Johnson, *Negroes and the Gun: The Black Tradition of Arms* (Amherst, NY: Prometheus Books, 2014); Akinyele Omowale Umoja, *We Will Shoot Back: Armed Resistance in the Mississippi Freedom Movement* (New York: New York University Press, 2013); Cobb, *This Nonviolent Stuff'll Get You Killed.*

3. Massachusetts Anti-Slavery Society, *Fifth Annual Report . . . 1837* (Boston: The Society, 1837), xxxix. See also Dillon, *Abolitionists*, 106–107.

4. Delany quoted in Rollin, *Life and Public Services*, 76.

5. Quarles, *Black Abolitionists*, 169; See also *Douglass' Paper*, June 15, 1855.

6. James Baldwin, "A Letter to My Nephew," January 1, 1962; see http://progressive.org/magazine/letter-nephew/.

7. Sinha, *Slave's Cause*, 589–590.

BIBLIOGRAPHY

ARCHIVAL SOURCES

American Antiquarian Society, Worcester MA
    Lydia Maria Child Papers
    Abby Kelley Foster Papers
Boston Public Library, Boston, MA
    American Anti-Slavery Society Agency Committee Minutes
    American Anti-Slavery Society Minutes
    Anti-Slavery Letters
    William Lloyd Garrison Collection
    Theodore Parker Papers
Butler Library, Columbia University, New York, NY
    Black Abolitionist Papers (BAP), microfilm
    John Brown Papers
    Sydney Howard Gay Papers
    Oswald Garrison Villard Papers
    Rare Book Division, Special Collections
Cornell University Library, Ithaca, NY
    Anti-Slavery and Civil War Collection
    Samuel J. May Anti-Slavery Collection
Historical Society of Pennsylvania, Philadelphia
The Dreer Collection
    Pennsylvania Abolition Society Papers
    Pittsburgh Gazette Papers
Houghton Library, Harvard University, Cambridge, MA
    Thomas Wentworth Higginson Papers
Library of Congress, Washington, DC
    Frederick Douglass Papers
    Robert Todd Lincoln Papers
Massachusetts Historical Society, Boston, MA
    Boston Female Anti-Slavery Society (BFASS)
    Henry Ingersoll Bowditch Papers
    William Lloyd Garrison Papers
    Horace Mann Papers
    Theodore Parker Papers

Moorland-Spingarn Research Center (MSRC), Howard University, Washington, DC
    John A. Copeland Papers
    Frederick Douglass Collection
    Gerrit Smith Papers
New-York Historical Society, New York, NY
    The Slavery Collection
        Massachusetts Antislavery Society Records
        Lysander Spooner Papers
New York Public Library, New York, NY
    Schomburg Center for Research in Black Culture
Ohio Historical Society, Columbus
    Boyd B. Stutler Collection of the John Brown Papers
Syracuse University Library, Syracuse, NY
    Gerrit Smith Papers
University of Detroit Mercy (UDM), Detroit, MI
    Black Abolitionist Archive
Virginia Historical Society, Richmond, VA
    Robert Carter Lee Papers
West Virginia State Archives, Charleston, West Virginia
    Boyd B. Stutler Collection

NEWSPAPERS

Anglo-African Magazine
Anti-Slavery Advocate
Anti-Slavery Bugle
Anti-Slavery Record
Atlantic Monthly
Boston Daily Advertiser
Boston Daily Courier
Boston Herald
Chicago Times
Chicago Tribune
Christian Recorder
Cincinnati Daily Commercial
Cincinnati Daily Times
Cincinnati Enquirer
Cleveland Plain Dealer
Colored American
Douglass' Monthly
Evening Journal
Frederick Douglass' Paper
Freedman's Journal
Harper's Weekly
Impartial Citizen

Liberator
National Anti-Slavery Standard
National Enquirer
National Era
National Reformer
New England Magazine
New Orleans Daily Creole
New York Daily Times
New York Herald
New York Independent
New York Tribune
North Star
Ohio State Journal
Pennsylvania Freeman
People's Press
Pine and Palm
Pittsburgh Gazette
Provincial Freeman
Syracuse Standard
Tribune
Toronto Globe
Valley Spirit
Voice of the Fugitive
Washington Post
Weekly Advocate
Weekly Anglo-African

BOOKS

Adams, Charles F. *Richard Henry Dana*. Boston: Houghton Mifflin, 1891.

Anderson, Osborne Perry. *A Voice from Harper's Ferry: A Narrative of Events at Harper's Ferry with Incidents Prior and Subsequent to Its Capture by Brown and His Men*. Boston, Printed for the Author, 1861.

Angle, Paul M. *"Here I Have Lived": A History of Lincoln's Springfield, 1821–1865*. Springfield, IL: Abraham Lincoln Association, 1935. Reprint, New Brunswick, NJ: Rutgers University Press, 1950.

Aptheker, Herbert. *Abolitionism: A Revolutionary Movement*. Boston: Twayne Publishers, 1989.

———. *American Negro Slave Revolts*. New York: International Publishers, 1974.

———. *Essays in the History of the American Negro*. New York, International Publishers, 1964.

———. *The Negro in the Abolitionists Movement*. New York: International Publishers, 1941.

———. *One Continual Cry: David Walker's Appeal to the Colored Citizens of the World 1829–1830*. New York, Published for A.I.M.S. by Humanities Press, 1965.

Bacon, Margaret Hope. *But One Race: The Life of Robert Purvis*. Albany: State University of New York, 2007.

Ball, Erica. *To Live an Antislavery Life: Personal Politics and the Antebellum Black Middle Class* Athens: University of Georgia Press, 2012.

Bakan, Abigail B. *Ideology and Class Conflict in Jamaica: The Politics of Rebellion*. Quebec: McGill-Queen's University Press, 1990.

Barnes, Gilbert. *The Antislavery Impulse, 1830–1844*. New York: D. Appleton-Century, 1933.

Barker, Gordon S. *Imperfect Revolution: Anthony Burns and the Landscape of Race in Antebellum America*. Kent, OH: Kent State University Press, 2011.

Basler, Roy B., ed. *The Collected Works of Abraham Lincoln*. 9 vols. New Brunswick, NJ: Rutgers University, 1953.

——, ed. *Abraham Lincoln: His Speeches and Writings, 1859–1865*. New York: World Publishing, 1946.

Bay, Mia. *The White Image in the Black Mind: African-American Ideas About White People, 1830–1925*. New York: Oxford University Press, 2000.

Beattie, Peter M., ed. *The Human Tradition in Modern Brazil*. Wilmington, DE: Rowman & Littlefield, 2004.

Bell, Howard H., ed. *Black Separatism and the Caribbean 1860*. Ann Arbor: University of Michigan Press, 1970

——. *Minutes of the Proceedings of the National Negro Conventions, 1830–1864*. New York: Arno Press, 1969.

——. *A Survey of the Negro Convention Movement, 1830–1861*. New York: Arno Press and *New York Times*, 1969.

Billington, James H. *Fire in the Minds of Men: Origins of Revolutionary Faith*. New York: Basic Books, 1980.

Blackett, R. J. M. *Building an Antislavery Wall: Black Americans in the Atlantic Abolitionist Movement, 1830–1860*. Baton Rouge: Louisiana State University Press, 1983.

——. *Making Freedom: The Underground Railroad and the Politics of Slavery*. Chapel Hill: University of North Carolina Press, 2017.

Boisrond-Tonnerre, Louis Félix. *Mémoires pour servir à l'histoire d'Haïti*. Port-au-Prince, Haiti: Editions des Antilles, 1991 [1804].

Bormann, Ernest G. *Forerunners of Black Power: The Rhetoric of Abolition*. Englewood Cliffs, NJ: Prentice-Hall, 1971.

Bowditch, Vincent Yardley. *Life and Correspondence of Henry Ingersoll Bowditch, by His Son*. Boston: Houghton, Mifflin, 1902.

Boyer, Richard O. *The Legend of John Brown*. New York: Knopf, 1973.

Bracey, John H., August Meier, and Elliott Rudwick, eds. *Blacks in the Abolitionist Movement*. Belmont, CA: Wadsworth Publishing, 1971.

Brown, William Wells. *The Black Man: His Antecedents, His Genius, and His Achievements*. New York: Thomas Hamilton, 1863.

——. *St. Domingo: Its Revolutions and Its Patriots. A Lecture, Delivered Before the Metropolitan Athenæum, London, May 16, and at St. Thomas' Church, Philadelphia, December 20, 1854*. Boston: Bela Marsh, 1855.

Burin, Eric. *Slavery and the Peculiar Solution: A History of the American Colonization Society*. Gainesville: University of Florida, 2008.

Burrows, Edwin G., Mike Wallace. *Gotham: A History of New York City to 1898*. Oxford: Oxford University Press, 1999.

Cairnes, John Elliott. *The Slave Power: Its Character, Career, and Probable Designs: Being an*

Attempt to Explain the Real Issues Involved in the American Contest. New York: Carleton, 1862. Reprint, Columbia, SC: University of South Carolina, 2003.

Campbell, Stanley W. *The Slave Catchers: Enforcement of the Fugitive Slave Law, 1850–1860.* Chapel Hill: University of North Carolina Press, 1970.

Carton, Evan. *Patriotic Treason: John Brown and the Soul of America.* New York: Free Press, 2006.

Chase, Franklin H., ed. *The Jerry Rescue.* Syracuse: Onondaga Historical Association, 1924.

Clausewitz, Carl von. *On War.* Abridged version translated by Michael Howard and Peter Paret, edited by Beatrice Heuser. Oxford: Oxford University Press, 2007.

Clavin, Matthew. *Toussaint Louverture and the American Civil War: The Promise and Peril of a Second Haitian Revolution.* Philadelphia: University of Pennsylvania Press, 2010.

Clifford, Deborah Pickman. *Crusader for Freedom: A Life of Lydia Maria Child.* Boston: Beacon Press, 1992.

Catherine Clinton. *Harriet Tubman: The Road to Freedom.* New York: Little, Brown and Company, 2004.

Cobb, Charles E., Jr. *This Nonviolent Stuff'll Get You Killed: How Guns Made the Civil Rights Movement Possible.* Durham, NC: Duke University Press, 2014.

Collison, Gary. *Shadrach Minkins: From Fugitive Slave to Citizen.* Cambridge, MA: Harvard University Press, 1997.

Commager, Henry Steel. *Theodore Parker.* Boston: Little, Brown, 1936.

Davis, David Brion. *Inhuman Bondage: The Rise and Fall of Slavery in the New World.* Oxford: Oxford University Press, 2006.

——. *The Problem of Slavery in the Age of Revolutions 1770–1823.* Oxford: Oxford University Press, 1999.

DeCaro, Louis A., Jr., *John Brown: The Cost of Freedom, Selections from His Life & Letters.* New York: International Publishers, 2007.

DeBow, J. D. B, *Statistical View of the United States: Embracing its territory, population—white, free colored, and slave—moral and social condition, industry, property, and revenue: The detailed statistics of cities, towns and counties: Being a compendium of the seventh census, to which are added the results of every previous census, beginning with 1790,* Washington, DC, 1854.

Delany, Martin. *The Condition, Elevation, Emigration, and Destiny of the Colored People of the United States.* Philadelphia: Author, 1852.

——. "Political Destiny of the Colored Race on the American Continent." In *Proceedings of the National Emigration Convention of Colored People,* held at Cleveland, Ohio, August 24, 1854. Pittsburgh: A. A. Anderson, Printer, 1854.

Dick, Robert C. *Black Protest Issues and Tactics.* Westport, CT: Greenwood Press, 1974.

Dillon, Merton L. *The Abolitionists: The Growth of a Dissenting Minority.* DeKalb: Northern Illinois University Press, 1974.

——. *Elijah P. Lovejoy, Abolitionist Editor.* Urbana: University of Illinois Press, 1961.

——. *Slavery Attacked.* Baton Rouge: Louisiana State University Press, 1990.

Dixon, Chris. *African America and Haiti: Emigration and Black Nationalism in the Nineteenth Century.* Westport, CT: Greenwood Press, 2000

Donald, David. *Charles Sumner and the Coming of the Civil War.* New York, Knopf, 1960.

Douglass, Frederick. *The Life and Times of Frederick Douglass: His Early Life as a Slave, His Escape from Bondage, and His History Complete.* New York: Citadel Press, 1983. First published 1881 by Park Publishing (Hartford, CT).

———. *Two Speeches by Frederick Douglass: West India Emancipation . . . And the Dred Scott Decision*. Rochester, NY: C. P. Dewey, August 4, 1857.

Duberman, Martin, ed. *The Antislavery Vanguard: New Essays on the Abolitionists*. Princeton, NJ: Princeton University Press, 1965.

Dubois, Laurent Dubois. *Avengers of the New World: The Story of the Haitian Revolution*. Cambridge, MA: Harvard University Press, 2004.

———. *Haiti: The Aftershocks of History*. New York: Henry Holt and Co., 2012.

Du Bois, W. E. B. *Black Reconstruction in America, 1860–1880*. New York: Harcourt Brace, 1935.

———. *John Brown*. Philadelphia: G. W. Jacobs, 1909.

Dumond, Dwight. *Antislavery: The Crusade for Freedom in America*. Ann Arbor: University of Michigan Press, 1961.

Dunbar, Erica Armstrong. *Never Caught: The Washington's Relentless Pursuit of their Runaway Slave, Ona Judge*. New York: Aria Books, 37Ink, 2017.

Egerton, Douglas R. *Gabriel's Rebellion: The Virginia Slave Conspiracies of 1800 and 1802*. Chapel Hill: University of North Carolina Press, 1993.

———. *Year of Meteors: Stephen Douglas, Abraham Lincoln, and the Election That Brought on the Civil War*. New York: Bloomsbury Publishing, 2010.

Elizur, Wright. *The Lesson of Santo Domingo: How to Make War Short and the Peace Righteous*. Boston: Williams, 1861.

Etcheson, Nicole. *Bleeding Kansas: Contested Liberty in the Civil War Era*. Lawrence: University Press of Kansas, 2004.

Fanon, Frantz. *The Wretched of the Earth*. New York: Grove, 2002. First translated by Constance Farrington (New York: Grove Press, 1963).

Fehrenbacher, Don E. *The Slaveholding Republic: An Account of the United States Government's Relations to Slavery*. Oxford: Oxford University Press, 2002.

Finkelman, Paul. *His Soul Goes Marching On: Responses to John Brown and the Harper's Ferry Raid*. Charlottesville: University Press of Virginia, 1995.

Fischer, Sibylle. *Modernity Disavowed: Haiti and the Cultures of Slavery in the Age of Revolution*. Durham, NC: Duke University Press, 2004.

Foner, Eric. *Free Soil, Free Labor, Free Men: The Ideology of the Republican Party Before the Civil War*. New York: Oxford University Press, 1970.

———. *Nothing but Freedom: Emancipation and Its Legacy*. Baton Rouge: Louisiana State University Press, 1983.

———. *The Story of American Freedom*. New York: W. W. Norton, 1999.

Foner, Philip S., ed. *Frederick Douglass: Selected Speeches and Writings*. Chicago: Lawrence Hill, 1999.

———. *The History of Black Americans*. Vol. 2, *From the Emergence of the Cotton Kingdom to the Eve of the Compromise of 1850*. Westport, CT: Greenwood Press, 1983.

———, ed. *The Life and Writings of Frederick Douglass*. 5 vols. New York: International Publishers, 1950–1975.

———, ed. *Proceedings of the Black State Conventions, 1840–1865*. Vol. 2: New Jersey, Connecticut, Maryland, Illinois, Massachusetts, California, New England, Kansas, Louisiana, Virginia, Missouri, South Carolina. Philadelphia: Temple University Press, 1980.

Ford, Lacy K. *Deliver Us from Evil: The Slavery Question in the Old South* Oxford: Oxford University Press, 2011.

Franklin, John Hope, and Loren Schweninger. *Runaway Slaves: Rebels on the Plantation, 1790–1860.* New York: Oxford University Press, 1999.

Frederickson, George. *The Black Image in the White Mind: The Debate on Afro-American Character and Destiny, 1817–1914.* New York: Harper & Row, 1971.

French, Scot. *The Rebellious Slave: Nat Turner in American Memory.* Boston: Houghton Mifflin, 2004.

Garnet, Henry Highland. *A Memorial Discourse by Rev. Henry Highland Garnet.* Philadelphia: Joseph M. Wilson, 1865.

Garrison, William Lloyd. *Thoughts on African Colonization: Or an Impartial Exhibition of the Doctrines, Principles and Purposes of the American Colonization Society; Together with the Resolutions, Addresses and Remonstrances of the Free People of Color.* Boston: Garrison & Knapp, 1832.

Gaspar, David Barry, and David Patrick Geggus, eds. *A Turbulent Time: The French Revolution and the Greater Caribbean.* Bloomington: Indiana University Press, 1997.

Geggus, David, ed. *Impact of the Haitian Revolution on the Atlantic World.* Columbia: University of South Carolina Press, 2001.

Genovese, Eugene. *From Rebellion to Revolution: Afro-American Slave Revolts in the Making of the Modern World.* New York: Vintage Books, 1981.

———. *Roll, Jordan, Roll: The World Slaves Made.* New York: Vintage Books, 1974.

Gillard, David, and David G. Hackett, eds. *Religion and American Culture.* New York: Routledge, 2003.

Goodman, Paul. *Of One Blood: Abolitionism and the Origins of Racial Equality.* Berkeley: University of California Press, 1998.

Grimsted, David. *American Mobbing, 1828–1861: Toward Civil War.* Oxford: Oxford University Press, 1998.

Hahn, Steven. *A Nation Under Our Feet: Black Political Struggles in the Rural from Slavery to the Great Migration.* Cambridge, MA: Belknap Press of Harvard University Press, 2003.

———. *The Political Worlds of Slavery and Freedom.* Cambridge, MA: Harvard University Press, 2009.

Harding, Vincent. *There Is a River: The Black Struggle for Freedom in America.* Orlando: Harcourt, Brace, 1981.

Harlow, Ralph Volney. *Gerrit Smith: Philanthropist and Reformer.* New York: Henry Holt, 1939.

Harris, J. Dennis. *A Summer on the Border of the Caribbean Sea.* New York: A. B. Burdick, 1860.

Harrold, Stanley. *Border War: Fighting over Slavery Before the Civil War.* Chapel Hill: University of North Carolina Press, 2010.

Hay, Melba Porter, ed., *The Papers of Henry Clay.* Lexington: University Press of Kentucky, 1999.

Hinks, Peter. *David Walker's Appeal to the Colored Citizens of the World.* University Park, PA: Penn State University Press, 2000.

———. *To Awaken My Afflicted Brethren: David Walker and the Problem of Antebellum Slave Resistance.* University Park, PA: Pennsylvania State University Press, 1997.

Hinton, Richard J. *John Brown and His Men: With Some Account of the Roads They Traveled to Reach Harper's Ferry.* New York: Funk & Wagnalls, 1894.

Hodges, Graham Russell Gao. *David Ruggles: A Radical Black Abolitionist and the Underground Railroad in New York City.* John Hope Franklin Series in African American History and Culture. Chapel Hill: University of North Carolina Press, 2010.

Hoffer, William James Hull. *The Caning of Charles Sumner: Honor, Idealism, and the Origins of the Civil War*. Baltimore, MD: Johns Hopkins University Press, 2010.

Holly, James Theodore. *A Vindication of the Capacity of the Negro Race for Self-Government, and Civilized Progress, as Demonstrated by Historical Events of the Haytian Revolution; and the Subsequent Acts of That People since Their National Independence*. New Haven, CT: Printed by W. H. Stanley and published for the Afric-American Printing Co., 1857.

Holt, Michael. *The Political Crisis of the 1850s*. New York: Norton, 1978.

Holt, Thomas. *The Problem of Freedom: Race, Labor, and Politics in Jamaica and Britain, 1832–1938*. Baltimore: Johns Hopkins University Press, 1992.

Horowitz, Tony. *Midnight Rising: John Brown and the Raid That Sparked the Civil War*. New York: Henry Hold, 2012.

Horton, James Oliver, and Lois E. Horton. *Black Bostonians: Family Life and Community Struggle in the Antebellum North*. New York: Holmes & Meier, 1979.

Hudson, Lynne. *The Making of Mammy Pleasant: A Black Entrepreneur in Nineteenth-Century San Francisco*. Urbana: University of Illinois Press, 2003.

Hunt, Alfred. *Haiti's Influence on Antebellum America: Slumbering Volcano in the Caribbean*. Baton Rouge: Louisiana State University Press, 1988.

Hunter, Carol. *To Set the Captives Free: Reverend Jermain Wesley Loguen and the Struggle for Freedom in Central New York 1835–1872*. Arlington, VA: Hyrax Publishing, 2013.

Humez, Jean M. *Harriet Tubman: The Life and the Life Stories*. Madison: University of Wisconsin Press, 2003.

Jackson, Maurice, and Jacqueline Bacon, eds. *African Americans and the Haitian Revolution: Selected Essays and Historical Documents*. New York: Routledge, 2010.

James, C. L. R. *American Civilization*. Oxford: Blackwell Press, 1993.

Jeffrey, Julie Roy. *Abolitionists Remember: Antislavery Autobiographies and the Unfinished Work of Emancipation*. Chapel Hill: University of North Carolina Press, 2008.

Johnson, Nicholas. *Negroes and the Gun: The Black Tradition of Arms*. Amherst, NY: Prometheus Books, 2014.

Kachum, Mitch. *Festivals of Freedom: Meaning and Memory in African American Emancipation Celebrations, 1808–1915*. Amherst: University of Massachusetts Press, 2003.

Karcher, Carolyn L., ed. *A Lydia Maria Child Reader*. Durham, NC: Duke University Press, 1997.

Kelley, Robin D. G. *Freedom Dreams: The Black Radical Imagination*. Boston: Beacon Press, 2002.

Kerr-Ritchie, J. R. *Rites of August First: Emancipation Day in the Black Atlantic World*. Baton Rouge: Louisiana State University Press, 2007.

Kousser, Morgan J., and James McPherson, eds. *Race, Region, and Reconstruction: Essays in Honor of C. Vann Woodward*. New York: Oxford University Press, 1982.

Kraditor, Aileen. *Mean and Ends in American Abolitionism: Garrison and His Critics on Strategy and Tactics, 1834–1850*. New York: Pantheon Books, 1969.

Langley, Lester. *The Americas in the Age of Revolution, 1750–1850*. New Haven, CT: Yale University Press, 1996.

Larson, Kate Clifford. *Bound for the Promised Land: Harriet Tubman, Portrait of an American Hero*. New York: Ballantine Books, 2004.

Lemcke, J. A. *Reminiscences of an Indianian*. Indianapolis: Hollenbeck Press, 1905.

Levine, Bruce. *The Spirit of 1848: German Immigrants, Labor Conflict, and the Coming of the Civil War*. Urbana: University of Illinois Press, 1992.

Levine, Robert S. *The Lives of Frederick Douglass*. Cambridge, MA: Harvard University Press, 2016.

Libby, Jean. *Black Voices from Harper's Ferry: Osborne Anderson and the John Brown Raid*. Palo Alto, CA: Libby, 1979.

Litwak, Leon. *North of Slavery: The Negro in the Free States, 1790–1860*. Chicago: University of Chicago Press, 1961.

Loguen, Jermain. *The Rev. J. W. Loguen, as a Slave and as a Freeman: A Narrative of Real Life*. Syracuse, NY: J. G. K Truair, 1859.

Loewen, James. *Lies My Teacher Told Me: Everything Your American Textbook Got Wrong*. New York: Touchstone, 1996.

Lubert, Steven. *The "Colored Hero" of Harper's Ferry: John Anthony Copeland and the War Against Slavery*. New York: Cambridge University Press, 2015.

Mabee, Carleton. *Black Freedom: The Nonviolent Abolitionists from 1830 Through the Civil War*. New York: Macmillan, 1970.

Malin, James. *John Brown and the Legend of Fifty-Six*. Philadelphia: American Philosophical Society, 1942.

Marable, Manning, and Leith Mullings, eds. *Let Nobody Turn Us Around: Voice of Resistance, Reform and Renewal*. Lanham, MD: Rowman & Littlefield, 2000.

Massachusetts Anti-Slavery Society. *Fifth Annual Report . . . 1837*. Boston: The Society, 1837.

May, Samuel J. *Some Recollections of Our Antislavery Conflict*. Boston: Fields, Osgood, 1869.

Mayer, Henry. *All on Fire: William Lloyd Garrison and the Abolition of Slavery*. New York: St. Martin's Griffin Press, 1998.

McCarthy, Timothy Patrick, and John Stauffer, eds. *Prophets of Protest: Reconsidering the History of American Abolitionism*. New York: New Press, 2006.

McPherson, James M. *Battle Cry of Freedom: The Civil War Era*. New York: Bantam Books, 1989.

McGlynn, Frank, and Seymour Drescher, eds. *The Meaning of Freedom: Economics, Politics, and Culture After Slavery*. Pittsburgh: University of Pittsburgh Press, 1992.

McKivigan, John R., and Stanley Harrold, eds. *Antislavery Violence: Sectional, Racial, and Cultural Conflict in Antebellum America*. Knoxville: University of Tennessee Press, 1999.

Morgan, Edmund. *American Slavery, American Freedom: The Ordeal of Colonial Virginia*. New York: W. W. Norton, 1975.

Morgan, Philip D. *Slave Counterpoint: Black Culture in the Eighteenth-Century Chesapeake and Lowcountry*. Chapel Hill, NC: Published for Omohundro Institute of Early American History and Culture, Williamsburg, Virginia, by University of North Carolina Press, 1998.

Murphy, Angela. *The Jerry Rescue: The Fugitive Slave Law, Northern Rights, and the American Sectional Crisis*. Oxford: Oxford University Press, 2015.

Newman, Richard, Patrick Rael, and Phillip Lapsansky, eds. *Pamphlets of Protest: An Anthology of Early African-American Protest Literature, 1790–1860*. New York: Routledge, 2001.

Oakes, James. *The Radical and the Republican: Frederick Douglass, Abraham Lincoln, and the Triumph of Antislavery Politics*. New York: W. W. Norton, 2008.

Oates, Stephan B. *To Purge This Land with Blood: A Biography of John Brown*. Amherst: University of Massachusetts Press, 1984.

Palmer, R. R. *The Age of the Democratic Revolution*. 2 vols. Princeton, NJ: Princeton University Press, 1959.

Parham, Althia de Puech, ed. *My Odyssey, Experiences of a Young Refugee from Two Revolutions by a Creole of Saint Domingue*. Baton Rouge: Louisiana State University Press, 1959.

Parrish, Issac. *Brief Memoirs of Thomas Shipley and Edwin P. Atlee*. Philadelphia: Merrihew & Gunn, printers, 1838.

Pease, Jane H., and William H. Pease. *They Who Would Be Free: Blacks' Search for Freedom, 1830–1861*. New York: Atheneum, 1974.

Penn, I. Garland. *The Afro-American Press and Its Editors*. Springfield, MA: Willey, 1891.

Peterson, Merrill, ed. *Thomas Jefferson: Writings*. New York: Library of America, 1984.

Phillips, Wendell. *Speeches, Lectures and Letters*. Boston: James Redpath, 1863.

Potter, David M. *The Impending Crisis, 1848–1861*. Completed and edited by Don E. Fehrenbacher. New York: Harper & Row, 1976.

——. *The South and the Sectional Conflict*. Baton Rouge: Louisiana State University Press, 1968.

Quarles, Benjamin. *Allies for Freedom: Blacks on John Brown*. New York: Oxford University Press, 1974.

——. *Black Abolitionists*. New York: Oxford University Press, 1969.

Rael, Patrick. *Black Identity and Black Protest in the Antebellum North*. Chapel Hill: University of North Carolina Press, 2002.

Rasmussen, Daniel. *American Uprising: The Untold Story of American's Largest Slave Revolt*. New York: Harper Collins, 2011.

Redpath, James, ed. *A Guide to Hayti*. New York: Haytian Bureau of Migration, 1861.

Remsen, Jim. *Embattled Freedom: Chronicle of a Fugitive-Slave Haven in the Wary* North. Boiling Springs, PA: Sunbury Press, 2017.

Renehan Edward. *The Secret Six: The True Tale of the Men Who Conspired with John Brown*. Columbia: University of South Carolina Press, 1997.

Reynolds, David S. *John Brown, Abolitionist: The Man Who Killed Slavery, Sparked the Civil War, and Seeded Civil Rights*. New York: Alfred A. Knopf, 2005.

Richards, Leonard. *"Gentlemen of Property and Standing": Anti-abolition Mobs in Jacksonian America*. New York: Oxford University Press, 1971.

——. *The Slave Power: The Free North and Southern Domination, 1780–1860*. Baton Rouge: Louisiana State University Press, 2000.

Richardson, Marilyn. *Maria W. Stewart: America's First Black Woman Political Writer*. Bloomington: Indiana University Press, 1987.

Ripley, C. Peter, ed. *The Black Abolitionist Papers*, vols. 1–5. Chapel Hill: University of North Carolina Press, 1985.

Rogozinski, Jan. *A Brief History of the Caribbean: From Arawak and Carib to the Present*. New York: Penguin, 2000.

Rollin, Frank A. *Life and Public Services of Martin R. Delany*. Boston: Lee and Shepard, 1868. Reprint, New York: Arno Press, 1969.

Rossbach, Jeffery. *Ambivalent Conspirators: John Brown, the Secret Six, and a Theory of Slave Violence*. Philadelphia: University of Pennsylvania Press, 1982.

Rugemer, Edward Bartlett. *The Problem of Emancipation: The Caribbean Roots of the American Civil War*. Baton Rouge: Louisiana State Press, 2008.

Runyon, Randolph Paul. *Delia Webster and the Underground Railroad*. Lexington: University Press of Kentucky, 1996.

Rus, Martin. *Night of Fire: The Black Napoleon and the Battle for Haiti*. New York: Sarpedon Publishers, 1994.

Savage, Kirk. *Standing Soldiers, Kneeling Slaves: Race, War, and Monument in Nineteenth-Century America*. Princeton, NJ: Princeton University Press, 1997.

Scheidenhelm, Richard, ed. *The Response to John Brown*. Belmont, CA: Wadsworth, 1972.

Sidbury, James. *Ploughshares into Swords: Race, Rebellion and Identity in Gabriel's Virginia, 1730–1810*. Cambridge: Cambridge University Press, 1997.

Sinha, Manisha. *The Slave's Cause: A History of Abolition*. New Haven, CT: Yale University Press, 2016.

Slaughter, Thomas P. *Bloody Dawn: The Christiana Riot and the Racial Violence in the Antebellum North*. New York: Oxford University Press, 1991.

Smith, David G. *On the Edge of Freedom: The Fugitive Slave Issue in South Central Pennsylvania, 1820–1870*. New York: Fordham University Press, 2012.

Smith, Ted A. *Weird John Brown: Divine Violence and the Limits of Ethics*. Stanford, CA: Stanford University Press, 2015.

Stampp, Kenneth M. *America in 1857: A Nation on the Brink*. Oxford: Oxford University Press, 1992.

Stauffer, John. *The Black Hearts of Men: Radical Abolitionists and the Transformation of Race*. Cambridge, MA: Harvard University Press, 2001.

——, ed. *The Works of James McCune Smith: Black Intellectual and Abolitionist*. Oxford: Oxford University Press, 2006.

Stepto, Robert B. *From Behind the Veil: A Study of Afro-American Narrative*. Urbana: University of Illinois Press, 1991.

Sterling, Dorothy. *Ahead of Her Time: Abbey Kelly and the Politics of Antislavery*. New York: W. W. Norton, 1991.

Still, William. *The Underground Rail Road: A Record of Facts, Authentic Narrative, Letters, & C., Narrating the Hardships, Hair-Breadth Escapes and Death Struggles of the Slaves in their Efforts of Freedom, as Related by Themselves and Others, or Witnessed by the Author; Together with Sketches of Some of the Largest Stockholders, and Most Liberal Aiders and Advisors, of the Road*. Philadelphia: Porter & Coates, 1872. Reprint, Medford, NJ: Plexus Publishing, 2005.

Strangis, Joel. *Lewis Hayden and the War Against Slavery*. New Haven, CT: Linnet Books, 1999.

Stewart, James B. *Holy Warriors: The Abolitionists and American Slavery*. New York: Hill and Wang, 1976.

Swain, Gwenyth. *Dred and Harriet Scott: A Family's Struggle for Freedom*. St. Paul, MN: Borealis Books, 2004.

Takaki, Ronald. *Violence in the Black Imagination: Essays and Documents*. New York: Oxford University Press, 1993.

Taylor, Nikki. *America's First Black Socialist: The Radical Life of Peter H. Clark*. Lexington: University of Kentucky Press, 2013.

Umoja, Akinyele Omowale. *We Will Shoot Back: Armed Resistance in the Mississippi Freedom Movement*. New York: New York University Press, 2013.

Villard, Oswald Garrison. *John Brown, 1800–1859: A Biography Fifty Years After*. Boston: Houghton Mifflin, 1910. Gloucester, MA: Peter Smith, 1965.

Voegeli, V. Jacque. *Free but Not Equal: The Midwest and the Negro During the Civil War*. Chicago: University of Chicago Press, 1967.

Walker, David. *Walker's Appeal, in Four Articles; Together with a Preamble, to the Coloured*

Citizens of the World, but in Particular, and Very Expressly, to Those of the United States of America. Boston: David Walker,1829.

Ward, Samuel R. *Autobiography of a Fugitive Negro: His Antislavery Labors in the United States, Canada, & England*. London: John Snow, 1855.

Webster, Daniel. *The Writings and Speeches of Daniel Webster*. Boston: Little, Brown, 1903.

Wells, Ida B. *Southern Horrors: Lynch Law in All Its Phases*. New York: New York Age, 1892.

Wheaton, Ellen Birdseye. *Diary, 1846–1857*. Boston: Marymount Press, 1923.

Wiencek, Henry. *An Imperfect God: George Washington, His Slaves, and the Creation of America*. New York: Farrar, Straus and Giroux, 2003.

Winks, Robin W. *The Blacks in Canada: A History*. Montreal: McGill-Queen's University Press, 1971.

Woodson, Carter G., ed. *The Mind of the Negro as Reflected in Letters Written During the Crisis, 1800–1860*. Washington, DC: Association for the Study of Negro Life and History, 1826.

Wright, Nathan. *Black Power and Urban Unrest: Creative Possibilities*. New York: Hawthorn, 1967.

Yee, Shirley J. *Black Women Abolitionists: A Study in Activism, 1828–1860*. Knoxville: University of Tennessee, 1992.

Yellin, Jean Fagan, and John C. Van Horne, eds. *The Abolitionist Sisterhood: Women's Political Culture in Antebellum America*. Ithaca, NY: Cornell University Press, 1994.

JOURNAL ARTICLES

A., R. "John Brown's Raid: Guns Against Slavery," *Progressive Labor Magazine* 12, no. 4 (Fall 1979): 14–53.

Anderson, Eric. "Black Émigrés: The Emergence of Nineteenth-Century United States Black Nationalism in Response to Haitian Emigration and Colonization, 1816–1840," *49th Parallel: An Interdisciplinary Journal of North American Studies* 1 (Winter 1999): 1–8.

Aptheker, Herbert. "Militant Abolitionism," *Journal of Negro History* 26, no. 4 (1941): 438–484.

———. "The Quakers and Negro Slavery," *Journal of Negro History* 25, no. 3 (July 1940): 331–362.

Belasco, Susan. "Harriet Martineau's Black Hero and the American Antislavery Movement," *Nineteenth-Century Literature* 55, no. 2 (September 2000): 157–194.

Brusky, Sarah. "The Travels of William and Ellen Craft: Race and Travel Literature in the Nineteenth Century," *Prospects* 25 (2000): 177–192.

Clavin, Matthew. "A Second Haitian Revolution: John Brown, Toussaint Louverture, and the Making of the American Civil War," *Civil War History* 54, no. 2 (2008): 117–145.

Davis, David Brion. "Slavery and the Post–World War II Historians," *Daedalus* 103 (Spring 1974): 1–16.

Demos, John. "The Antislavery Movement and the Problem of Violent 'Means,'" *New England Quarterly* 37, no. 4 (December 1964): 503–504.

Dixon, Chris. "An Ambivalent Black Nationalism: Haiti, Africa, an Antebellum African-American Emigrationism," *Australasian Journal of American Studies* 10, no. 2 (December 1991): 10–25.

Drescher, Seymour. "Servile Insurrection and John Brown's Body in Europe," *Journal of American History* 80, no. 2 (1993): 499–524.

Forbes, Ella. "'By My Own Right Arm': Redemptive Violence and the 1851 Christiana, Pennsylvania Resistance," *Journal of Negro History* 83 (1998): 159–167.

Furstenberg, François. "Beyond Freedom and Slavery: Autonomy, Virtue, and Resistance in Early American Political Discourse," *Journal of American History* 89, no. 4 (March 2003): 1295–1330.

Geffert, Hannah N. "John Brown and His Black Allies: An Ignored Alliance," *Pennsylvania Magazine of History and Biography* 126, no. 4 (October 2002): 591–610.

Goldstein, Leslie Friedman. "Violence as an Instrument for Social Change: The Views of Frederick Douglass, 1817–1895," *Journal of Negro History* 61, no. 1 (1976): 61–72.

Halstead, Murat. "The Execution of John Brown," *Ohio State Archaeological and Historical Quarterly* 30, no. 3 (July 1921): 290–299.

Hofstader, Richard. "U. B. Phillips and the Plantation Legend," *Journal of Negro History* 29 (April 1944): 109–124.

James, John A. "The Optimal Tariff in the Antebellum United States," *American Economic Review* 71, no. 4 (September 1981: 726–734.

Johnson, Michael P. "Denmark Vesey and His Co-Conspirators," *William and Mary Quarterly*, 3rd ser., 58, no. 4 (October 2001): 915–976.

Kachum, Mitch. "Antebellum African Americans, Public Commemoration, and the Haitian Revolution: A Problem of Historical Mythmaking," *Journal of the Early Republic* 26, no. 2 (Summer 2006): 249–273.

Knight, Franklin W. "The Haitian Revolution," *American Historical Review* 105, no. 1 (February 2000): 103–115.

Landon, Fred. "Canadian Negroes and the John Brown Raid," *Journal of Negro History* 6, no. 2 (April 1921): 174–182.

———. "The Negro Migration to Canada After the Passing of the Fugitive Slave Act," *Journal of Negro History* 5, no. 1 (January 1920): 22–36.

Lechner, Zachary J. " 'Are We Ready for the Conflict?' Black Abolitionist Response to the Kansas Crisis, 1854–1856," *Kansas History: A Journal of the Central Plains* 31 (Spring 2008): 14–31.

Murphy, Angela. " 'It Outlaws Me, and I Outlaw It': Resistance to the Fugitive Slave Law in Syracuse, New York," *Afro-Americans in New York Life and History* 28, no. 1 (January 2004).

Pease, William, and Jane Pease. "Confrontation and Abolition in the 1850s," *Journal of American History* 58 (1972): 923–937.

———. "Walker's Appeal Comes to Charleston: A Note and Documents," *Journal of Negro History* 59, no. 3 (1974): 287–292.

Shiffrin, Steven H. "The Rhetoric of Black Violence in the Antebellum Period: Henry Highland Garnet," *Journal of Black Studies* 2, no. 1 (September 1971): 45–56.

Sidbury, James. "Plausible Stories and Varnished Truths," *William and Mary Quarterly*, 3rd ser., 59, no. 1 (January 2002): 179–184.

Sinha, Manisha. "The Caning of Charles Sumner: Slavery, Race, and Ideology in the Age of the Civil War," *Journal of the Early Republic* 23, no. 2 (Summer 2003): 233–262.

Smith, Robert P. "William Cooper Nell: Crusading Black Abolitionist," *Journal of Negro History* 55, no 3 (July 1970): 182–199.

Sokolow, Jayme. "The Jerry McHenry Rescue and the Growth of Northern Antislavery Sentiment During the 1850s," *Journal of American Studies* 16, no. 3 (December 1982): 427–445.

Stewart, James B. "Peaceful Hopes and Violent Experiences: The Evolution of Reforming and Radical Abolitionism, 1831–1837," *Civil War History* 17 (1971): 293–309.

Tate, Gayle T. "Free Black Resistance in the Antebellum Era, 1830–1860," *Journal of Black Studies* 28, no. 6 (July 1998): 764–782.

———. "Prophesy and Transformation: The Contours of Lewis Woodson's Nationalism," *Journal of Black Studies* 29, no. 2 (November 1998): 215–217.

Thompson, Thomas Marshall. "National Newspaper and Legislative Reactions to Louisiana's Deslonde Slave Revolt of 1811," *Louisiana History* 33 (Winter 1992): 5–29.

Toplin, Robert Brent. "Upheaval, Violence, and the Abolition of Slavery in Brazil," *Hispanic American Historical Review* 49, no. 4 (1969): 639–655.

Watts, Dale. "How Bloody Was Bleeding Kansas?," *Kansas History: A Journal of the Central Plains* 18, no. 2 (Summer 1995): 116–129.

Wyatt-Brown, Bertram. "William Lloyd Garrison and Antislavery Unity: A Reappraisal," *Civil War History* 13 (1967): 11–12.

DISSERTATIONS

Bell, Howard Holman. "A Survey of the Negro Convention Movement, 1830–1861." PhD diss., Northwestern University, 1953.

Boggus, Michael. "Nat Turner's Revolt and the Demise of Slavery." MA thesis, Southern Illinois University at Carbondale, 2006.

Boom, Aaron M. "The Development of Sectional Attitudes in Wisconsin, 1848–1861." PhD diss., University of Chicago, 1948.

Cooper, Afua Ava Pamela. " 'Doing Battle in Freedom's Cause': Henry Bibb, Abolitionism, Race Uplift, and Black manhood, 1842–1854." PhD diss., University of Toronto, 2000.

Fisch, Audrey A. "Uncle Tom in England: The Black American Abolitionist Campaign, 1852–1861." Ph. diss., Rutgers University, New Brunswick, NJ, 1993.

Gordon, Dexter Barrington. "Black Ideology in American Black Abolitionist Discourse: The Materialization of a Constitutive Rhetoric." PhD diss., Indiana University, 1998.

Karlsson, Ann-Marie Elisabet. "Signs in Blood: Racial Violence and Antebellum Narratives of Resistance." PhD diss., University of California, Berkeley, 1995.

Rhodes, Jane. "Breaking the Editorial Ice: Mary Ann Shadd Cary and the Provincial Freeman." PhD diss., University of North Carolina at Chapel Hill, 1992.

Scott, Julius. "The Common Wind: Currents in Afro-American Communication in the Era of the Haitian Revolution." PhD diss., Duke University, 1986.

Scroggins, Marvin Keith. "Educational Leadership Modalities of Afrocentric Alliance Building: The Political Theory of Henry Highland Garnet." EdD diss., School of Intercultural Studies, Biola University, 1993.

Sepinwall, Alyssa Goldstein. "Regenerating France, Regenerating the World: The Abbé Grégoire and the French Revolution, 1750–1831." PhD diss., Stanford University, 1998.

Simmons, Adam Dewey. "Ideologies and Programs of the Negro Antislavery Movement, 1830–1861." PhD diss., Northwestern University, 1983.

Ward, William Edward. "Charles Lenox Remond: Black Abolitionist, 1838–1873." PhD diss., Clark University, 1977.

INDEX

Numbers in boldface refer to figures.

abolitionist movement, 156; after emancipation, 162–163; antiblack sentiments of white abolitionists, 84–85; black abolitionists born into slavery, 36, 39, 62, 67, 165n5, 187n61; Brown and, 109–110; Burns court decision and, 73, 75; caning of Sumner and, 91–92; Christiana Resistance and, 58; Civil War and, 156, 158–159; colonization movement and, 167; dissolution of Union and, 149–150; Douglass/Garnet dispute and, 39–40; Douglass/Garrison dispute and, 43–44; Dred Scott decision and, 100–103; economic opposition to, 166n15; emigration to Haiti and, 151–154; equality and, 32–34, 82, 95, 104, 110, 156, 158, 161; Free Soil Party and, 83–85; Fugitive Slave Law and, 52, 64–67; funding of, 110–111, 113; Garrison and, 20–24; Harpers Ferry raid and, 125–126, 145; historiography of, 3, 157–158; importance of Kansas to, 85–86, 92–95; influence of American Revolution on, 4–6, 44, 77, 123–124, 141–143; influence of Haitian Revolution on, 5–6, 15–16, 18–19, 44, 47, 77, 172n104; Jerry Rescue and, 64–67; Kansas-Nebraska Act and, 85–86; lack of political support, 138; leadership of black abolitionists, 9–12, 30, 34, 44, 106–107, 109, 157–158, 165n5; Lincoln and, 132, 143–145, 150; as minority movement, 85; moral suasion and, 3, 7, 23, 159, 161; nonviolence and, 6–7, 22–27; proslavery legislative acts and, 80–81; Quaker influence on, 21, 95, 174n33; Radical Political Abolition Party, 87–89; religious foundation of, 21, 23–24, 39; Republican Party and, 83, 143–145; seen as failure, 157; Slave Power and, 86, 158; use of

political power by, 3, 27, 87–90, 92; Walker and, 17–20; women's contributions to, 8–9, 29–30. *See also* abolitionist movement, violence and

abolitionist movement, violence and, 2–6, 8, 11, 30, 80, 82, 105, 136, 140–141, 147–148; American Revolution and, 77–78, 141–143; anti-abolitionist violence, 7, 28–30, 40–41, 145–148, 166n14; black abolitionist leaders and, 8–10, 30, 44, 82, 97, 103; black liberation ideology, 40, 88, 109, 133; black militancy, 52, 82, 96–99, 104, 161; Brown and, 93, 118, 141, 147–148; changing strategies of, 7–8, 161–162; civil disobedience, 34–35, 49, 64; Civil War and, 149–150, 156; declining support for nonviolence, 36, 43, 45–47, 94–96, 136, 161–162; discomfort of white abolitionists, 62; Douglass and, 41, 43–44, 69, 103–104, 117, 130, 148; Dred Scott decision and, 101–103; emancipation through revolution, 4–6, 15, 96, 108, 123–124, 141–143, 154, 156; emigration and, 154; equality and, 52; Garnet and, 36–38, 45–46; Garrison and, 96, 130, 142–143; Harpers Ferry raid and, 107, 130–131, 133, 145, 181n3; historiography of, 157–158; influence of Haitian Revolution, 15–16, 18–19, 47, 77, 108; Kansas violence and, 81–82, 87, 93–94; leadership of black abolitionists and, 109; Lovejoy and, 31–32; political and economic hardship and, 34; political violence and, 161; practical abolitionism, 35; Radical Political Abolition Party and, 88–89; religion and, 19; Remond and, 48–49; resistance to Fugitive Slave Law, 8, 49, 53, 59, 69–75, 78–79; against slave-catchers, 11, 60, 104; slave revolts and,

Free Soil Party, 82–85, 88–90; Fugitive Slave Law and, 65
Fugitives and Their Friends, 69
Fugitive Slave Law, 3, 7–8, 48, 49–52, 86, 149; anti-kidnapping act of 1847 and, 58, 174n33; black militancy and, 49, 99, 104; Christiana Resistance and, 58; enforcement of, 73; Jerry Rescue and, 61, 63–67; Lincoln and, 150; resistance to, 53, 59–63, 65–67, 78–79; resistance to in Massachusetts, 69–75; self-defense and, 49, 78, 81; strengthened in 1850, 50–51; Sumner and, 71; white abolitionists' resistance to, 64–65
Furstenberg, François, 4

Gabriel (Prosser), 106
Gabriel (slave in Richmond), 15, 167n3
Gag Gang, 54
"gag rule," 31
Garner, Margaret, 104
Garnet, Henry Highland, 8, 15, 36–40, 80, 109, 168n7; "Address to the Slaves" speech, 17, 36–39, 45, 110; criticism of, 179n66; Douglass and, 38–40, 117; Dred Scott decision and, 103; Haiti and, 47, 151; Harpers Ferry and, 119, 127; influence on Brown, 107, 110; refusal to participate in Harpers Ferry, 119; as slave, 187n61
Garnett, Henry, 60
Garrison, William Lloyd, 6–7, 20–24, 52; American Antislavery Society cofounded by, 20, 22; black leaders criticize, 17, 96, 137, 138; black leaders support, 23–24; Douglass and, 43–44; on Fugitive Slave Law, 69, 73; Haitian Revolution and, 47; on Harpers Ferry, 130; ideological turn, 143, 150; Liberator published by, 20, 21; May confesses ideological turn to, 65; Meionaon Hall speech, 142–143; pacifism of, 21–22, 29, 31–32, 96; as Quaker, 17, 21; on Radical Political Abolitionists, 88; Stearns and, 95–96; Turner and, 26–27; Walker and, 21, 23, 24, 27, 143; work seen as threatening, 21–22
Geffrard, Fabre-Nicholas, 151
German Coast rebellion, 15
Gloucester, Elizabeth, 110
Gloucester, James Newton, 110
Gloucester, John, 119–120
Goldman, Leslie Friedman, 40

Goodell, William, 31
Goodman, Andrew, 160
Gorsuch, Edward, 55–57, 58
Great Awakening, second, 6, 20
Greeley, Horace, 85
Green, Robert, 61
Green, Shields, 120–123, 125
Grigby, Barnaby, 75–77, 76, 176n92
Grigby, Mary Elizabeth, 75–77
Grimes, Leonard, 91

Haiti, 5, 108, 186n46; black emigration to, 17, 150–155, 168n9, 186n46; Haitian revolution as inspiration for abolitionist movement, 5–6, 15–16, 18–19, 44, 47, 77, 172n104; as inspiration for Harpers Ferry raid, 107–108, 119; slave rebellions and, 17, 26
Halstad, Murat, 127
Hamilton, Robert, 151–152
Hamilton, Thomas, 151–152
Hamlin, Hannibal, 144
Hardy, Neal, 41
Harper, Frances Ellen Watkins, 8, 86
Harpers Ferry raid, 106, 115–116, 120–124, 142; aftermath of, 123–125, 127–128, 184n61; black hesitation to participate in, 120, 124, 126–127; black leaders views of, 129–131; black women and, 111, 113, 116–117; conflicting interpretations of, 124–127; funding of, 113, 115, 117, 181n3; historians' treatment of, 107; influence of black abolitionists on, 106–107, 111, 133–134, 180n2; memorialization of, 131–134, 141, 145; repercussions of, 128–129. See also Brown, John
Harriet (wife of Hayden), 68–69
Harris, John, 37
Harris family, 150
Harvey, Esther (wife of Hayden), 67–68, 70
Harvey, Joseph, 67
Hayden, Lewis, 8, 67–73, 68, 108
Henry, Patrick, 4, 165n8
Henry, William (aka Jerry, runaway slave), 63–64
Henry Highland Garnet Guards, 98–99
Henson, Josiah, 69
Higginson, Thomas Wentworth, 72
Hinks, Peter, 19
Hinton, Frederick A., 23
Hinton, Richard J., 125
Hodges, Graham Russell Gao, 35

ACKNOWLEDGMENTS

Fellow alumna, Toni Morrison, said it best: "I tell my students, 'When you get these jobs that you have been so brilliantly trained for, just remember that your real job is that if you are free, you need to free somebody else. If you have some power, then your job is to empower somebody else. This is not just a grab-bag candy game.'" If I could add to Morrison's wisdom, I would say it is not only your job to bring others along, but to thank those who helped you get where you were going. It gives me great joy to roll call those who have freed me, empowered me, and shared their intellectual candy.

My love for history was cultivated at Howard University. I remain eternally grateful for the rich education I received and the numerous professors who poured their wisdom down on me. The classes I took in the beloved Frederick Douglass Hall taught me how to think, how to value who I am, and how to create a path forward to achieve my dreams. Most importantly, Howard taught me how to lift while climbing.

At Howard, my path to research began with the Ronald E. McNair Scholars Program. There I was paired with the indomitable Dr. Edna Greene Medford, who introduced me to the archive and Howard's most precious gem: the Moorland-Spingarn Research Center. It was in the fall of 2002 that Dr. Medford and I sat in a small room in Founders Library. Donning white gloves, she opened a manila envelope that held an old and original letter. The letter was written to a woman named Rosetta, and it was signed, "Affectionately, your father, Frederick Douglass." That was the first time I realized what historians did and that I was going to be one. I used the sources I found in the archive and wrote a research paper. Dr. Medford gave me an opportunity to present my research at a national conference on the same stage as Nettie Douglass Washington, a descendent of Frederick Douglass and Booker T. Washington. I still have the kind letter Nettie Douglass Washington wrote me after I presented. It was also at that conference where I received my first informal invitation to graduate school. To Crystal Evans, and the entire Ronald E. McNair

Scholar cohort and team of mentors and writing coaches, this book is the fruit of our labor. It is a shared success. To Edna Medford, Greg Carr, Priscilla Ramsey, Joseph Reidy, Yanick Rice Lamb, and Korey Brown, thank you for your invaluable mentorship.

Every trip I took to the Moorland-Spingarn Research Center transformed my thinking on history. My appetite for history remains insatiable. As an undergrad, I even started a campaign to get the hours of operation increased. Though I was not successful, it taught me a valuable lesson about the activism required to ensure archives, historical societies, and all those who serve in the preservation of history be protected from the dangers of budget cuts and politics. Many thanks to the wonderful Joellen ElBashir, Ida Jones, and the late Donna Wells, all of whom I had the privilege of working with in the photographs department. I can confidently say I became a historian at MSRC.

The summer before I began graduate school I spent at two months at the University of Iowa as part of the Summer Research Opportunity Program. I am grateful for the mentorship of Leslie Schwalm and the time we spent working on Emancipation Day celebrations. Leslie and Diana Sproles, your example of kindness and rigor has remained a part of my journey. In Iowa, I built lifelong friendships that have enriched me both professionally and personally. Natalie Leger, you have made me better at everything. I remain in awe of your brilliance. Terence Nance and James Bartlett have always encouraged me to strive for more. You remind me how wonderful it is to be black and dope.

My time at Columbia University was transformative. My beloved and esteemed advisor, Eric Foner, has taught me so much about what it means to be a historian and to write for the people. Your generosity, accessibility, and guidance opened up a world of opportunities for me. Thank you for helping to shape the ideas of this book. At Columbia, there are many who helped to hone my thoughts and writing when it came to black abolitionists and violence. I am grateful to Barbara J. Fields, Sam Roberts, Farah Jasmine Griffin, Frederick Harris, Christopher Brown, and Natasha Lightfoot. To the late Manning Marable, I will never forget how you affirmed me and gave me the confidence to speak and write and to see my work as its own form of necessary activism. To the Institute for Research in African American Studies (IRRAS), thank you and Shay Bryd-Harris for being a haven to students of color. I would not have survived without my Black Historians Matter (BHM) family. Thank you to Zaheer Ali, Samir Meghelli, Elizabeth Hinton, Russell Rickford, Adrienne Clay, Megan French-Marcelin, Betsy Herbin, Horace Grant, Zinga Fraser, Amanda Alexander, and Toja Okoh.

There are several fellowships that have been instrumental in aiding in the research and completion of this book. I would like to thank the John & Louise Fellowship Award, the George E. Haynes Fellowship Award, and the GSAS Merit Fellowship. The Gilder Lehman Fellowship allowed me to complete much needed research in New York City. I am also grateful to the funds provided for travel from the George N. Shuster Faculty Fellowship at Hunter College, the Faculty Fellowship Publication Program, Hunter College's President Fund for Faculty Advancement, and the Presidential Travel Award. I would also like to thank the feedback I received from the workshop, Emerging Perspectives on Race & Gender in the Nineteenth Century United States, at Pennsylvania State University. I am also grateful for the McNeil Center for Early American Studies and the University of Pennsylvania for providing me a platform to present my chapters in progress. Many thanks to Samuel W. Black; parts of Chapter 2 was published in Black's award-winning edited collection, *The Civil War in Pennsylvania: The African American Experience.*

Over the better part of a decade, I have been able to present my work at numerous conferences and invited talks. I am grateful for useful feedback from Manisha Sinha, Matthew Clavin, John Stauffer, Tim McCarthy, Jessica Marie Johnson, Judith Geisberg, the late Stephanie Camp, David Waldstreicher, Angela Murphy, Sara Gronningsater, David Blight, Noelle Trent, Eola Dance, dann J. Broyld, Jim Downs, Catherine Clinton, Donald Yacovone, Martin Blatt, Ryan McNabb, and Jean Libby. No collaboration has stretched my ideas and thinking more than the Dark Room for Race and Visual Culture. To Kimberly Juanita Brown, thank you for your unending solidarity and brilliant mind. To all of the members of the Dark Room, you have shown every woman scholar of color what it looks like to be excellent. Here's to global domination!

For two years, I spent time as a visiting professor at Gonzaga University. A very special thanks to Tracy Ellis Ward, Ann Ostendorf, Inga Laurent, Jessica Maucione, Keya Mitra, Becky Bull Schaefer, Betsey Downey, Rudy Mondragon, Shawn Washington, David Garcia, Ylisse Bess, and my awesome students: thank you for making me a better educator. Go Zags! Spokane, Washington, is also where I formed some of my strongest friendships. To Nyasha GuramatunhuCooper and Rebecca Carew, life was made so much easier by your laughter, wisdom, reality checks, and necessary trips to Post Falls, Idaho. Suwanee Lennon, Charity Park, Sheba Caldwell, Faye Baptist, Sandy Wade, and Kimberly Wynn, thank you for your unending support.

From 2012 to 2014, I was a Harvard College Fellow in the Department of

African and African American Studies at Harvard University. Much of the writing and editing of this book took place among a community of outstanding intellectuals. The mentorship and partnerships I built were pivotal in my career. Many thanks to Evelyn Brooks Higginbotham; I cannot think of an academic who does not owe some part of their professional success to your generosity. Many thanks as well to Henry Louis "Skip" Gates Jr., Marcyliena Morgan, Marla Frederick, Evelynn Hammond, Carla Martin, Larry Bobo, Jacob Olupona, Tommie Shelby, Vincent Brown, Laurence Ralph, Cassandra Fradera, Emily Owens, Carolyn Roberts, Charrise Barron, Funlayo Wood, Grete Viddal, Lisanne Norman, Adam McGee, and Sara Bruya. I would like to extend a special thanks to everyone at *Transition Magazine* for collaborating to give my research a voice. To my former Harvard students, you continue to enrich my teaching and your success shines like a beacon to others. A very special thanks to Eziaku Nwokocha, Rachel Bryd, Fay Alexander, Evelyne Alexander, Travis Anderson-Hamilton, Shakkaura Kemet, and Kayci Baldwin.

The History Department at Hunter College and the larger CUNY system has given me nothing but support. I remain grateful to Donna Haverty-Stacke, Rick Belsky, Manu Bhagavan, Mary Roldan, Angelo Angelis, Eduardo Contreras, Benjamin Hett, Elidor Mëhilli, Dániel Margócsy, Daniel Hurewitz, Karen Kern, Jon Rosenberg, Laura Schor, Iryna Vushko, Jill Rosenthal, and John Jones. Special thanks to my graduate assistants Luke Reynolds, John Winters, and Arin Amer. I am also appreciative of the graduate students at CUNY who helped to reshape much of Chapter 4. Your comments were vital. While at Hunter, I was blessed with the opportunity to mentor three amazing Ronald E. McNair Scholars. To Ashley Dennis, Tatiana Nelson, and Shakeya Huggins, the harvest is plenty, but the laborers are few. I can't wait to see the awesome things you will accomplish. The field is waiting for you! To Vilna Treitler, a special thank you for your support in my writing and scholarship.

Throughout the writing of this book, I formed an incredible friendship with Erica Ball. Together, we published two edited collections and bonded over our shared passion for history, justice, and collaboration. Thank you for giving me your time, your feedback, and your intellectual kinship. I also remain indebted to the mentorship and friendship of Erica Armstrong Dunbar. Thank you for counsel, your candid feedback, and your perfect example of what it means to write for the marginalized.

At Wellesley College, I am grateful to my colleagues Filomina Steady, Layli Maparyan, Selwin Cudjoe, Ophera Davis, Kathryn Lynch, Andy Shennan,

Ann Velenchik, Brenna Greer, Nikki Greene, Ryan Quintana, Irene Mata, Petra Rivera-Rideau, Jenn Chudy, Soo Hong, Laura K. Gratton, Smitha Radhakrishnan, and so many others who have encouraged me and offered their support. A special thank you to President Paula Johnson, your leadership has inspired me. In a short time, my students at Wellesley have refined my teaching and even pushed my research process. I am grateful for each class in which they renew my hope for the future.

Writing can often be a solitary and even demoralizing process, but I remain thankful to a host of scholars and dear friends who keep me encouraged, balanced, and present: Nafissa Cisse-Egbuonye, Patrice Clark, Madelina Young-Smith, Crystal Sanders, Deirdre Cooper Owens, Mary Phillips, Tara Bynum, Tamika Nunley, Marylou Fulson, Christy Cox, Jan Cox, Nikki Taylor, Andrea Watkins-Hairston, Brook Nappo, Robyn Spencer, Tikia Hamilton, Leah Wright Rigueur, LaShawn Harris, Amberia Sargent, Tiffany Gill, John and Quinita Ogletree, Kimberly Muse, Staci Stubbs, Anne MacFarland, Vanessa Holden, Natanya Duncan, Marcia Chatelain, Kendra Field, Tyler Perry, Yetunde Zannou, Leah Byzewski, Grace Nieh Howes, Charlene Shortte, Felicia Scott, and Sonia Marrero.

This project would not be complete without the skillful mind of Robert Lockhart at Penn Press. Thank you Bob for your kindness and patience in making *Force and Freedom* forceful. Many thanks to Lily Palladino, Gail Schmitt, and the entire UPenn team for bringing this project together. A special thanks to Kennie Lyman for your initial edits as well. I am also grateful to be a part of the America in the Nineteenth Century series edited by Steven Hahn, Brian DeLay, and Amy Dru Stanley.

Family support has been everything to me. The following have cheered me on and promised to buy the book even when they did not quite know what I was writing about! I will always be indebted to my parents William and Norvella Carter and my amazing squad of siblings: Camille Carter, Jerome and Mia Oberlton, China and Frank Jenkins, Crystal and George Rose, Valerie and Jamaal McNeil, and Victoria and Kevin Jones, along with a host of nieces and nephews. This book is also dedicated to the loving memory of Tracie Oberlton and William Charles Carter II. I know you are proud beyond measure. Thank you Aunt Betty, Aunt Rosa, and Grandma Leona for your love and support. Thank you to my in-laws Cheri and Edward Jackson, Edward and Elizabeth Jackson, Jeanae Jackson, Joshua Jackson, and Rachel Jackson.

It is very hard to write a book. It is even harder to write a book with young children at home. The village that helped raise this book extends to the village who helped to raise my children, William Charles Carter Jackson and Josephine Piper Carter Jackson. I could not have finished my writing and spent time away from home had it not been for a team of people who gave me the constant assurance that my children were safe, healthy, and happy. I owe a debt of gratitude to Sydney Scott; Children's Lighthouse in Cypress, Texas; and two very important women: Michelle Harding and Shalon Persadh. Michelle and Shalon, thank you for being light, love, and fostering a safe haven.

Finally, to my darling husband, Nathaniel Emmitt Jackson, thank you for never letting our dreams escape us. Thank for you being there even when we were apart. This book is the culmination of so many hard-won battles. Everything that is good about this book comes from your unending encouragement.

CPSIA information can be obtained
at www.ICGtesting.com
Printed in the USA
LVHW041630220721
693425LV00003B/330